From Esk to Tweed

From Esk to Tweed

Harbours, Ships and Men of
the East Coast of Scotland

BRUCE LENMAN

Blackie
Glasgow & London

Published by
Blackie & Son Limited
Bishopbriggs, Glasgow G64 2NZ
5 Fitzhardinge Street, London W1H 0DL

ISBN 0 216 90030 1

Printed in Great Britain by
Thomson Litho, East Kilbride, Scotland

Preface

A single, modestly-sized volume is scarcely adequate for this topic. A high degree of selectivity has therefore proved essential. I have not tried to write an exhaustive antiquarian inventory. Many small ports have been relatively neglected. Rather have I tried to account for the rise and fall of the port industry, shipowning and shipbuilding, and fishing, in the context of social and economic change between 1750 and the present day.

Many people helped me in my research. To name them all would be impossible, but I am particularly beholden to Dr Wray Vamplew of the University of Edinburgh, Mr John Hume of Strathclyde University and Mr Robert Smart of St Andrews University, for generous help and stout support under difficult circumstances. For permission to reproduce illustrations I must express sincere gratitude to the University of Aberdeen, for prints in the George Washington Wilson Collection; the Department of Geography of the University of Dundee; the University of St Andrews for material in the Valentine Collection; the Edinburgh Public Libraries; Dundee Public Libraries; the D. C. Thomson Organisation of Dundee; Mr John Hume; and Mr S. Turner of the Photographic Department of Dundee University.

I owe particular thanks to the staff of Dundee Harbour Trust; to Captain White, lately Harbourmaster of Arbroath; and to the Admiral Superintendent and Mr J. Biggerstaff,

5

Yard Services Manager, H.M. Dockyard Rosyth. Clackmannan County Education Committee and the Department of Agriculture and Fisheries for Scotland have both furnished information. Mr James Ford of the Department of Geography of the University of Dundee drew the maps and I am deeply grateful both to him and to Professor S. J. Jones of that department, who agreed to make Mr Ford's services available to me.

My greatest debt is to my wife and family who have borne so cheerfully the strains and stresses of the last few years and who have sustained me through them.

University of St Andrews   Bruce Lenman
September 1974

Contents

List of Illustrations

PLATES

8

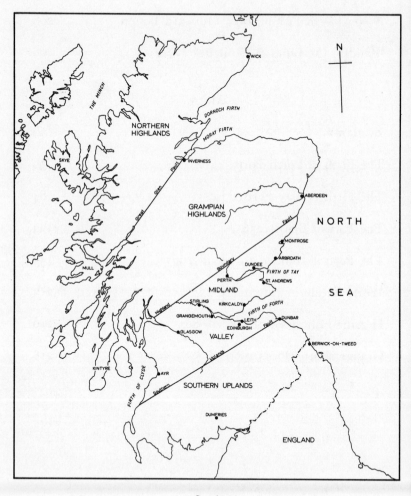

Scotland

CHAPTER I

The Ports of Eastern Scotland South of Stonehaven before 1800

THE PHYSICAL SETTING

Between Montrose and Eyemouth the eastern coastline of Scotland includes the two great indentations of the Firth of Tay and the Firth of Forth, and it has four hinterland areas which lie in three of the four main geological divisions of which mainland Scotland consists. The only major geological division not represented in the hinterland is that of the Northern Highlands, with its very ancient rocks, nearly all of which are metamorphic. This is to say that they have undergone extensive physical and chemical change during periods when they were exposed to a combination of rising temperature and lateral stress generated by mountain-building movements in the earth's crust. A second geological division, separated from the first by the fault in the earth's crust called the Great Glen which runs from Inverness to Fort William, is however well represented. It too consists of metamorphic rocks of great age, though younger than the first. They make up the Grampian Highlands which are separated from the rocks of a third geological division by the Highland Boundary Fault, which runs in a north-east, south-west direction behind all the ports of this coastline from Montrose to Perth. The Grampian Highlands are today a dissected plateau with a general level between 2,000 and 3,000 feet, but the immediate hinterland of most of the ports on this coastline is the Midland Valley of Scotland, consisting of layered rocks of Old Red Sandstone and Carboniferous Systems gently folded by earth movements and pierced by volcanic rocks which now outcrop as the Sidlaw, Ochil, and Campsie Hills. This valley is drained by the Clyde in the west and the Tay and Forth in the east. It runs from the Highland Boundary Fault in the north to the Southern Uplands Fault in the south, a fault which also runs in a north-east, south-west direction, reaching the coast to the east of Edinburgh, and marking the start of the last great geological division of Scotland, the Southern Uplands. These consist of tightly folded fossil-bearing layered rocks younger than those of the Grampian Highlands, but older than those of the Midland Valley.

It is almost impossible to exaggerate the importance of these basic geological facts for the history of the ports which have developed along this part of the east coast of Scotland. The nature of their agricultural hinterlands is largely governed by the predominant type of rock there, for the rocks of the different geological divisions of Scotland when sub-jected to the action of atmospheric and biological agents break down into very different soil-types, ranging from the relatively infertile soils derived from the quartzites, schists, and gneisses of the southern Grampian Highlands, to the very fertile soils overlying the Old Red Sandstone of the Midland Valley, to the good grazing land which cloaks much of the Southern Uplands. Equally important for the develop-ment of ports on the east coast was the presence or absence in their hinterland of the carboniferous rocks bearing pro-ductive coal seams. There are only three important coal-fields, all clustering round the Firth of Forth: the Fife coal-field which is concentrated in south-west Fife and Clack-mannan; the West Lothian coal-field which lies west of Edinburgh and is essentially a western outcrop of the great Central coal-field of Scotland; and the Midlothian and East Lothian coal-field which lies east of Edinburgh.[1]

In the same way, the effects produced by long-term sculpture of the earth's surface by the agencies of weathering and erosion have had a profound effect on the history of the development of the ports of this coast, nowhere more strikingly illustrated than in the ports of the two great firths. The Tay and its tributaries, for example, drain 2,510 square miles of central Scotland, the seventh largest drainage basin in Britain, and the river system is, in terms of volume of water discharged, the foremost British river, discharging more water than the combined Thames and Severn basins. Despite its relative lack of falls and rapids and its relatively low gradient, the Tay is also the fastest flowing major British stream after the Spey. A natural consequence of this is that the Tay carries a formidable volume of sediment. Indeed the Tay estuary can almost be described as an estuarine delta, so extensive are the great sandbanks and reed-fringed islands in it.[2] In the same way, the Forth river system deposits great quantities of sediment in its firth. As it happens, the greatest weight of sedimentation is on the south side of the Firth of Forth, which on balance has had the greater concentrations of population and economic activity, and therefore the greater need for port facilities. Though the presence of great areas of slob land or mud flat exposed at low tide has encouraged various schemes for land reclamation on the south shore of the Forth, it has added enormously to the difficulty and expense of harbour construction. The same is true of the Tay, where the largest port, Dundee, lies on the north side of the widest part of the estuary, but where the main tidal channel has always tended to hug the south shore. A further difficulty for modern engineers contemplating bridging or tunnelling activity in either firth is posed by the fact that the rock underlying the modern sediments is not at an even depth across both estuaries. On the contrary, there is a great buried river channel under both the Tay and the Forth, and their major tributaries. This channel was cut well below present sea-level during ice-age conditions when sea-level all over the world was lowered, and it is infilled with silt, mud, and other unstable elements which suddenly replaced the solid rock strata.

As late as the seventeenth and eighteenth centuries many of these difficulties were still not immediate problems be-

cause of the small size of contemporary shipping and because
of the comparatively undeveloped nature of harbour facilities on this coast, itself a tribute to the smallness of both ships
and the volume of maritime trade. This can be strikingly
demonstrated by the report written by Thomas Tucker on
the settlement of the revenues of excise and customs in Scotland in 1656. Tucker was an English civil servant, Register
to the Commissioners for the Excise, who was sent to Scotland to assist in settling the administration of the customs
and excise there after Scotland had been formally united
with England by an ordinance of Lord Protector Oliver
Cromwell in 1654. Admittedly, Tucker was writing at a time
when the fortunes of some of the east coast ports were at a
low ebb due to the upheavals of the civil wars. Thus the
burgh of Dysart, situated on the south coast of Fife, not far
east of Kirkcaldy, plaintively informed Tucker in 'Ane state
of the condition of the burgh of Dysart' that;

> The said burgh being ane antient and flourishing burgh
> royall, bearing all portable chairges with the rest of the
> burrowes till the year of God 1644 and 1645 they came
> to decay by the intestine and unnatural war against
> Montrose where the most part of the skippers and
> traffiquers were killed and destroyed. . . .

The Marquis of Montrose, the royalist commander in Scotland after 1644, as well as cutting a swathe through the
manpower of the Fife ports, especially at the battle of
Kilsyth, sacked Dundee. Other royalists raided Montrose,
and then in a further cycle of civil conflict Cromwell's troops
sacked both Kirkcaldy and Dundee. Nevertheless, it is very
interesting to notice that in the returns of shipping belonging
to burghs on the east coast between Montrose and Eyemouth, Tucker records ownership of vessels over ten tons
burthen only for Leith, Kirkcaldy, Dundee, and Montrose
(Crail recorded a single vessel of sixty tons). The largest ship
recorded was of two hundred tons burthen, and this was
exceptional, for of the eighty odd vessels recorded twenty-
seven were between ten and thirty tons, twenty-one between
thirty-one and fifty-one tons, and eighteen between fifty-two

and ninety-two tons. In other words, a ship of over a hundred tons burthen was a rare exception.

Not surprisingly, harbour facilities were not particularly elaborate. Even Leith, which Tucker recognised as 'the cheife port of all Scotland', had simply 'a convenient drye harbour into which the Firth ebbs and flowes every tyde; and a convenient key on the one side thereof, of a good length, for landing of goods.' There was no increase in the size of boats recorded as being owned by the burghs on this stretch of coastline in the register containing the state and condition of every burgh within the Kingdom of Scotland, which was compiled for the information of the Convention of Royal Burghs and submitted to that ancient Scottish representative body in 1692.[3] Of course, before the Union of 1707 brought Scotland under the English Acts of Navigation, a good deal of the trade of Scottish ports would be carried in European, particularly Dutch, bottoms, but even the general tendency towards an increase in the size of merchant vessels throughout the eighteenth century failed to produce any dramatic changes in harbour facilities on this stretch of the Scottish coast.

When Defoe wished to paint the economic potential of the Edinburgh-Leith area in glowing terms in the early eighteenth century he argued that its inhabitants had '. . . a very fine harbour for their trade, a good road in the Firth for their ships of burthen, . . .'[4] and this is significant for it underlines the point that all harbours in the Forth were tidal until the early nineteenth century. Large ships, particularly when threatened by an unfavourable wind, had to find a sheltered roadstead to anchor in. In practice such anchorages are few and far between on the east coast of Scotland. Because of its peculiar configuration which means that it narrows sharply at its mouth, which in any case has a substantial bar in the shape of two great banks of sand, the Firth of Tay is relatively sheltered near Dundee, but the Firth of Forth is a very different proposition. It is open, and only the fact that the prevailing winds are south westerly, and therefore off-shore, can have rendered it tolerable for much of the shipping activity in it up to the nineteenth century. When a bad storm did occur the best sheltered anchorage available was in Saint Margaret's Hope at North Queensferry, on the other side of the firth from Leith. It is said that at times a hundred ships could be seen taking refuge there.[5]

The Main Ports of the Coast

To understand the economic, as distinct from the physical background to the ports of this coast in the eighteenth century, it is essential to distinguish between fishing and the import and export of commodities. Fishing is very much a subject in its own right and best treated along with shipbuilding. Furthermore, in considering the significant ports involved in the import and export of commodities it is convenient to break them down into three groups; the Tayside ports, the ports of the northern shore of the Forth, and the ports stretching from the south side of the Firth of Forth down to Eyemouth. None of these groups is wholly coherent from every point of view but they are all meaningful enough to be convenient divisions. Each group will be dealt with in turn, starting with the most northerly.

The Tayside Ports

By most criteria, the Tayside ports were in steady decline between 1612 and 1705. Between those two dates the contribution made by the royal burghs of the Firth of Tay to burghal taxation dropped from a quarter of the assessments to one eighth. A good part of this decline, which was unusually heavy compared with the royal burghs of most other Scottish regions, can be accounted for by the decay of Dundee's capacity to pay tax. In 1612 she had been responsible for eleven per cent of the total tax assessment, the second highest percentage of any burgh. By 1705 Dundee stood fourth equal with Perth and was responsible for four per cent of the total tax assessment. It has been suggested that economic decline had already set in in Dundee before the

civil wars, but in fact the only major contraction in her overseas trade was concentrated in the French trade after 1620,
which was only one of a complex of overseas trades, and it
seems clear that the civil wars, which brought two devastating sacks upon Dundee, were decisive, though the town
made no serious recovery for half a century after they were
over. Perth, Arbroath, and Montrose all had smaller drops
in taxable capacity, partially compensated for by a slight
increase in wealth between 1697 and 1705. St Andrews, however, which can by a slight effort of imagination be treated
as the most southerly of this group of ports, experienced un-
paralleled decline. During the civil wars St Andrews had
been a seat of government and a serious rival to Perth. By
1705 St Andrews had faded into a straggle of houses near the
university with no serious trade nor shipping, paying a mere
tenth of her contributions in 1649. By the beginning of the
eighteenth century, therefore, the significant ports of Tayside were, as they remained in the twentieth century, from
north to south Montrose, Arbroath, Dundee, and Perth.

The reasons for this steady decline are not far to seek. The
Tayside ports had no mineral-bearing hinterland, so their
early seventeenth-century export pattern was the classic one
of exporting the agricultural products of their hinterland,
corn, hides, salmon, and wool with some coarse woollen cloth
constituting the only substantial item of manufactured goods
exported. This is not to say that the area did not have
sophisticated craftsmen. Dundee, for example, had a famous
school of armourers, but it had never built up an exporting
industry. In exchange for their exports the Tayside ports imported two categories of goods. One was natural products
in which contemporary Scotland was deficient, such as
timber and iron from Scandinavia, flax and in bad years
grain from the Baltic, and wine and salt from France. The
second category of goods imported were manufactures, of
which luxuries tended to come from France, necessities from
the Netherlands. Tayside never had a very large direct trade
with the Netherlands, so to secure imports ranging from soap
to dyestuffs, and from hardware to onions, the area had to

deal coastwise with ports like Leith which imported very large quantities direct from the Netherlands.

Across these trade routes politics repeatedly thrust barriers after the Union of the Crowns of Scotland and England in 1603. At once Scotland's small trade with Spain and Portugal (united under the Spanish crown) was complicated by the fact that James the Sixth and First inherited Elizabeth's Spanish war. Subsequently Charles the First waged war on France, while both Oliver Cromwell and Charles the Second waged war on the Netherlands. When William of Orange ousted James the Second and Seventh, he cemented relations between Scotland and the Netherlands at the cost of leading Scotland, with the rest of the British Isles, into a great war with France. On top of these disturbances came civil war in the middle of the seventeenth century and the tremendous problems of adjustment which followed the Parliamentary Union of England and Scotland in 1707. An important consequence of the Union was that Scotland was included within the English commercial system, which meant that the Scots had access to English colonies, but another consequence was that legal barriers were raised against many older Scottish overseas trades. For example, the export of wool to the Netherlands was simply illegal under English law, mainly to deprive the Leyden cloth industry, a serious rival to the East Anglian woollen industry, of vital raw material. After 1707, despite a great deal of smuggling, the new laws and the new customs service enforcing them managed severely to reduce the export of wool and coarse woollens from ports like Dundee to the Netherlands.

Only with the great expansion in the Scots linen trade in the eighteenth century did the major Tayside ports begin to recover their lost economic impetus. However, the rise of the linen trade was a relatively slow process. It was greatly assisted by the help given by a state-sponsored body, the Commissioners and Trustees for Improving Fisheries and Manufactures in Scotland, which was set up in 1727, but not until the failure of the last Jacobite rebellion in 1746 were political conditions in Scotland stable enough to encourage rapid economic growth. In 1727–8 officials of the Board of Trustees inspected and approved of 2,183,978 yards of linen cloth valued at £103,312. 9s. 3d. (£103,312·46). By 1767–8 the figures were up to 11,795,437 yards and £599,669. 4s. 2d. (£599,669·21) respectively and thereafter there was steady long-term growth giving figures of 20,506,310⅛ yards and £854,900. 16s. 2¼d. (£854,900·81) for 1787–8 and 36,268,530½ yards and £1,396,295. 19s. 11½d. (£1,396,296·00) for 1821–2.[7] The important point about all this growth for the Tayside ports was that it was, with one substantial exception, concentrated in their hinterland. The exception was the linen industry of south Fife where Dunfermline specialised in very fine linens and Kirkcaldy in canvas. Apart from that, Scots linen was largely produced in eastern Perthshire and in the counties of Angus and Kincardine, and north Fife. Here the speciality was relatively coarse linens especially the kind known as osnaburgs which appear to have been introduced first in Arbroath through the agency of the Wallace family, but which rapidly more than replaced the old plaiden or coarse wool manufacture in east-central Scotland. A commentator of the 1770s said;

> Dundee used to be celebrated for the manufacture of plaiden, which was exported undressed and undyed to Sweden, Germany, etc, for clothing the troops in these countries, but this was superseded by the manufacture of Osnaburgs in 1747, and it is now the staple of the county of Angus. In 1773 4,488,460 yards of linen were stamped.[8]

Even if the choice of 1747 as a turning point is clearly too absolute, the general point is sound. Scotland's linen industry became concentrated on the east-central area and it was predominantly a coarse linen trade.

The importance of water-transport to this rapidly expanding industry was very great. Though flax was grown in Scotland, it was never grown in sufficient quantities to meet all the demands of Scottish industry. In any case, flax is a labour-intensive crop which makes heavy demands on the soil, so it was logical to import flax and hemp from the Baltic provinces of the Russian Empire where land and labour were cheap and abundant. The flax went into coarse linens, the hemp into ropes. By the early nineteenth century, when we have fairly reliable figures for imports of flax and hemp into Dundee by sea, the figures have a steadily upward trend.[9]

Year	Total Tons Imported	Year	Total Tons Imported
1815	2,187	1822	9,791
1816	2,866	1823	7,924
1817	4,724	1824	9,000
1818	4,927	1825	13,902
1819	3,471	1826	8,270
1820	4,958	1827	14,049
1821	6,452	1828	15,106

Before 1838 raw material could only reach east-central Scotland from overseas by ship. There was no question of bringing it in by rail from a distant port, because there were no railways.

This situation first revitalised and then seriously strained the capacity of the ports of the region. Montrose coped with the situation with less difficulty than most of the other significant ports because the harbour there was naturally rather a good one, and industrial growth in the port and its hinterland was not as spectacular as elsewhere. Partly this was because Montrose had always been very consciously the capital of the surrounding agricultural region. The local landowners had country houses in the town, and the merchant class was closely linked to the landlord or laird class. Indeed many of the estates immediately adjacent to Montrose, some of which had very valuable salmon fishing rights attached to them, eventually because the property of the bigger town merchants. Furthermore, the existence of the extraordinary South Esk Basin, three miles in diameter, which lies behind the town, not only acted as a primitive town sewerage system, but also enabled eighteenth century landowners whose properties abutted on to the basin to bring vessels of fifty to sixty tons burthen up to the east and west side of the basin without serious risk. This greatly facilitated the import of coal and lime for heating and land-improvement.

Montrose remained essentially a port for its rich agricultural hinterland, importing Scandinavian wood and iron, as well as coal and lime from elsewhere in Britain, and exporting grain and salmon. In 1745 a company began to manufacture canvas in the town, with sufficient success to encourage other firms to start up, until during the war of the American Revolution Montrose looked as if it was on the verge of very rapid growth. Actually the canvas manufacture was over-extended, and in the post-war slump after 1783 the Montrose canvas industry collapsed, leaving the town with a small manufacture of osnaburgs, a small thread industry, and an even smaller rope trade.

In 1789 Montrose was therefore still a significant east-coast port with a merchant fleet of fifty-three vessels whose total tonnage amounted to 3,543 tons. Apart from its export of agricultural produce and import of timber, iron, coal and lime, it imported flax and hemp from the Baltic, and it exported the finished products of its textile industry, be they yarn or cloth or ropes or thread, mostly along the coast to London where they were sold to merchant houses who looked after their subsequent distribution. This dual development of North Sea and coastal shipping was typical of the smaller ports of the east-coast linen area, and reflected, of course, the rudimentary state of the roads which were the only alternative transport medium within Britain. Montrose's harbour which lies on the north side of the broad estuary of the South Esk in the middle of which stands the island of Inchbraoc, included in the late eighteenth century a wet (or tidal) dock, where ships were built and repaired, not only for Montrose but for other ports as well. In 1783 'several gentlemen and merchants of Montrose' established a marine insurance agency in the town. Clearly Montrose was still well ahead of nearby ports like Arbroath which in 1789 had a much smaller merchant fleet. In the last analysis, however, Montrose's lack of really dynamic industrial development was to undermine its relative position among the east coast ports.[10]

Arbroath, which was technically an outport within the Montrose customs area, showed more long-term ability to take advantage of the expansion of the linen trade. It already had a tradition of textile manufacture, in the early eighteenth century, on which it rapidly capitalised. The building known as the Abbey House because of its associations with the great abbey which dominated medieval Arbroath, became a thread factory controlled by Wallace Gardyne and Company who, about 1738, were the first to make osnaburgs in Scotland—a development which gave a lead to the whole east-central area. By 1772 the town was producing sailcloth as well as osnaburgs, and by 1790 sailcloth had emerged as the local speciality in a town which was already the principal producer of sailcloth in Scotland. Overall, Arbroath's production of coarse linens was then about a quarter of that of Dundee. As early as 1742 the Town Clerk of Arbroath recorded that weavers were as numerous as all other trades put together. The repercussions of all this on the harbour were bound to be profound for Arbroath needed to import flax and hemp from the Baltic as well as to export finished goods by coast, mainly to London. Furthermore, because Arbroath, like Montrose, acted as a supply port for the eastern end of the Strathmore Valley, which runs between the Grampian Highlands and the coastal hills from Perth to Montrose, it imported goods like flax seeds. Because of their relatively high value and small bulk these could easily be distributed to rural parishes like St Vigeans, Arbirlot, Craig, Dunnichen, Farnell, Guthrie, Kinnell, Lunan and Monikie where flax was being grown in substantial, if not adequate quantities in the late eighteenth century.

The early eighteenth-century harbour of Arbroath had changed very little indeed from medieval times, when the

Abbot of Arbroath Abbey and the citizens of the burgh had gone into partnership to build a wooden pier about 1194. This solitary pier, much restored and rebuilt, remained Arbroath harbour until 1725. As such, it was very unsatisfactory, for there was no natural harbour and just north of the town the Old Red Sandstone of the Midland Valley of Scotland rears up in spectacular sea-cliffs. The pier was inadequate as shelter for vessels when dangerous surges swept along the shore, so it was decided in 1725 to build a new harbour a little to the west of the old. It was a small, stone harbour, with quays all round it except at the entrance, which was a mere thirty-one feet wide. Even so modest an exercise strained the resources of the town and the harbour was still tidal, which meant it was quite dry at low tide, though at spring tides there was a depth of fifteen to sixteen feet at the entrance, and at neap tides nine or ten feet. (Spring tides are the highest, neap tides the lowest in the year.) To protect shipping in very bad weather there was a gate arrangement, similar to the one which can still be seen in Crail harbour in Fife. Fourteen or fifteen strong beams of wood were let down into grooves on either side of the narrow entrance to Arbroath harbour and held down at the top by iron bars. This was all done with the aid of a crane, which could dismantle the gate in quarter of an hour.

Though still well behind Montrose as a port in the late eighteenth century, Arbroath, with its growing industry and improved harbour, was clearly an up-and-coming maritime centre. This was reflected in the growth of its merchant fleet. In 1781 the town owned only seventeen or eighteen vessels amounting in all to about 900 tons. By 1789 Arbroath owned twenty-nine ships whose tonnage totalled 1,539. By the early 1790s the number of ships had reached thirty-two, the tonnage 1,704, and there were ships on the stocks which would soon push the last figure over 2,000. For a town which had had very little overseas trade in 1725, this was an impressive achievement.[11]

Of the Tayside ports, however, Dundee was to be by far the most significant for the simple reason that it emerged as what A. J. Warden was to call 'the centre and great seat of the Linen manufacture in Scotland.' Precisely why it achieved this status is a complex question. For most of the eighteenth century the Scots linen manufacture was a dispersed one leaning heavily on domestic labour. There were no great factories. Indeed, the first substantial production units in the industry were found in the finishing trades where extensive physical and chemical treatment of the cloth or yarn was only possible if abundant water-power was available and if a substantial investment was made in machinery, chemicals and buildings. Notoriously Dundee was deficient in water-power resources to the point where the local bleach-fields, which subjected cloth and yarn to all the normal finishing processes, were concentrated on the Dighty Water, a stream which runs in a west-east direction several miles north of Dundee before it turns south to enter the Firth of Tay at Monifieth. As far as water-power is concerned Perth was far better endowed than Dundee, for the Tay and its tributary the Almond provided a plethora of sites around and in Perth where the water-wheels which were the most important source of mechanical power before the end of the eighteenth century could be set up.

Even the dispersed nature of the preparatory trades and the spinning and weaving could just as well have been turned to, say, Perth's advantage, as Dundee's. After flax had been imported, or produced by a local farmer, the next three processes it had to undergo were usually executed by small groups of people. The preparation of the fibre for spinning was done in small workshops presided over by a master heckler. Heckling was a process whereby the woody element in flax was broken and then combed out. After further combing by many-toothed combs or 'cards' the fibre was usually spun into yarn by female labour working at home, and then woven, occasionally in small workshops but more often by an individual male weaver in his own home. Much of this activity was scattered through the rural parishes of Strathmore, where labour abounded, or in the small market towns of the valley like Brechin, Kirriemuir, Forfar, Alyth,

24

Coupar Angus and Blairgowrie. Before the construction of good roads over the Sidlaw Hills in the late eighteenth century, Dundee did not enjoy particularly good communications with Strathmore, and Perth was in many ways the natural port for the southern end of Strathmore, as was Montrose for its northern part.

The emergence of Dundee as the industrial capital of all Tayside was in large measure a nineteenth-century phenomenon, but by the end of the eighteenth century Dundee had already established a clear lead amongst Tayside linen towns. Factors contributing to this seem to have included the town's relatively substantial population, its possession of concentrations of mercantile wealth which could be turned to industry when directed by progressive financial institutions like banks, a field in which Dundee was early off the mark, and the web of credit and contacts which its financial resources enabled it to cast over its hinterland. Even if the importing merchant sold his flax to the craftsmen, as he seems to have done as often as he retained control over the raw material, credit was essential, if only because a weaver finished a web of cloth a very long time before it could be sold to a consumer in, say, the West Indies. Pre-existent financial strength, or access to it, was an enormous asset.[12]

Another factor reinforcing Dundee's position was undoubtedly her harbour. As a feat of engineering it was no more prepossessing than other contemporary Tayside harbours. On 23 December 1700 the Magistrates of Dundee had petitioned the Scots Parliament for the right to impose special local taxation to be used for the building and repair of the harbour. The request does not appear to have been granted. Nevertheless, there was a steady and mounting demand for harbour facilities based on the exceptional buoyancy of the local linen trade and on a steady volume of grain exports from the immediate hinterland of Dundee. This last factor should not be underestimated. South of the Sidlaws there were within reasonable distance of Dundee three different kinds of agricultural area capable in normal years of producing a grain surplus. First there were the southward-facing lower slopes or braes of the coastal hills. Then there were the light sandy coastal soils based on old raised beaches produced by ancient falls in sea-level. Finally in the area called the Carse of Gowrie, which lies between Dundee and Perth and which consists largely of consolidated river-sediment, there were occasional higher areas, usually centred on an outcrop of andesite, a local volcanic rock, which due to their superior drainage and rich soil were very fertile. In eighteenth-century Europe regional grain short- ages due to bad harvests were a recurring phenomenon, and one from which an enterprising Scots grain exporter could derive much advantage. When there was a dearth of grain in Dundee itself, of course, local mobs attacked granaries and grain-exporting ships as they did in 1720, 1729, and 1772–3.

By the 1740s Dundee was being recognised as the leading Scottish centre for coarse linens manufactured from the relatively low-grade Baltic flax. By 1759 Brice of Exeter could say in his geographical dictionary that;

> Dundee is one of the best ports for trade in all Scotland particularly for foreign, yet has it considerable inland business also, especially for corn and Linen cloth, which makes the country round about rich and populous, being maintained by the great quantities of goods which the merchants of Dundee buy for exportation.

The last point made in the quotation underlines the im- portance of rural cloth and yarn production and of access to this production by Dundee merchants. In fact by the time the Reverend Robert Small came to write his *Statistical Account* of Dundee in 1792 he could remark that the town could expect to derive signal benefits from the excellent turn- pike roads lately constructed and continuing to be extended through all the principal districts of Angus, and the neigh- bouring parts of Perthshire. He added that though the town of Dundee had taken no share in the trouble or risk of this undertaking, which was the concern of the country gentle- men, the town was likely to be the principal beneficiary. The roads were practical for the short and medium distance haulage of cloth, but for sending cloth as far as London, to the great merchant houses who distributed it as far afield as the American and West Indian colonies, coastal shipping was still the only economic proposition.

On top of the substantial volume of business for the port which flowed to and fro along the new road network, the town itself had by 1792 a formidable concentration of industry. Osnaburgs and other coarse fabrics were produced, largely for export. Between November 1788 and November 1789 4,242,653 yards of these were stamped by Board of Trustees officials in Dundee and valued at £108,782. 14s. 2d. (£108,782·71), of which about a quarter represented the value of goods brought into Dundee from its hinterland. Dundee itself actually exported a fair amount of sacking to neighbouring parishes. Bagging for cotton wool was by definition an export line, and Dundee also had in 1792 a thread manufacture, a rope manufacture, and even a small cotton manufacture. On top of textiles there were extensive tanneries, a tobacco and snuff manufacture, a sugar refinery and a glass works.

The tonnage cleared inwards from foreign ports to Dundee had been 1,280 in 1745 when the outward tonnage was 500 for foreign ports, 3,000 for coastal. By 1791 the figures had soared to 10,520 for inward foreign; 1,276 outward foreign; 40,923 inward coasting; and 20,055 outward coasting. On 5 January 1772, 116 vessels navigated by 698 men and with a tonnage of 8,550½, belonged to the port. Of these thirty-four were employed in foreign trade, seventy-eight in coasting, and four in the whale-fishing.[13]

By 1730 Dundee had obtained an Act of Parliament entitling it to levy a duty of two pennies Scots (or one sixth of a penny sterling) on every Scots pint of ale or beer sold within the town. The revenue accruing from this was to be expended mainly on repaying the public debt of the town and on repairing the harbour, which the preamble to the act described as choked and unsafe due to silting and the decayed state of the piers. As a certain amount of revenue could also be derived from the shore dues levied on vessels using the port,

Dundee had funds for serious work on its port. By 1736 the Town Council had set up a specialist committee for harbour matters which was contemplating a plan for a general re-furbishing and improvement of the harbour at a cost of £1,751. 10s. 0d. (£1,751·50). The plan was drawn up by an architect called Dowrie, and it seems to have been proceeded with piecemeal. Even by the end of the eighteenth century the result was not particularly impressive, for the harbour still consisted essentially of a tidal harbour protected by piers, some stone, some timber, with a scouring basin closed by gates lying just north of it. Water was trapped there at high tide to be released at low tide in the hope that it would scour at least some of the sediment which was still a major problem. In his account of the harbour Robert Small states that in order to obtain a through-scour from tidal currents some of the piers had been pierced by arches. It is clear from the records of shore dues that at least part of this operation was financed from that source. The results were still very un-satisfactory.[14]

If, however, Dundee had its troubles, they were quite minor compared with the problems facing its most serious rival, Perth. Perth stands at the very limit of tidal action in the Tay. It became also the lowest point at which the river was bridgeable. Its harbour originally lay just above Mon-creiff Island, a substantial obstacle in the middle of the river. For a variety of reasons, only small vessels could use Perth harbour. Basically this was because of the size and frequency of sandbanks in the Tay estuary, which is also rendered hazardous by reed-fringed islands of which Mugdrum Island and Moncreiff Island are only two. All these difficulties became more acute further up the estuary in the direction of Perth, and there was the additional hazard of a number of fords, some artificial, some possibly natural, at least in origin when they may have been dykes of intrusive igneous rock running across the line of the stream. There is still a good example of the latter at Stanley, just north of Perth. In the late eighteenth century boats of sixty to a hundred tons could reach Perth, but at the upper end of this range a spring tide became very desirable if they were heavy laden.

Yet if industrial activity tended to act as a stimulus to port development, Perth was likely to find this restriction increasingly annoying. By the 1790s there were 1500 looms in the city and suburbs producing linens and cottons to the annual value of £100,000. In addition, Perth acted as a gathering centre for yarn and cloth from a large rural area, and linen worth £120,000 was annually purchased by dealers in its market. Around Perth lay a complex of bleach-fields and water-powered sites into which in the late eighteenth century the booming cotton manufacture of Scotland's west coast was buying its way in what was to prove a generally unsuccessful attempt to expand in the Perth area. Despite all this Perth had virtually no direct exports to foreign countries. She imported about £30,000 per annum of goods from abroad, mostly flax, flax seed, wood, iron, and in bad years grain, but if these goods came in a ship over a hundred tons burthen they had to be unloaded several miles down the river and shipped up to Perth by lighter.

Like Dundee, Perth was at the heart of a complex of turnpike roads whose capacities were complementary to the rapidly expanding coastal trade of the port, which consisted of little more than a reinforced and built-up river bank. In 1781 209 vessels cleared outwards from Perth and 581 inwards. In 1791, 319 vessels cleared outward, 588 inward. The most valuable outgoing commodities would be cloth and yarn, mostly destined for London, while there was a substantial range of imports including in addition to those already mentioned increasing quantities of lime and stone for agricultural and building purposes.[15]

So despite its apparent vigour Perth harbour suffered from a variety of difficulties. By any standards Dundee was already in the late eighteenth century the largest and most important Tayside harbour, though it was not nearly so clear then as it was to become in the nineteenth century, that it was also the one with much the greatest potential for development. Perth and Montrose had really reached and passed their peak of relative importance by 1800.

The Ports of the Northern Shore of the Firth of Forth

The ports of the northern shore of the Forth fall into two groups. At the eastern end of this stretch of coastline lie a group of ports; Crail, Kilrenny, the two Anstruthers, and Pittenweem, which were essentially fishing ports and which are best dealt with in a general consideration of the east coast fishing industry. From Dysart westwards, however, there lay a string of linen, coal, and salt ports; Dysart, Kirkcaldy, Kinghorn, Burntisland, Inverkeithing, Culross, and Alloa, to name only the more significant ones. In terms of the taxable capacity of the royal burghs on this stretch of coast, the story in the seventeenth century is one of uneven decline. Dysart, for example, plunged downwards in the assessments, while Kirkcaldy actually increased its share of the assessments until 1683, when it joined a general tendency for all these royal burghs to register sharp falls in their capacity to bear taxation. Partly this decline is probably misleading, for though the royal burghs were important along this stretch of coast, they were intermingled with ports which were burghs of barony, like Leven, Methil, Wester Wemyss, and Aberdour. The distinction between the two kinds of burgh hinged on whether the Crown or a baron had been the immediate feudal superior when the burgh gained its original charter of privileges. Originally the royal burghs, in exchange for bearing a share of national taxation, were endowed with a monopoly of overseas trade. It was always difficult for them to enforce this, and in the period 1660–1707 the burghs of barony managed to persuade the Scottish Parliament formally to breach the royal burghs' monopoly of overseas trade, granting the other burghs extensive rights in the field, in exchange for a contribution to burghal taxation. The whole business was a confused sequence of legislation and counter-legislation, enforcement and evasion. In Fife, a mile from the declining royal burgh of Dysart in the 1690s, one could find the port of Wester Wemyss, which had been licensed as a burgh of barony in 1511, and which was in a flourishing state. It exported not only coal from the lands of its superior, the Earl of Wemyss, but also salt, which was produced in great quantity near the shore, using low-grade coal to evaporate sea water held in great iron pans.[16]

The whole question of the economic fate of the south Fife ports in the eighteenth century is a complex one, for no group of ports complained more bitterly of the effect of foreign wars and the Act of Union. Certainly ports like Kirkcaldy and Burntisland, which depended heavily on hiring out their ships for use in the European carrying trade, were hard hit, when Britain went to war with Louis the fourteenth's France, because the wars disrupted traditional trade patterns. However, there would probably have been a readjustment in the trade of the Fife ports anyhow for two reasons. One was that protectionism was very much on the increase amongst European states, and nowhere more rampant than in France. The other was that the Netherlands were ceasing to be the most profitable market for some Scottish exports. Undoubtedly the restrictive legislation constituting the Old Colonial System of England did cut across links between the Fife ports and the Netherlands when Scotland came within the Old Colonial System after 1707. Nevertheless there would have been a swing towards the London and Baltic trades on the part of Scottish traders in any case.

The south Fife ports went through a difficult period in the late seventeenth and early eighteenth centuries. When he visited Inverkeithing about 1707 Defoe referred to its 'spacious harbour which has lately been much neglected for want of trade'. The spaciousness derived mostly from the natural configuration of Inverkeithing Bay, and the man-made facilities consisted merely of a pier or two. Nevertheless, trade had so picked up by 1738 that Inverkeithing Town Council agreed to lengthen the main pier by sixty feet. This revival of trade occurred in nearly all the south Fife ports as the century went on, though it affected them in different ways and at different times. Thus Dysart, which was not endowed by nature with so good a site for a harbour as Inverkeithing, seems to have sensed a notable improvement in maritime trade after about 1756. The town lay on the edge of a coalfield, but it had other interests in the shape

31

of a vigorous linen industry. By the early 1790s there were 700 to 750 looms in the town producing nearly 800,000 yards of coarse linens or ticks per annum valued at just under £40,000. There was not enough trade from Dysart itself fully to occupy the twenty-three square-rigged vessels and two sloops belonging to the port. Not more than a dozen large ships could lie in the harbour at one time and when a storm blew up from the east, Dysart harbour was very exposed. Its ships were often hired out for the carrying trade when they were not importing flax or exporting coals. In the last analysis the town lacked the financial strength to cope with the deepening and improving of the harbour, and the construction of a dry dock which were clearly called for.

Coal was by far the most important commodity on which the south Fife ports rebuilt their prosperity in the second half of the eighteenth century, though nearly all of them had coal-fired salt pans near the shore from which they exported salt. Thus the parish of Wemyss had two harbours, one at Wester Wemyss, and one at Methil. The latter had been built about 1650 by David, Earl of Wemyss, for exporting his coal. Both were tidal harbours protected by piers in the late eighteenth century, though Wester Wemyss had recently acquired a small basin behind it in which water was trapped to scour the harbour proper at low tide. By the 1790s Wester Wemyss was exporting annually 6,000 tons of coal mainly to Hamburg and Dutch ports like Amsterdam and Middleburg where it was regarded as ideal fuel for light-houses. In addition to coal, however, these two ports exported 40,000 bushels of salt annually to northern Scotland. Imports were, predictably, about ten cargoes of Scandinavian and Baltic timber and iron per annum. A larger Fife coal port like Inverkeithing could be exporting in the late eighteenth century 25,000 tons of coal annually, and as many as forty or fifty ships at a time could be seen lying ready to load there. Most of the coal came from the nearby Halbeath Collieries, linked from the early 1780s to Inverkeithing by a waggon way which greatly facilitated coal exports. To cope with an increasing flow of coal, there had to be some improvement even in a naturally good harbour like Inverkeithing, but before 1800 it consisted only of some modest pier building, and the cutting in 1790 of a new approach channel through a reef in the bay at a cost of £400.[18]

Further west along the coast from Dysart, Kirkcaldy, a town which had been particularly hard hit by the seventeenth-century civil wars and by the effects of the Union of 1707, had by the early 1790s gone some way towards restoring its prosperity. Though it had been very dependent on maritime trade in its hey-day in the early seventeenth century, it was not blessed with a good harbour. Indeed, a commentator in the late eighteenth century recorded the harbour as one of the town's disadvantages, on the grounds that it was narrow, incommodious, and much exposed to heavy seas during easterly gales. As these storms frequently caused extensive damage, the town's financial resources were only adequate to keep the harbour in repair, and could not be expected to stretch to the substantial works necessary to improve it. Kirkcaldy was unimportant as an exporter of coal and salt.

Like Dundee, Kirkcaldy was a substantial urban unit compared with nearby ports, and however much events had hindered development, it retained a capacity for economic expansion, given favourable conditions. Throughout the eighteenth century it built up its linen industry, specialising in lines whose names showed their Dutch origin—striped hollands, Dutch checks, Dutch ticks, Flanders checks and ticks. Wars, particularly wars which interrupted communications with Kirkcaldy's best markets, which were in America and the West Indies, inflicted repeated set-backs, but by the 1790s the manufacturers of Kirkcaldy controlled over 800 looms producing some 900,000 yards of cloth per annum worth about £45,000. Every year the Kirkcaldy manufacturers also bought in about £30,000 of cloth from neighbouring districts. As Fife grew only a seventh of the flax it required, Kirkcaldy imported a great deal of flax from Riga. In the late eighteenth century it was also importing a good deal of linen yarn from Bremen and Hamburg.

33

Interestingly enough, very little of this yarn was used in Kirkcaldy. Instead, it was re-distributed to landward towns like Dunfermline, Falkland, Auchtermuchty, and even Perth, which specialised in coarse linens.

With a steady import of wood, iron, flax, yarns, and foodstuffs, and an export of cloth both by coast and abroad, allied to a long tradition of participation in the carrying trade, Kirkcaldy had a growing merchant marine. In 1760 it had only three ships whose tonnage total was 110. In 1772 it had eleven ships whose total tonnage was 515. By 1782 the figures were twelve and 750 respectively and by 1792 they were up to twenty-nine and 3,700. Between its expanding shipping, and its solid industrial base, Kirkcaldy had the makings of a favourable setting for further harbour development.[19]

On the coast between Kirkcaldy and Inverkeithing lie the harbours of Kinghorn and Burntisland. Both had been significant ports in the sixteenth and early seventeenth centuries, playing an important role in the import-export trade of Scotland and having, like other Fife ports, a particularly close relationship with the Netherlands. By the end of the eighteenth century both had been left behind by history. Kinghorn's major industry was a service to Leith on the other side of the Forth which employed no less than nine boats of about fifty to sixty tons apiece, whereas the whole of the rest of the town's shipping in the 1790s was reduced to a couple of coasting sloops. Until the 1790s there was no profitable textile industry to stimulate the local economy, while the local coal export went through other ports. Only around 1794 did the water-power, represented by the stream which flowed through the town from the nearby Loch of Kinghorn, attract manufacturers who wished to set up small spinning mills using the machinery devised by English innovators like Arkwright, and Kendrew and Porthouse of Darlington.

To set the crown on its decline, Kinghorn had spread the few advantages it had far too thinly by electing to develop two harbours. The original one was the old Kirk-harbour, so called because of its proximity to the church, but about

1760, because this harbour was deemed inconvenient for the boats plying to Leith, another harbour was built at Petty-cur, about half a mile south-west of the town. Unfortunately this new development turned out to be terribly susceptible to silting from the west, so the creation of first one scouring-basin, which proved inadequate, and then another, became essential. The upshot was that Kinghorn was left with two unsatisfactory harbours, neither of which could deal with a vessel of over 150 tons, whereas if all the expenditure at Petty-cur had been sunk into improving the Kirk-harbour, Kinghorn might have acquired a very considerable asset.[20]

Burntisland's story was broadly similar. Before 1707 it had had a substantial export of malt to England and northern Scotland, but this faded without any compensating development of industry, partly because of taxation burdens. Even in the 1790s there was no coal export, and no textile industry. Apart from a sugar refinery and a works manufacturing sulphuric acid, Burntisland was innocent of development. This is extremely interesting, for the town was blessed with what was generally considered to be an unusually fine harbour, with an exceptional depth of water even at low tide, and great potential for development, especially for the construction of dry docks. It seems clear that, though a good harbour was a great asset for any east coast town in the age of accelerating economic growth which was dawning in the late eighteenth century, it was not enough by itself to attract industrial development. The town had to have a certain dynamic of its own, or it had to be the outlet for substantial interests in its hinterland.[21] Burntisland was a curious case of a small port with virtually no hinterland, so its prospects remained bleak until the railway age.

West of the expanding coal port of Inverkeithing there lay in the late eighteenth century a string of harbours of very different kinds. North Queensferry, for example, poised on the Ferryhill peninsula one and three quarters of a mile down the coast from Inverkeithing, was purely a debarcation point for the ferries from Queensferry on the south side of the Forth, which at this point narrows to one and an eighth miles broad. Beyond it lay several other small harbours whose very names sometimes explain their function. Limekilns obviously at one stage in its history employed local coal for firing lime-kilns as well as the more usual salt pans, but in the late eighteenth century it was enjoying unwonted prosperity, along with two other small harbours which lay close to it, Charleston and Torryburn, as one of the ports of Dun-fermline. In Dunfermline there occurred a steady evolution in the linen industry which began making coarse linens, then gradually turned its attention to finer lines until table linen became the staple manufacture of the town. As early as 1749 there were some 400 looms in the parish, and though as late as 1778 only a score of looms in Dunfermline can be shown to have been producing the fine linen called damask, a series of technological break-throughs between 1778 and 1825 con-firmed the ascendancy of the fine lines. Carts conveyed Dunfermline's products to its three small harbours and returned with goods imported through the harbours. As a result Torryburn alone boasted thirteen vessels in the 1790s with a total tonnage of 1,000. Dunfermline merchants actually built a ferry boat for the service between Torryburn and Borrowstounness on the south side of the Forth where they disposed of much fine linen. Charleston, Limekilns, and Torryburn were all adequate harbours in the days when 200 to 300 tons was the largest size of ship seen in the Forth trade. Once an increase in ship size necessitated massive dock improvements, they were at a disadvantage, and their survival depended on a mobilisation of resources for im-provement at which only Charleston proved very effective.[22]

Already in the late eighteenth century there lay to the west of these busy little harbours a port left behind by history. Culross had once been a thriving centre of industry and trade with extensive collieries and a monopoly of the manufacture of iron cooking girdles. However, the coal seams which out-cropped near Culross became exhausted, while the under-ground workings designed to pursue them under the Forth proved unstable. The town's monopolistic rights on cooking girdles were undermined by the Court of Session in 1727, and the Culross craftsmen were hopelessly out of date compared with the large-scale production methods for domestic ironware adopted by organisations like Carron Company which started up on the opposite shore of the Forth in 1759. As the harbour had never been particularly good Culross lost its import as well as its export trade, becoming a sixteenth-century Scots burgh preserved in the aspic of economic atrophy, for the future delight of historians of architecture.[23]

Four miles to the north-west of Culross lies the port of Kincardine-on-Forth, which along with Alloa, brings to an end the succession of ports along the northern shore of the Forth. Kincardine was largely built on reclaimed marsh land filled in with ashes provided by the coal used to fire many local salt pans. At the beginning of the eighteenth century it had less than ten boats, all occupied in carrying salt to Leith and in bringing back wood and iron for the salt pans. Around 1735 there were thirty-five salt pans in the parish producing salt from sea-water and coal. Local shipowners subscribed to build what was known as the High Pier. By 1740 there were sixty vessels of from fifteen to sixty tons belonging to the village. The 1780s were a difficult time for the port because of the decline of the salt export and failure in local distilleries, but in 1786 there were ninety-one ships belonging to Kincardine with a total tonnage of 5,461. Many engaged in the carrying trade. They imported wood, iron, flax, and linseed from the Baltic and Holland, and barley from England and the Carse of Gowrie while exporting coals from Alloa and Clackmannan and other mining areas on or near the Forth, to Dundee, Perth, Norway and Sweden. Despite the failure of its staple trade, and the modest nature of its harbour, Kincardine survived because of the enterprise of its shipowners, in the days of small ships. Significantly, those parts of the town which intrigue contemporary architectural historians include much early nineteenth-century work, giving Kincardine a good century or two of a run for its money over Culross.[24]

In view of the economic implications, it is perhaps a matter

for self-congratulation to Alloa that it offers comparatively
little to enthusiasts for Scottish domestic architecture from
the seventeenth to the early nineteenth century compared
with Culross and Kincardine. As a river-port, a seat of manufacture, and the chief town of the small county of Clackmannan, Alloa has had a history of fairly continuous development. The key to its eighteenth-century prosperity lay
in its coal exports from the collieries which lie immediately
behind it, some of which were to be linked to the harbour by
an early waggon way. Among the local coal owners the Earl
of Mar stood pre-eminent. Though the holder of the title
committed political suicide by leading, with outstanding
lack of success, the Jacobite rebellion of 1715, the family contrived to cling to its estates. From his exile the Jacobite earl
encouraged his family to embark on the manufacture of glass
at Alloa as another outlet for the family coal. The glass
business was eventually sold to a group of capitalists, and
has survived to this day. Industrial survival is in fact one of
the keynotes of Clackmannan's economic history, for it is one
of the few Scottish counties where the old Scottish east coast
woollen manufacture survived into the nineteenth century as
a vigorous, exporting trade.

Under the circumstances, Alloa was likely to have a busy
and improved harbour by the 1790s, and this was indeed the
case. There was a good natural depth of water, at neap tides
from twelve to fifteen feet, and at spring tides from seventeen to twenty-two. In essence the harbour consisted of a pow
or creek formed by a pier of rough-hewn stone and the shore,
with the rivulet which ran through the north-east end of the
town running into it and ineffectually scouring the accumulations of silt. Acts of Parliament were passed in 1754, 1786,
and 1803 allowing local bodies to improve the harbour with
the aid of a small duty levied on ships using it. By the 1790s
not only had the pier been rebuilt and the pow dredged, but
there had also been built a little above the harbour an
excellent dry dock for ship repairs with gates thirty-four and
a half feet wide and sixteen feet of water at spring tides. With
its buoyant export trade, and the usual timber and iron

staples as the foundation of its import trade, Alloa was in confident mood in the late eighteenth century, a mood symbolised by the decision to start building a 'new town' adjacent to the older areas in 1786.[25]

In general, it is difficult to find a unifying factor common to the ports on the north shore of the Forth, comparable with the influence of the linen trade on Tayside. The Forth ports fall into groups like the fishing harbours of the eastern corner or East Neuk of Fife; the linen centres like Kirkcaldy and Dysart; the coal ports like Inverkeithing, Wemyss and Alloa; and a host of minor harbours, some with a great future like Methil in the parish of Wemyss, which was still minute in the 1790s, and some like Culross which had been moribund for a long time by then. Quantitatively the future lay with coal. Salt was in decline, partly because of its poor quality, partly because of competition from English rock salt. Port development in the nineteenth century largely hinged on the export of coal. Nevertheless it is important to recognise that most of these ports had recovered from the immediate post-Union depression by the middle of the eighteenth century.

The Ports of the Southern Shore of the Forth to Eyemouth

From the shore of Stirling a string of ports stretched down the east coast of Scotland as far as Eyemouth. Of them all, Stirling was perhaps the least significant, for though Stirling was for long the lowest bridge point on the Forth, the river below it was so obstructed by fords and rocky shallows that vessels of over seventy tons burthen could not hope to reach it.[26] At the opposite extreme stood Leith, which was by far the most important of east coast, let alone Forth ports. Its significance derived almost entirely from the fact that it was the port of Edinburgh, the capital city, and in the seventeenth and eighteenth centuries the richest city in Scotland. Spared the massacre and plunder which was the lot of so many east coast burghs in the seventeenth century, Edinburgh not only remained the richest Scottish burgh, but also became richer relative to the others after the middle of the seventeenth century. In Edinburgh lay the focus of much fashionable life, of the law, the church, and until 1707 of parliamentary activity. Naturally, Leith, which until well into the nineteenth century was separated by green fields from Edinburgh was pre-eminently an importing port. In terms of exports it was not nearly so significant. Because Edinburgh was the only royal burgh, and also the dominant economic influence in Midlothian, Edinburgh's port was naturally the only port of consequence in the county.

If, however, Edinburgh-Leith merits consideration as a unit in its own right, the other ports on the southern side of the Forth naturally fall into two groups. First there are the ports to the west of Leith, the ports of Stirlingshire and West Lothian. In the eighteenth century several ports on this stretch of coast were taking advantage of the seventeenth-century developments which had turned them into a trading outlet to the North Sea for Glasgow and other western burghs like Ayr and Dumfries. Great quantities of imported goods in particular flowed through Bo'ness for subsequent cartage west. On top of this, the southern shore of the Upper Forth has as hinterland one of Scotland's old-established coalfields whose prosperity generated the usual exports of salt and coal, as well as a good volume of import demand. The second group of ports are those to the west of Leith, the ports of East Lothian and Berwickshire. Though the royal burghs of East Lothian fared badly after about 1650, the coast of the county boasted a string of burghs of barony and regality developed by private proprietors as outlets for the coal, salt, and corn which the agriculturally rich, but coal-bearing land of East Lothian produced in substantial quantities. The extension of the coast to the southern frontier of Scotland was not particularly rich in ports, and of these the more southerly ones like Eyemouth were essentially import-export points for a largely agricultural hinterland.

First then, we turn to Leith, and to its relationship with Edinburgh. That relationship has not always been a happy one. Indeed when the Protestant Lords of the Congregation were attacking their Roman Catholic Regent, Mary of

Guise, and her French troops, who had fortified themselves in Leith, they referred in a pronouncement in 1559 to the long-standing hatreds known to exist between Edinburgh and the town of Leith. The basis of this hostility is, however, often misunderstood, for it is usually thought to be rooted in the fact that Edinburgh became the feudal superior of Leith, largely by royal grant. This is, of course, true. The Stewart kings were always anxious to appease their politically significant capital city, and it was easy enough to gratify the desire of Edinburgh Town Council to replace the lairds of Restalrig and the Abbot and monks of Holyrood as feudal superior of Edinburgh's port of Leith. This happened in stages of which one significant one came in the reign of James the Third when Edinburgh Town Council was given sole right to the customs of Leith. Mary of Lorraine, in an attempt to win support in Leith, promised to give the town some legal standing to resist Edinburgh by erecting it into a burgh of barony, but by 1560 she had lost her war, and Edinburgh resumed its siege of Leith's legal autonomy by offering the crown loans against possession of the feudal superiority, or virtual ownership of Leith. Finally in 1603 James the Sixth confirmed the grip of Edinburgh over Leith as feudal superior in what was known, in Edinburgh, as the Golden Charter.

In fact, all these manoeuvres merely set the seal on a situation which would have arisen anyhow, and ensured that Leith was prevented from trying to organise any sort of counter-attack. Edinburgh was the only royal burgh in Midlothian. In exchange for its contribution to the revenues of the crown, it enjoyed a monopoly of trading rights, not only within its own bounds, but also over a wide stretch of territory around. The precise boundary of this surrounding territory is a matter of debate, but it was always clear that Leith lay within it, and her inhabitants were in theory forbidden to buy or sell except in the market places of Edinburgh, by virtue of Edinburgh's inherent status. This inevitably had serious consequences for Leith which from the sixteenth century had more intercourse with foreign lands

41

than any port in Scotland. There were other ports on this stretch of coast which were equally thirled or tied to an inland royal burgh. Good examples are Blackness on the upper Forth, which was the port and possession of Linlithgow, and Aberlady, in East Lothian, which was the port of Haddington. Neither Blackness nor Aberlady were however of any real consequence by the eighteenth century, whereas Leith, the principal port of the realm, and the granary and warehouse of its capital was so vigorous that an observer once remarked;

> were Leith a free and independent town Edinburgh would soon empty itself into Leith which has occasioned its suffering great hardships to prevent its engrossing the trade and commerce of Edinburgh.

In practice Edinburgh aimed at conserving a monopoly of trade in the hands of its own burgesses, and used as its principal instrument for doing this its control of local government in Leith. From 1567 down to the passing of the Municipal Reform Act of 1833, the Bailies, or principal magistrates, of Leith were appointed by the Town Council of Edinburgh, so for 266 years the shipowners and craftsmen of Leith in particular regarded the great merchants who used their port as in a sense an alien aristocracy sustained by outside authority. Nevertheless, the Edinburgh authorities, for reasons of enlightened self-interest, had every motive to try to uphold the primacy of Leith amongst the ports of Scotland, even at the cost of sinking money into harbour improvement.[28]

As early as 1710 the Corporation of Edinburgh humbly petitioned Queen Anne to instruct the Royal Navy to set about constructing a wet dock and a dry dock at Leith for the convenience of building, fitting and careening ships of war and trading vessels. The Corporation no doubt hoped to avoid most of the expense of port improvement by this patriotic device, but the government was not so easily gulled. When port improvement works did start at Leith in 1717 the government confined its assistance to prolonging for nineteen years a duty of two pennies Scots (or one-sixth of a penny Sterling) payable on every pint of ale and beer sold in the city. As it was, the improvements, whose most notable feature was a new stone pier on the line of an old wooden one, though poorly executed, were very expensive and doubled Edinburgh's town debt to £50,000. Yet the harbour was still encumbered with a dangerous bar of shifting sand after the improvements were completed about 1730. Already the urgency of improvement and the parlous state of Edinburgh's finances were apparent. In 1753 an act was passed for deepening and widening the harbour of Leith, but as the statute provided no means of defraying the expense involved, nothing was done. When the city fathers of Edinburgh devised an even more ambitious scheme of dock development, to be financed by additional levies on shipping, the shipowners of Leith showed such signs of militant resentment that their overlords withdrew the scheme.[29]

The need for improvement at Leith harbour was becoming very acute, for after about 1745 there had been a spectacular increase in the volume of shipping using the port. This was largely a response to an increase in the tempo of economic life in Edinburgh and Leith. Underlying factors included improvements in landward transport ranging from the replacement of the sleds which were the common vehicle in Edinburgh until the late seventeenth century by wheeled carts, to the creation of a network of turnpike roads after the passing of enabling legislation in 1751. Banking played a part, because banks could offer credit. The Bank of Scotland had been founded in Edinburgh in 1695, and it was followed by the Royal Bank of Scotland in 1727. Eventually branch banks were established in Leith, the first being a branch of the British Linen Company, itself founded in 1746 mainly because the two older Scottish banks were very slow to develop branch banking. New industries established themselves in Leith such as oil works, and sugar refining. Older Leith industries, such as glass making, greatly expanded, mainly because of an increasing demand for bottles. In 1712 the combined populations of Edinburgh and Leith were about 48,000, but by 1754 the figure had risen by nearly a fifth to over 57,000. The harbour not only grew with the population it served, but also far outstripped the rate of demographic growth. Despite its poor situation at the head of a flat, sandy, and muddy shore, with its inadequate facilities, the port of Leith saw its volume of trade increase sevenfold in the twenty-five years after 1745.

In 1788 an Act of Parliament was passed empowering the Town Council of Edinburgh to build a wet dock twenty acres in extent at Leith, near the old harbour. There were provisions for further improvements and Edinburgh was authorised to borrow £30,000 for these purposes, partly on the security of the port revenues. In retrospect this last provision was momentous, but at the time the most remarkable phenomenon associated with this act was how little it achieved apart from a bridge and a few street improvements. It would have ranked as the non-event of Leith's late eighteenth-century history, had it not been for a wholly futile joint stock company founded in 1791 to cut a canal from Leith to Lanark.[30]

The author of an account of Edinburgh and Leith published in the *Old Statistical Account of Scotland* in 1793 remarked that in 1791 the registered tonnage of shipping using Leith was 130,000. He added that, 'magnificent plant have been formed for enlarging the present harbour, which is found much too small for the number of ships resorting to it.' The writer then went on to drive home his point by underlining the huge volume of goods moving in and out of the port. Several hundred Leith ships alone were involved in the Baltic trade, taking back to Leith not only the usual wood and iron, but also much tallow for the candle manufacture. When there was a bad harvest in the fertile corn fields of the Lothians, as there was in 1783, great quantities of grain would be imported through Leith to feed its people and those of the capital. Coal from other Forth ports came into Leith in appreciable quantities. Even though Leith harbour was a major outlet for the industries of Leith, like sugar and glass, and for those of Edinburgh, like brewing and printing, there was always a fair number of ships leaving Leith in ballast, so dominant was the import trade. Nevertheless by 1790 Leith had reached a point of crisis which other eastern ports in Scotland reached. Improvement was imperative if the harbour was to retain its importance and expand, but the financial soundness of the unreformed Edinburgh Town Council was so dubious as to cast doubt over any serious progress.[31]

On the coast of Stirlingshire and West Lothian there had already been extensive changes in the relative importance of the various ports long before the eighteenth century. Stirling itself had in the thirteenth century ranked with Perth as one of the two busiest harbours in Scotland, and one of the two most lucrative from the point of view of Scotland's king, who levied dues on seaborne traffic there. By the eighteenth century not only had Stirling ceased to be of any real consequence as a port, but the attempt by another ancient royal burgh, Linlithgow, to play Edinburgh to Blackness's Leith had also foundered, partly on the inadequacies of the harbour of Blackness, and partly on the intransigence of the rising port of Bo'ness (or Borrowstounness to give it its full title). Bo'ness was fortunate enough to secure the backing of the powerful Duke of Hamilton who first helped it to fight off Linlithgow's opposition to it achieving the status and privileges of a burgh of barony, and then helped Bo'ness to secure the transfer of the local custom house from Blackness to Bo'ness. This last move was an acknowledgement of a very rapid phase of growth during which Bo'ness, a mere handful of houses in the sixteenth century, developed into the second most important port on the east coast of Scotland by 1750. In large measure this expansion was the result of Bo'ness's role as window on the North Sea for the merchants of Scotland's west coast. However, Bo'ness itself was to experience something of the sense of being left behind by developments, even though it was never to decline to the level of the ossified port of Blackness, with its decaying warehouses and deserted shore.[32]

It was the arrival of the canal age in Scotland which raised up the rival port of Grangemouth to steal away much of the glory of Bo'ness. The father of eighteenth-century canal engineering was the Englishman James Brindley (1716–72) who developed a network of canals in the Midlands and North of England, linking the Staffordshire potteries and the Cheshire salt works with the outside world, as well as Manchester and its surrounding area with Liverpool and the Mersey. Topographically, Scotland was much less favourable to large-scale canal construction than England, but the idea of linking the Firth of Clyde and the Firth of Forth by means of a canal across the narrow 'waist' of Scotland was so obvious that it had been mooted in the seventeenth century before being first seriously surveyed on behalf of the British government by one Alexander Gordon in 1726. No action followed until the Board of Trustees for Fisheries and Manufactures in Scotland commissioned the Yorkshire engineer John Smeaton, who had finished the Eddystone Lighthouse in 1759, to make a fresh survey in 1763. His report, submitted in 1764, set in motion a protracted period of argument and lobbying over the course and scope of the proposed scheme. At first the rich tobacco merchants of Glasgow, anxious to re-export American tobacco to the continent and conscious of the assistance which a Forth and Clyde canal would offer to this operation, were furious because the proposed course of the canal ignored Glasgow. Once the Glasgow interests had used the weight of their money to take control of the canal project, Edinburgh took fright and threw its influence into the balance against the project. As parliamentary legislation was essential if the canal was to be built, the possibilities of lobbying were immense.

Ironically Bo'ness, which of all established ports suffered most in the long run from the canal, soon sensed the danger inherent in the fact that the proposed eastern outlet of the canal was several miles up the Forth from it, near the mouth of the River Carron. As early as 1767 the merchants of Bo'ness, in a bid to preserve their port's relative importance on the Forth, petitioned for a canal from Carronshore to

Bo'ness of the same width and depth as that from Glasgow to Carronshore, and the promoters of the Bill whose passage was essential if the main canal project was to be embarked upon chose to compromise. When the bill became an Act in 1768, it provided for a canal from Carronshore to Bo'ness, but this was to be executed by an independent company with a capital of £5,000 or £8,000. This proved a gross under-estimate and by 1796 the shareholders of the company set up to construct the Carronshore to Bo'ness canal decided to cut their losses and abandon the half-finished work.[33]

Thus by 1791 there was a rapidly-growing community called Grangemouth at the eastern terminal of a canal which ran across Scotland to connect with Glasgow and the upper reaches of the Clyde, and was navigable by vessels of seventy tons. Since 1759 there had existed just north, a short distance up the Carron, the iron works of Carron Company. This company had originally been founded by two Englishmen, Samual Garbett and John Roebuck, and a Scot, William Cadell. After a major financial crisis due to over-extension of financial commitments in 1772, the company went on to become a stable concern producing a wide variety of goods on a scale without parallel in contemporary Scotland. The basic product of the Carron furnaces was pig iron, but from the start finished goods like ploughshares, axle bushes, pots and pans, and agricultural implements were churned out in bulk. By the last quarter of the eighteenth century the firm had developed strong interests in five main fields—the production of cylinders, cast-iron pipes, stoves and grates, nails and ordnance. In the last-named field, after a difficult start during which the Board of Ordnance showed deep suspicion of the quality of Carron guns, Carron Company established perhaps its most lucrative trade which was duly crowned by the immense success of the short-barrelled quick-firing gun called the Carronade. Obviously the proximity of such a heavy industrial complex, with bulk imports of raw materials and a substantial export trade was bound to affect the development of Grangemouth. On the other hand, the outlet of the canal was south of the natural mouth of the

Carron and Grangemouth was sited around the canal outlet.

Ideally Carron Company would have liked the eastern outlet of the canal to be the mouth of the Carron, and when this proved impractical the company placed pressure on the promoters of the canal to have a subsidiary canal built linking the main canal to the works at Carron. The canal promoters accepted the idea in theory, only to kill it by endless procrastination. Eventually Carron Company, which never owned more than a handful of ships itself but which made heavy use of shipping facilities, bowed to the inevitable and built itself a wharf at Grangemouth. From an early stage in the history of Carron Company a director of the firm established a shipping company legally distinct from Carron Company but geared to its needs for bulk imports of iron ore and limestone and for the export of finished products.[34] Altogether the proximity of Carron works was a useful supplement to the basic trade of Grangemouth which, like that of Bo'ness, consisted of importing grain in bad years and Baltic products at all times. Especially during war, Glasgow and other merchants preferred to import Baltic tallow, hemp, wood, and iron through the Forth rather than run the risks of storms and privateers which attended a passage round the North of Scotland. Both Bo'ness and Grangemouth suffered from the interruptions to the Baltic trade which followed the outbreak of war with France in 1793, but by then Grangemouth was well established and clearly held an edge of advantage on its older rival.[35] For a town only founded in 1777, this was an achievement.

The only other harbour of real consequence on the southern shore of the Forth west of Leith around 1790 was that of South Queensferry. It was not particularly impressive as a harbour, even by late eighteenth-century Scottish standards, consisting of little more than a pier for the ferry. Apart from the ferry South Queensferry had no economic importance. Its one manufacture, soap, had virtually collapsed by 1789, and its reliance on the ferry to and from Fife was so apparent that its inhabitants actually raised the money to repair the crumbling ferry pier in the 1790s.[36]

48

East of Leith the ports and harbours of the coast divided, as has been said, into two groups. First came a group of East Lothian ports of which Port Seton, Prestonpans, Morison's Haven, Cockenzie, and Musselburgh were the most significant, which were essentially outlets for the grain, coal, and salt of their immediate hinterland, as well as points through which commodities like Norwegian timber, much in demand in the local coal mines, could be imported. Really no distinction can be drawn between Port Seton, Morison's Haven, and Prestonpans, for they were part of a single complex of which Prestonpans was the industrial heart and Morison's Haven and Port Seton the ports. Prestonpans, though a coastal town, lacked a decent harbour, but it had by the second half of the eighteenth century become an industrial centre.

As the name suggests, Prestonpans had early become celebrated for salt. By the 1790s four of the ten existing salt-pans in the parish were out of use, but the remaining six produced a fair volume of salt. In addition to this the Cadell family started up near the parish church in the 1750s a manufacture of stoneware pottery which by the 1790s employed seventy men and boys. There was also a smaller pottery manufacture at Morison's Haven. In 1749 there was set up at Prestonpans the first sulphuric acid works in Scotland. It was set up by Dr John Roebuck, who had studied chemistry and medicine at Edinburgh and Leyden, and who undoubtedly was aware of the possibilities of selling his acid as a bleaching agent to the expanding linen industry of Scotland. One must not exaggerate the importance of this development of industry. Prestonpans seems to have existed as a centre of salt manufacture as early as the twelfth century, yet in the early nineteenth century its basic pattern was still that of a single street parallel with the beach in so rough a way as to earn the taunt that it was 'zig-zag at both ends and crooked in the middle'.

Nevertheless, Port Seton, about a mile to the east of Prestonpans, was before 1707 and for some years after it a busy little port importing goods from the Baltic, the Nether-

49

lands, France, and America, and exporting not only the goods of its own immediate hinterland, but also some of the products of the North of England. Smuggling goods across the border into England, and exporting to France English goods like wool whose exportation was forbidden were the keys to the profitability of this trade which naturally declined after 1707. Losses at sea could not be replaced when profits were sagging, so by 1743 the trade had virtually collapsed. Morison's Haven had by the 1790s largely replaced Port Seton as the outlet for Prestonpans. Its name derived from the former proprietors of the estate of Prestongrange, but its real importance hinged on a sheltered harbour with ten feet of water at most tides. Morison's Haven exported some coal, a deal of salt, pottery and sulphuric acid, the produce of Prestonpans and the area around. Imports included grain and raw materials for the acid and pottery works. It is interesting to note that for the pottery alone clay had to be brought from Devonshire, flint from Gravesend and white and red lead from London, Hull, and Newcastle.[37]

Neither Musselburgh nor Cockenzie possessed the economic vitality of Prestonpans. Musselburgh, which lies only a few miles to the east of Edinburgh, derived its importance almost entirely from acting as a centre for the surrounding area, and, in association with the nearby harbour of Fisherrow, as an import-export point. The one exception to this generalisation was the presence of a large distillery which, despite the proximity of good grain-growing land, needed to import much of its raw material. Despite the vigour of several collieries around Musselburgh, there was no great volume of coal exports in the 1790s, and harbour dues derived from fish, grain, wood and iron, all of which entered in fair quantities. Cockenzie, which lies a mile or two to the east of Prestonpans, was still in the 1790s an important producer of salt. The produce of several flourishing nearby collieries was used for this manufacture. Apart from the export of salt, and the import of wood and iron, trade was dull.[38] All the coal and salt harbours east of Edinburgh wore a somewhat downtrodden air in the late eighteenth century, for their merchant shipping had fallen almost entirely into the hands of others, often Edinburgh merchants.

Only at North Berwick, twenty-two miles along the coast to the east of Leith and beyond Haddington's decaying port of Aberlady, can it be said that a new sequence of ports and harbours began. In the late eighteenth century there was definitely a group of county ports of which North Berwick, Dunbar and Eyemouth were the most significant which lay beyond the immediate sphere of the influence of Edinburgh-Leith, in a way that the coal and salt ports did not. North Berwick, with some 700 inhabitants in the early 1790s, was not a particularly important town. It had no manufactures, and the only substantial trade from its port consisted in the export of grain grown in its fertile hinterland. Dunbar was altogether a more important place with a harbour which had been substantially improved in the early eighteenth century. Prior to that Dunbar harbour, like most other harbours on the southern shore of the Forth, consisted of a pier on a muddy shore, and it could cope with only a few small ships. The improvements consisted of enlarging and improving the harbour by digging into solid rock to a depth of eight feet, and then constructing extensive quays. Though the harbour remained small and difficult of access, the parish minister hailed the improvements in the *Old Statistical Account* as 'the very making of the town and its trade'. With the help of the Convention of Royal Burghs, Dunbar financed a new west pier at the end of the century, and in the same period constructed a large and convenient dry dock.[39] Indeed what is now known as the Old Harbour of Dunbar appears to have assumed roughly its present form by 1730, and the late eighteenth-century improvements increased the efficiency of a busy port complex which in addition to the usual range of Baltic imports was a notable grain port, exporting in good years, importing in bad. The survival into the second half of the twentieth century of the early eighteenth-century grain-store called Spotts Granary, at the Old Harbour, is a monument to this phase in Dunbar's story.[40]

Eyemouth was hardly a port of the calibre of Dunbar in

the late eighteenth century. It more resembled North Berwick in its relatively unimproved state, and in the limited character of its trade in the late eighteenth century. It exported grain, chiefly barley and oats, and numbers of sheep and cattle. Though the absence of coal under the soil of Berwickshire might lead one to look for an import of coal, this did not occur, because Eyemouth was less than twenty miles from the nearest English collieries, and it was normal, especially after the development of a turnpike road system from 1772, to import coals by cart.[41]

SHIPBUILDING AND FISHING

Of these two topics shipbuilding is the easiest to summarise, for ships were still small and wooden, and wherever there was an import of Baltic timber there could be, and usually was by the late eighteenth century, a shipyard. Even Perth built ships of sixty to seventy tons burthen, and in the ports on the northern shore of the Forth vessels only a little larger were built and used in such distant trades as the West Indian and the American. This undifferentiated shipbuilding industry scattered along the coast represented a great step forward compared with the seventeenth century and earlier when Scotsmen often went abroad for their ships, but clearly any substantial increase in the size of vessels, let alone any major increase in complexity in the technology involved in building them, was likely to lead to specialisation and decline in those smaller ports which could not keep pace with change.

Fishing was a more complex tale on the east coast, even though the central fact about the North Sea fisheries in the first half of the eighteenth century was simplicity itself. This was that the Dutch virtually monopolised the herring fishery, which was by far the most lucrative one off the shores of Scotland. From the seventeenth century the British Crown sought to break this monopoly by a mixture of naval force and state-sponsored corporations like the Association for the

Fishing which received its charter in 1632, and the Royal Fishery chartered in 1661. Neither was very successful because Scotsmen could not mobilise enough capital to compete with the hundreds of specialised Dutch herring boats or busses which moved down the east coast and into the Firth of Forth with the herring shoals, often under escort of Dutch warships. The Board of Trustees for Fisheries and Manufactures offered premiums to encourage Scotsmen to invest in equipment for deep-sea fishing, but by the 1740s the board had lost heart due to lack of response, and a series of Acts of Parliament after 1745, which also offered subsidies, proved no more successful. Scots fishermen were still in the 1790s largely confined to coastal fishing, except in the field of whale fishing where a series of acts from 1733 onwards offered sufficiently handsome subsidies to awaken a real response. In 1750 the continuous traceable history of Scottish Arctic whaling began when some Edinburgh merchants financed a whaler sailing out of Leith. By 1754 there was a Dundee Whale Fishing Company with its own whaler. Rising demand for oil in the late 1780s led to further growth. By 1788 Dundee had three whalers, Leith six, and Dunbar five. Though the whaling industry's most rapid growth still lay in the future, these whalers of 200 or 300 tons, represented a real success for subsidised economic growth.[42]

Whaling apart, it was the inshore fishing for lobsters and white fish like cod, ling, turbot and whiting that mattered. On the south shore of the Forth oyster beds or scalps were very important. The shallowness of these waters suited oysters admirably. At Aberlady, for example, though vessels of sixty to seventy tons could reach the pier at spring tides in the 1790s, low tide revealed two miles of mud.[43] North of the Tay lobsters were the regional speciality, and Montrose had a unique position as a bulk exporter of river salmon. On top of this geographical specialisation there was a great deal of specialisation between coastal communities. The larger ones did not do much coastal fishing. Dundee and Arbroath are good examples, but the latter had just north of it the specialised fishing village of Auchmithie, and this

53

satellite relationship with a larger town was common amongst the many small fishing communities scattered down the coast. On the whole, the white fishing was in a sluggish state at the end of the eighteenth century, as a glance at any of the entries in the *Old Statistical Account* for the fishing towns of the East Neuk of Fife confirms. Whether it be Crail, Elie, Pittenweem, or the Anstruthers, the tale is the same. The number of ships sailing out of these ports was much lower than it had been in the seventeenth century, and though they had quite reasonable harbours and a strong inshore fishing tradition, none of them felt particularly prosperous.[44]

CONCLUSION

By the end of the eighteenth century the ports of this coast were surprisingly unimproved, and yet clearly on the verge of rapid change, if only because the tempo of economic life in Scotland was accelerating as never before. That acceleration was bound to put heavy strain on port facilities, partly because of the importance of overseas trade, and partly because of the immense need for coastal shipping in an age when land transport over long distances was prohibitively expensive. Turnpike roads were local in impact.

Apart from a degree of specialisation between fishing and non-fishing communities, specialisation was not a dominant feature of the ports of this coast even as late as 1800. There was a wide distribution of roughly comparable port facilities, as well as a wide distribution of ancillary activities such as shipbuilding. Technological change had not yet become a disruptive factor. Grangemouth had, however, failed to avert the growth of Bo'ness after the construction of the Forth and Clyde canal, and Perth had tried and failed to take advantage of the new canal technology with abortive schemes for linking it with Loch Earn and, more realistically, Strathmore.[45] In these two examples we perhaps see the first signs of that tide of selective development in the wake of economic and technological change which was to set the pattern of the nineteenth century.

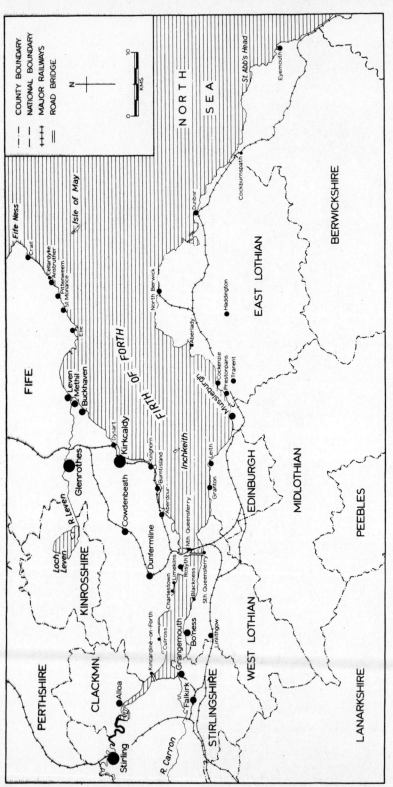

The Firth of Forth Ports

CHAPTER II

The First Era of Massive Improvement

INTRODUCTION

The early nineteenth century was a period when extensive developments in port facilities on the east coast of Scotland south of Stonehaven had become inevitable. After a period of stagnation during the wars with France between 1689 and 1713, there had been a steady growth in the size of the British mercantile marine throughout the eighteenth century. During two periods the overseas trade of Britain virtually doubled during that century. The first lay between the years 1735 and 1760, when the governing factor in the increase in overseas trade was a great expansion in trade with the British colonial empire. On the whole, it was ports on the west coast which were in a position to reap the maximum benefit from this opportunity. Between 1785 and 1800, however, another spectacular expansion in overseas trade was based more on the expansion of a few key manufacturing industries within Britain, amongst which textiles took pride of place. The Scottish east coast linen industry naturally participated in this economic growth, as did the coal and iron industries which lay on the shores of the Forth. The increasing prosperity of adjacent industrial areas was inevitably reflected in Edinburgh, Scotland's social and administrative capital, which in its turn generated more demand for shipping space because of its increasing consumption of

57

imported commodities. Many of the products of Scottish east-coast industries were first shipped to London before distribution overseas. Many of the goods imported for consumption in the urban centres on and inland from the coast came by sea from elsewhere in Britain. There was, therefore, a substantial increase in coastal as well as in overseas shipping using the ports between Montrose and Eyemouth.

It was possible for a port to be over-ambitious in its construction of docks in the early nineteenth century. The classic illustration is Bristol, which between 1804 and 1809 created a new course of over two miles for one stretch of the River Avon, turning the old course into a princely floating harbour. However, Bristol subsequently quite failed to make use of the full potential of its new harbour. Although Bristol had industries, they were largely of a processing and refining nature natural in a port which was a vast distribution centre for the Irish and colonial trades. In an age when manufacturing industry and its canal communications were beginning to dominate economic life, Bristol was just left behind. Ports like Dundee and Leith, not to mention a dozen or so smaller ones on the same stretch of coast, entered the nineteenth century in a much happier position. There was strong and steady growth both in manufacturing industry, and in consumption, in their hinterlands, and apart from the odd cyclical depression, it seemed reasonable to expect that growth to continue indefinitely.[1]

The main problem was which ports would contrive to extract the maximum of advantage from this economic growth. As all existing harbour facilities were to a greater or lesser extent inadequate to deal with a really large volume of trade, there was a premium on improvement. Where there was an element of rivalry between adjacent ports, the first to improve its facilities would clearly forge ahead. Improvement, however, cost money on a scale which gave the larger ports a substantial advantage provided they could overcome the very tangled political problems which were inseparable from any attempt to embark upon ambitious public works. The main obstacle to efficiency was the unreformed system of local government which the early nineteenth-century Scots burghs inherited from the eighteenth century. As both Leith and Dundee are admirable examples of just how tangled those problems could be, their histories in this the first, and perhaps the greatest age of substantial port improvement on the coast, provides a natural core for this chapter.

IMPROVEMENTS IN THE FIRTH OF FORTH PORTS

The early nineteenth century was a period when the profession of civil engineer was emerging as a very important one in an industrialising Britain, and several of the early giants of the profession were active on the east coast of Scotland. John Smeaton is a case in point. He had been a consultant on the Forth and Clyde canal project from 1764. He furnished the designs for the new bridge over the Tay at Perth, which was opened in 1772, and which, after widening, is still carrying a heavy load of modern traffic. It was Eyemouth, the most southerly of the Firth of Forth harbours, which first called on Smeaton's talents for the task of improvement. In an age of sail Eyemouth, situated at the mouth of the Firth of Forth, was a convenient harbour of refuge for ships prevented by contrary winds from pursuing their voyage deeper into the firth or further north up the east coast of Scotland. Its own harbour, as Smeaton himself pointed out, lay at the corner of a bay and was so oriented that ships could work in and out of it at all times of the tide, or lie at anchor secure from all winds except those from the north or the north-east. Although such winds were infrequent on a coast where the prevailing wind is westerly or south-westerly, they could be dangerous, and Smeaton supplied plans for a breakwater pier which was erected in 1770 and which protected the harbour from north-easterly gales.

Because Smeaton utilised an existing ledge of rock for the foundation of his pier, its cost was kept down to £2,500. For that sum Eyemouth secured not only a safer but also a larger harbour, which was further improved between 1770 and 1841 by clearing away rocks and shingle, and by building wharves. Apart from its use as a harbour of refuge, Eyemouth had a fair volume of coastal trade. By the 1840s its once reasonably prosperous, if never very large, fishing industry was in decay and herring and white fish were no longer being sent in any quantity to Leith. However, there had been a resurgence of corn production in the immediate hinterland necessitating the construction of new granaries adjacent to the harbour by 1841, and sustaining a fair volume of trade out of the port. Eyemouth's improvement had been relatively painless, relatively cheap, and relatively advantageous to most other ports in the Firth of Forth, for apart from its own purely local imports and exports, Eyemouth was simply a sea tavern conveniently placed on an otherwise hostile shore to offer succour, in the age of sail, to vessels foiled by adverse winds.[2]

Not all port improvements could be regarded with equanimity by other ports in the Firth of Forth. Where ports were not too far apart, there was bound to be an element of rivalry leading to competitive schemes for improvement. An example of this is the group of coal ports on the northern shore of the Firth of Forth. The front runner as far as progressive improvement was concerned was probably Inverkeithing. The burgh continued its record of close co-operation with the Halbeath Colliery Company. The two bodies combined to deepen the harbour substantially in 1805. In 1821 a new east pier was constructed. By 1825 there was further pier construction and extension, some of it at the expense of the Halbeath Company which ran its existing waggonway for horse-drawn waggons right on to one of the piers. Around 1836 twenty vessels ranging in tonnage from twenty to a hundred tons belonged to the port and foreign and English vessels which came in for coal often discharged bark, timber and bones. In addition to the coal exports of the Halbeath Company, another 23,000 tons of coal were on average exported through Inverkeithing every year between

1839 and 1844 by the following companies; the Cowden-beath Colliery, Dunfermline Colliery, Hill of Beath Colliery, Dunfermline Coal, and Townhill Colliery. By 1838 further attempts were being made to improve the entry to the harbour, and by the time the railway age reached Inverkeithing with the conversion of the Halbeath Company's line from a waggonway to a railway in 1840, it was clear that further increases in the size of ships would necessitate even more drastic development.[3]

With improvement in the air at the coal ports, it is not surprising that the great civil engineer John Rennie, a native of East Lothian educated in Dunbar, should have been called upon to report on several of their harbours in the early nineteenth century. Around 1807 Rennie was working on Berwick harbour when he was asked to survey the possibilities of improving Charleston harbour. That small harbour had been built up close to the existing harbour of Limekilns mainly because of the exertions of the Earl of Elgin, whose seat of Broomhall lay a mere three quarters of a mile to the east. It was meant to be the principal outlet for the lime, limestone, coal and ironstone from the Elgin estates, and from 1778 the Earl of Elgin had sunk a good deal of money in laying out the harbour and village. However, the further improvements suggested by Rennie in his report were never executed.

This was something which quite often happened after Rennie had produced a report on possible improvements in a Scottish east-coast port. The reason was simple—cost. Thus improvements Rennie suggested at St Andrews harbour would have cost that small town nearly £19,000, so the remarkable fact is not that the whole scheme was never executed, but that part of it was. Another port which called on Rennie's services was Alloa, where he surveyed during 1808 and where he recommended a programme of improvement and dock construction which when executed cost nearly £36,000.[4] The fact that Alloa, like Inverkeithing, could rise to such formidable expenditure was significant. Inverkeithing raised the money by co-operation between the burgh and private companies. Alloa took the more dramatic step of transferring harbour development to a board of trustees who by Acts of Parliament of 1754, 1786, and 1803 were empowered to rebuild and develop the port.

Such a body was much more likely to command respect than the unreformed governments of the Scottish burghs, which before 1833 were corrupt and self-perpetuating oligarchies. In Kirkcaldy, another important port on the northern shore of the Forth, a compromise had been reached by a statute of 1829. The actual management of the harbour was by this act placed in the hands of a body of trustees or commissioners. Their composition reflected the major groups interested in harbour development, for in addition to the provost of Kirkcaldy, two bailies, the dean of guild and the treasurer, all representatives of the town council, they included three representatives of the shipowners and shipmasters, as well as three merchants, and two representatives of the landed interest of Fife. The revenue of the harbour remained the property of the town, whose main source of revenue it was. On the other hand the commissioners were a very real watchdog to ensure that harbour interests were not neglected, and the state of Kirkcaldy's finances was not such as to compel the town council to starve the harbour of development funds. In fact development was rather slow at Kirkcaldy, but when it became apparent that any further delay in improving port facilities might lead to a substantial loss of trade to adjacent and more progressive ports, a civil engineer called James Leslie, from Dundee, was called in. Despite the fact that his plan for extending the east pier was to cost £10,000, the town council also agreed to long-term plans for spending £20—£30,000 on further improvements, and the construction began in the 1840s.[5]

The process of transferring control of a major port, either managerial or financial or both, from an unreformed town council was, of course, a much more difficult proposition when that council's finances were so disastrous that plundering the harbour revenues was essential to avoid municipal bankruptcy. Under such circumstances the rising commercial and manufacturing interest, excluded from the municipal oligarchy and desperate for the port improvement which was essential if crippling transport bottlenecks were not to arise, was usually determined to keep the oligarchs' hands off the very large sums involved in major reconstruction, not to mention the increased revenues that would flow from an increased volume of trade after the improvements. Equally, the oligarchy was bound to fight to hold on to the only buoyant source of revenue available to mitigate the effects of the ages of peculation and incompetence which had brought most major Scottish towns to declared or undeclared bankruptcy by the third decade of the nineteenth century.

Leith had the misfortune to be hopelessly entangled with the ruinous finances of the city of Edinburgh. At the same time, pressure for extensive harbour improvement at Leith was irresistible when other ports on the southern shore of the Forth were steadily investing in better port facilities. Grangemouth was fortunate in having the resources of the Forth and Clyde canal behind it. In 1836 Parliament gave its approval to legislation entitling the directors of the canal to construct a dock at Grangemouth. Opened in 1843, it acquired, over the course of the years, the epithet of the Old Dock. With it, Grangemouth left the era of purely tidal harbours behind.[6] Grangemouth's great rival, Bo'ness also indulged in extensive harbour construction in the first four decades of the nineteenth century. Because of the extensive stretches of mud-flat along the southern shore of the Forth, serious improvement was bound to involve heavy expenditure. Bo'ness harbour consisted of two great piers carried out into the firth. The western pier, which was the one first erected, had its extremity bent towards the east, and the eastern pier approached close enough to that extremity to leave only a narrow entrance to an almost completely sheltered basin. Though the basin was still tidal in the 1840s, it was equipped with a smaller scouring basin at its landward end where water collected at high tide could be released at low tide to clean out the harbour. To achieve all this construction Bo'ness taxed itself by local Acts of Parliament. By the Act

63

of 1816 (which was valid for twenty-five years) a shilling in the pound was levied on the value of all houses in the town for the good of the harbour. In addition, and for the same purpose, a long-standing duty of two pennies Scots (a sixth of a penny Sterling) on every pint of ale and beer sold in the town was renewed. Anchorage duties of twopence halfpenny per ton on coasters and threepence halfpenny on foreign vessels were also confirmed. In exchange for devoting these revenues to improvement Bo'ness expected a bigger flow of trade and was extremely jealous when a nearby rival port like Bridgeness secured the privilege of exporting the products of the Duke of Hamilton's collieries.[7]

Edinburgh did in fact call in John Rennie, to advise them on improvements to Leith docks. His report, submitted in 1799, recommended extensive pier and dock construction. He argued that half-measures would be ineffective and that there was no chance of gaining a permanent or uniform depth in a harbour much subjected to silting, or of protecting the entrance against sand bars, without pushing a great pier out across the shore and well into low water on the east side of the entrance. He also recommended a whole suite of docks on the west side of the existing anchorage with a deep-water entrance near the fishing village of Newhaven which lies about a mile north-west of Leith. His plan was adopted by Edinburgh town council, who were authorised by an Act of 1799 to borrow £80,000 on the security of the rates for the task.

A great deal of Rennie's conception was executed. Two wet-docks were built giving Leith for the first time docks with a permanent depth of water regardless of the tide. In 1800 the eastern wet-dock next to the old tidal harbour was begun, to be completed in six years, and in 1810 the middle dock was begun, to be finished in 1817. As the name suggests, these were the first two of a suite of three docks recommended in Rennie's plans. Each was 100 yards long and 250 yards broad, so they both encompassed ten acres or so of water and together could offer shelter to 150 ships of the period. Complementary to these new docks were three new graving

Steam crane, Victoria Dock, Dundee. This crane was built by James Taylor, Engineer, Birkenhead, in 1874. Originally designed to lift a maximum of ninety tons, it was still in use with reduced loads in 1971, but was dismantled shortly afterwards

Hydraulic crane, with control tower, Leith Docks. This is Brown's Patent Hydraulic Crane No. 169. The photograph was taken in 1971, but the crane is much older, certainly pre-1900

docks for ship repair, each 136 feet long and 45 feet wide at the bottom, which were constructed just north of the new docks.[8]

Like most of his major contemporaries in the field of civil engineering, Rennie was something of a perfectionist, especially as far as materials were concerned. Almost as soon as parliamentary sanction for his schemes had been obtained Rennie was expressing strong preferences for particular quarries as the source of stone for his works. The Earl of Hopetoun's quarry near Rosyth was one, and the Earl of Morton's quarry near Aberdour another. Apart from the basic rent of such quarries, Edinburgh had to rent ground for the construction of accommodation for both men and horses.[9] Executed to Rennie's exacting standards, it is perhaps not surprising that the cost of the Leith harbour improvements soon far outstripped the financial provision envisaged by the legislation of 1799.

As early as 1807 those responsible for the immediate oversight of the works were pointing out to the Edinburgh authorities that the liquid funds required to keep construction going had virtually dried up, and the town council was compelled to embark on a hunt for ready cash in the course of which it secured loans from various sources including not only private individuals, but also the Board of Ordnance. Already in 1807 it had become necessary to select priorities amongst the various items in the improvement programme.[10] In the event, only part of the dock programme was completed, and that at staggering expense. A select committee of the House of Commons reported in 1819 that the two wet-docks had cost about £175,086; the three graving docks £18,198; drawbridges necessitated by the new docks £11,281, and the areas for the sites of the new docks and ancillary features like warehouses £80,543. These sums alone totalled £285,108, without including another £8,000 required for constructing a drawbridge over the water of Leith in order to preserve the line of a new street leading from the foot of the Tolbooth Wynd to the centre of the first wet-dock.[11]

Inevitably, Edinburgh had to borrow more and more money as these works progressed. Mostly it borrowed from the government. In 1800 legislation authorised the lending of £25,000 to Edinburgh at five per cent per annum on the security of the rates. By 1805 further subvention had become essential. By 1817 Edinburgh had spent over £300,000 on Leith dock improvements, and was heavily in debt to the government. Indeed, the point had been reached where further massive improvement was financially impossible. In 1818 estimates were obtained for the cost of completing Rennie's original scheme, with its further extension of the docks westward and a deep-water entrance at Newhaven. The cost was estimated at £322,565, while an alternative plan of a sea-wall and a canal between the docks and Newhaven was estimated to be likely to cost £192,000. Neither sum was tolerable.

On the other hand, by neglecting Rennie's recommendations about the entrance to the harbour, the Edinburgh authorities had left themselves a problem which could scarcely be ignored. Sand bars continued to render access to the harbour difficult and dangerous. John Paterson, the engineer who supervised the execution of Rennie's plans suggested in 1818, with Rennie's approval, the construction of a short pier on the east side of the entrance. This improved the situation without really solving the problem and after much debate amongst consulting engineers in the early 1820s Edinburgh corporation accepted the advice of William Chapman, a Newcastle engineer, that tinkering with the problem would only make it worse, and that only an extension of the eastern pier of 1500 feet, combined with a new breakwater running out from the north-west of the dock wall in an east-north-east direction would be adequate. There was to be a 200 foot gap between the end of the extended pier and the end of the breakwater. Within the roughly triangular shape thus formed twenty-three acres of water would be enclosed, reasonably sheltered from silting from either east or west. The Martello Tower, which had been a seaward landmark at Leith since the Napoleonic wars would be passed by the newly-extended east pier, and the total estimated cost was such that fresh legislation was necessary to raise funds. Work began on the piers in 1826. By 1829 when they were finished £47,000 had been spent on them.

This was Edinburgh's last fling as far as serious improvement at Leith was concerned. Edinburgh's finances were quite out of hand. An Act of 1825 had authorised the government to advance another £240,000 to the city authorities, but there were ominous conditions attached which gave the government claims on all the real property belonging to the city of Edinburgh, which included Leith docks, as security for principal and interest. In addition, Edinburgh had to surrender part of the docks and shore to the Admiralty for the use of the Royal Navy.[12]

Bankruptcy was staring Edinburgh in the face. No situation could have been better calculated to exacerbate feeling between the city and its reluctant vassal the port of Leith. In a desperate attempt to recover some of the cost of harbour improvements from the users of the port, the Edinburgh authorities piled dues on both ships and cargoes. By the time a ship had paid beaconage, anchorage, berthage, flaggage, pilotage and dock dues, it was with a sinking heart that its master or proprietor approached the separate set of charges on his cargo. The expansion of the trade of ports like Grangemouth was greatly assisted by the exorbitant level of shore dues at Leith. To crown it all, Edinburgh town council produced a remarkable scheme whereby Leith harbour was to be sold to a private joint-stock company, which was to take over the existing debt and try to liquidate it by, amongst other devices, higher rates on shipping.

Probably this move was triggered off by a strong remonstrance to Edinburgh town council by Leith shipowners. The remonstrance was submitted in April 1824, and in it the shipowners complained that though dues were high and the harbour neglected, the corporation was known to be creaming off a substantial part of the revenue of the port for the purposes of the general finances of the city of Edinburgh.

The joint-stock company proposal would have eliminated the manifold problems created by Edinburgh's ownership of Leith docks, but only by presenting the docks with even harsher masters, many of whom, it emerged, were members of Edinburgh town council. Fortunately for Leith, the fact that Edinburgh's city fathers were proposing to sell Leith docks to themselves proved damning to the legislative proposals they laid before Parliament. Instead of obtaining its desired Act, Edinburgh had in 1826 to submit to the first serious loosening of its grip on Leith docks.[13]

The critical factor forcing Edinburgh to come to terms was the need for further government loans. It was clear that these would not be forthcoming without a radical reform of the administration of the port. It seems that Edinburgh authorities meant to secure further loans in the last days of one parliament, on the understanding that they would accept reforms, and then obstruct any attempt to introduce reform measures in the next parliament. Due to the vigilance of the Leith interests, this ploy failed and in 1826 an Act vested the administration of the docks in twenty-one commissioners. These were to have the right to spend £1,000 per annum on the harbour and a like sum on the docks, but beyond that the finances of the port remained in the hands of Edinburgh, which was heavily represented amongst the commissioners. The whole arrangement was still unsatisfactory. Edinburgh and Leith interests were so nicely balanced on the commission that deadlock was commonplace. Improvement virtually ceased in 1829. The impasse could only be broken by the final plunge which carried Edinburgh town council down into insolvency. That plunge was less than four years away at the end of 1829.

The early 1830s were difficult years for the oligarchy in control of Edinburgh town council. They were saddled with a debt of quarter of a million pounds to the government because of Leith dock improvements. The interest rates on that debt were in fact rather high. On top of this, Edinburgh town council had a whole series of recurring financial commitments which it had to try to service out of a revenue patently inedequate for the demands made on it. It owed the clergy of the established church in the city, for example, substantial annual payments, about which there had been bitter litigation between 1810 and 1814. Part of the shore dues of Leith went to the clergy. Edinburgh was also obliged to give money to the University, which was a child of the town council, and to the city schools. The scale of this expenditure may be gauged by the claim made by the town council that between 1807 and 1833 it expended about £25,000 from the revenue of Edinburgh on the University, not to mention £10,010 paid in salaries to the professors out of the proceeds of a local duty on ale in the same period. Not surprisingly, by the 1820s not only was the town council reluctant to undertake very necessary street improvements in the old town of Edinburgh, but it also refused to sponsor legislation setting up an independent commission to do the job, unless a voluntary subscription was raised to guarantee it against loss of money in the event of failure to secure the legislation. Such canniness, if commendable, was too late. In 1833 the city of Edinburgh went bankrupt.[14]

Already the passing of a great reform Bill in 1832 had spelled the doom of the old order in Scotland. The prosperous middle class had finally scaled the heights of political power. The business and shipping interest in Leith regarded the long history of Edinburgh's control over their docks as part and parcel of the malversion, mismanagement, and corruption countenanced in the unreformed Scots burghs by an unreformed parliament. They argued that despite the vast sums spent on the port, the registered tonnage sailing from it had only increased from 20,000 in 1808 to 25,674 in 1826, and had then fallen back to 23,328 in 1832. The finances of the docks were in chaos, dues were high, and Alloa and Grangemouth were benefitting from the situation at Leith. Leith would have liked a sharp break with Edinburgh. It seems genuinely to have feared the fate which had overtaken Bristol, where immensely expensive dock improvements were known to be grossly under-used.[15]

On top of all this, it was widely recognised that changes

in the nature of the ships using Leith docks would render further construction work essential. There were no revolutionary changes in the structure of the British mercantile marine in the first half of the nineteenth century. In 1850 the vast majority of British ships were still small wooden vessels driven by sail. However, steam power was slowly becoming commoner in this period. On the whole, the early steamships were designed to carry passengers and mails, because their engines were so heavy and required so much coal that there was little space left for cargo. Leith was always an important port for the coastal packets which at an average of three to four days were by far the quickest means of travel between Scotland and London before a complete rail network was built up in Britain. By 1835 it was clear that facilities for the new steam packets were essential. There was also a general tendency for the size of the ships using the port to increase. This only became dramatic after about 1860 when the combination of iron hulls and the compound engine made very large steamships an economic proposition, but already by the mid 1830s the facilities planned by Rennie in the late eighteenth century were proving on the small side.

The final settlement between Edinburgh and Leith turned out to be a very complex matter. The government, itself a major interested party, was advised on the question by the then vice-president of the Board of Trade, Henry Labouchère. Labouchère, who in 1859 was created Lord Taunton, came from a great Franco–Dutch commercial family and his report was broadly sympathetic to the claims of Leith. He recommended that the historic connection between Edinburgh and Leith should be severed and that the property and management of the port of Leith should be vested in an independent body of commissioners. When he submitted his report in 1836 Labouchère clearly felt that the government would have difficulty in reconciling the conflicting claims of the taxpayer, Edinburgh, Leith and the creditors of Edinburgh. In this he proved correct, and his hope that the parties involved could be propelled towards quick agreement by an offer on the part of the government to waive some of its own claims to repayment of loans or the interest on them proved delusive. The rock on which his proposals foundered was the obduracy of Edinburgh's creditors who pointed out that Labouchère's detailed proposals suited everyone but them. In particular they objected to the removal of Leith from involvement in Edinburgh's bankruptcy subject to a payment equal to £6,000 annually to the city of Edinburgh. They pointed out that Leith docks were part of the property of the city of Edinburgh, and therefore in law belonged to Edinburgh's creditors, subject to the debt to the British government being settled. There was no denying the validity of this claim in law, so the final settlement, which was eventually embodied in legislation in 1838, was the product of further negotiations. The three men who carried the negotiations through to success were the Solicitor General, Andrew Rutherford, the city treasurer of Edinburgh, Duncan McLaren, and Sir William Rae.

Leith docks were placed in charge of an independent Dock Commission. There were to be eleven commissioners, five appointed by the government, three by Edinburgh and three by Leith. From 1833 Leith had had its own town council, which by a quirk of fate was never in its near century of existence to have direct jurisdiction over Leith docks. The government agreed to write off a good deal of what Edinburgh owed it. Leith docks were burdened with an annual payment of £7,680 to the city of Edinburgh part of which helped pay the salaries of the Edinburgh clergy. The rest was to be divided between the schools of Edinburgh, including its University, and the creditors of the city. Apart from this the new Dock Commission was to be free to spend the revenues of the port on the upkeep and improvement of the harbour. Only if there was a surplus left over after these purposes had been served, was it to go to reducing the outstanding debt to the government. In addition, the commissioners were authorised to abolish, reduce, equalise and consolidate the rates and duties leviable at the harbour.[16]

By 1845 the new commissioners had used their powers greatly to extend the east pier, and to deepen the harbour substantially by further dredging. By 1847 they were promoting parliamentary legislation designed to reduce and rationalise the rates and duties. The reason for the delay was that, despite the legislation of 1838, the dock commissioners were advised in the late 1830s that they lacked the legal power to cut through the complex of existing charges. By 1847 the situation was intolerable. Not only were the charges numerous and complex, but they were all levied in terms of Scots currency, which no longer existed. A mere handful of men, none of them merchants or seamen, understood the system. Freight charges to Leith were so high that even Dundee was cutting into Leith's share of the Baltic trade. However, by 1846 the Leith commissioners were already worrying about railway lines in the docks, and Leith was entering a new age—the railway age.[17]

IMPROVEMENT IN THE FIRTH OF TAY PORTS

The history of early nineteenth-century improvement in the harbours of Tayside differs in one vital respect from what was happening in the ports of the Firth of Forth at the same period. In the Forth the biggest single port was Leith, but Leith found improvements a difficult process because of the involvement of the harbour with the affairs of the unreformed town council of Edinburgh. If anything, Leith lagged slightly behind other Forth harbours in improving its facilities. It preserved its importance mainly because of the sheer size of the flow of traffic generated by Edinburgh, and because when improvements did come, they came on a scale which no other Forth port could match. On Tayside Dundee was the most important urban unit, as well as the most important port. In Dundee, however, the grip of the unreformed town council over the docks was loosened at a relatively early stage and Dundee in many ways led the way on Tayside in practical dock improvement.

As in Leith, it was the need for improvement which brought the disputes over control of the docks to a head in Dundee. By 1815 it was generally agreed that something must be done about the still purely tidal harbour. The town council was dominated by Alexander Riddoch, who first became Provost of Dundee in 1788, and who ruled it thereafter for the best part of thirty years. For technical reasons Riddoch's spells as Provost lasted two years. A crony would relieve him for two years, and then Riddoch resumed his sway for another two. Originally a merchant, Riddoch became a manipulator of the property of the town, not altogether without an eye to his own advantage. Admittedly, he considerably improved the street system of the town without imposing additional local taxation burdens on its inhabitants. He widened its principal street, the Nethergate. He also improved access to the harbour area by opening up Crichton Street and Castle Street, which ran south from the Nethergate towards the harbour. However, it was alleged at the time and afterwards that nearly all these activities were connected with his own private speculations in property. No iron man, Riddoch was all the more formidable as the leader of a self-perpetuating oligarchy because he combined wise moderation with a flair for cloaking his financial activities in a fog of obscurity.[18] As leader of the town council Riddoch had accepted the need for harbour improvement to the point of calling in the great civil engineer Robert Stevenson to submit to the town council proposals for modernising and extending harbour facilities at Dundee. As a local wag put it in a somewhat scurrilous poetical broadside;

> Fye, let us a' to the meetin',
>   For there's to be wrangling there,
> For Riddoch's to have a new Harbour
>   And gentle John's in the chair;

73

> And there's to be lang Resolutions
> And flourishing speeches nae few,
> And spirited questions and motions
> And fustian and rant, till we spew.[19]

It was, however, fury rather than sickness (or spewing) that the town council's proposals roused in the hearts of the business community. Stevenson's report itself was quite straightforward. He stressed that the existing harbour 'will be found extremely incommodious, and but ill-adapted to the thriving and extensive trade of Dundee'. He found the harbour poorly designed from the point of view of coping with the problem of silting, which was a very serious drawback in the lower reaches of the Tay. This fact was all the more damaging in that the draught of ships had been steadily increasing due to changes in design calculated to give a vessel a better grip on the water. A depth which would once have been sufficient for a 300 ton ship would not, by 1815, suffice for one of 100 tons. Of the 3,000 feet of quays in Dundee harbour, a mere 500 feet could cope with vessels requiring the full rise of the tide to float them. The existing scouring basin was too small, badly placed and ineffective. Stevenson suggested that most of the existing upper harbour be turned into a proper wet dock controlled by sluices. The new wet dock could then be turned into a large scouring basin. Eventually the lower harbour could also be made into a wet dock, but in the short run Stevenson felt that it was more important to further improve landward access to the harbour area.

Stevenson emphasised the vital importance of dock construction by quoting the cases of Liverpool and Lancaster. The latter had failed to create adequate wet docks. Liverpool had invested heavily in wet docks and despite the difficulty of navigation on the Mersey, its trade had soared, while that of Lancaster had gone into rapid decline. The moral for Dundee was plain to see. Stevenson ended by estimating the cost of his immediate proposals at £21,000. A second wet dock would cost nearly another £35,000.

74

He suggested that to help raise such sums dock dues should be levied, as they were at Leith. With 130,000 tons of shipping using the port every year, the dues would be lucrative.[20]

The analogy with Leith was unfortunate. The prospect of Dundee's vital harbour facilities becoming a pawn in the financial calculations of the town council did not amuse local merchants, and when the council began to promote a Bill in parliament, there was uproar in Dundee. A committee of merchants was formed which called in a rival civil engineer in the shape of Thomas Telford, perhaps the greatest of all Scots civil engineers in an age when great Scots civil engineers abounded. Telford submitted his own plan for the harbour. His instructions from the committee urged him to ignore all vested private property interests. This was a hit at Riddoch, who owned property in the harbour area. The committee also waxed eloquent on the shortcomings of the existing harbour, pointing out that facilities for a substantial trade like the lime trade simply did not exist. They urged Telford to devise a plan which would not only cope with the existing volume of shipping using the port, but which would also make allowances for substantial future expansion. All this Telford did in a plan which was exhibited to the committee of merchants to their great satisfaction.

Like Stevenson, Telford recommended the creation of a large wet dock, but in other respects he was more ambitious, recommending substantial extension of existing piers and dredging and other works to improve the entrance to the harbour from the river. His plan was such that the work could be carried out in consecutive stages without interrupting the general trade of the port. Almost at once the town council laid siege to Telford who duly modified his plan in response to council pressure until it became a report which was rather ambiguous about the vital wet dock, and exceedingly deferential to Riddoch's vested property interests. These took the shape of ownership of a shipyard so sited as seriously to impede any substantial improvement. The legislation which the council was promoting in Westminster proposed to set up commissioners to execute the improvements. The new body was to be wholly dominated by members of the town council. It was to have power to raise moneys on the security of the rates, but the precise nature of the proposed harbour improvements was left very vague.

The committee of merchants bitterly opposed this proposed legislation on four grounds. One was the lack of any firm plan of the proposed improvements. Another was that the Bill safeguarded existing property rights to the point of restricting possible improvements. A third was that a great part of the money which it was proposed to raise under the Bill was to be applied to the repayment of the general debts of the council. Finally, the merchants complained that the different groups most interested in the improvement of the harbour were quite inadequately represented on the proposed body of commissioners who were to execute the improvement.[21]

Relations between the mercantile community and the council rapidly deteriorated after this, with angry allegations being voiced that Riddoch's shipyard had originally been public property, which Riddoch had to all intents and purposes stolen by establishing squatters' rights over a long period when he controlled the town council.[22] In a situation where the oligarchic, secret, and financially irresponsible nature of town government was being challenged, the local political radicals enjoyed a field day.

The leading radicals in Dundee all belonged to the business community. They included Robert Rintoul, editor of the local newspaper the *Dundee, Perth and Cupar Advertiser*; James Saunders, a Dundee solicitor; and David Blair, a merchant in the local linen trade. Meeting in George Miln's bookshop, they co-ordinated a campaign for a different piece of legislation which would take control of the harbour out of the hands of the town council, and place it in the hands of a genuinely autonomous body of commissioners. The trade guilds of Dundee provided a convenient framework for the agitation which also secured the services of George Kinloch of Kinloch, a landed gentleman from Strathmore of radical sympathies who approached Mr Maule, then Member of Parliament for the county of Forfar, on behalf of the guilds. Later, George Kinloch went to London to sponsor the Bill advocated by the guilds. Its eventual passing marked the end of an epoch in the history of the harbour of Dundee, for the new Dundee Harbour Commissioners, though including seven nominees of the town council, also included thirteen elected representatives of other interests. These included local merchants, manufacturers and shipowners, as well as the landed interest of Dundee's hinterland.[23] This Act of 1815 envisaged the return of the harbour to council control after twenty-one years during which the new commissioners would execute substantial improvements in accordance with plans drawn up by Telford.

In the first fifteen years of the new commission's existence nearly £163,000 was expended. Though the financial records give an impression of a rather hand-to-mouth existence, with a perpetual hunt for loans,[24] the credit of the commissioners was buoyant, because within a decade the tonnage using the harbour doubled. The council was not allowed to plunder harbour revenues for its own general purposes, though Riddoch's property had to be bought over by the Commissioners. In 1825 Dundee's first wet dock was opened on the site of the old, tidal lower harbour. It was six and a quarter acres in extent and was called the King William the Fourth Dock. The old upper harbour remained tidal, but its western side was completely sealed off from the river to keep out silt moving downstream and was then extended eastwards by over 500 feet to form a new receiving basin in front of the new wet dock. The new tide harbour was completed by November 1820. An old graving dock left high and dry by the improvements was bought by the commissioners, closed, and replaced by a vastly superior new one at the south-eastern end of the King William the Fourth Dock.

By 1829 a new wave of agitation for improvement and change was swelling under the leadership of rising textile dynasts like the Baxters, who had come into Dundee from Glamis to found a great linen firm. There were two main economic motives behind this agitation and both were connected with the expanding textile trade. First, during the peak period of flax imports from the Baltic in spring and early summer, the single existing wet dock could not hold all the flax ships. Many had to discharge in the tidal harbour risking damage to their hulls if grounded at low water. Secondly, colliers could never find berths in the King William Dock which meant they were grounded at low water in the tidal harbour. This restricted the size of colliers, but demand for coal was soaring with the widespread adoption of steam engines as sources of power in the Dundee linen mills. Larger colliers were more economic, and held out a prospect of cheaper fuel, provided further improvement could be made to the harbour.[25]

The Dundee Harbour Commission decided that an adequate response to these pressing requirements was only possible after further legislation, so they began to draft a bill for the purpose. Central to its structure was the extension of the life of the commission itself beyond the date at which, under the legislation of 1815 and supplementary legislation of 1819, it was due to return the harbour to the control of the town council. At once the town council expressed bitter hostility at what it saw as a breach of contract and attempted theft of part of the corporate property-rights of the town. The commissioners replied with considerable venom that the harbour was essentially the achievement of the acumen and finance of the merchants, manufacturers, and shipowners of Dundee. If it was returned to the control of the town council the commissioners forecast that most of its revenue would be creamed off for the general needs of the council, leaving the harbour facilities to stagnate through lack of funds. After a bad-tempered public debate, and much rival lobbying, the Dundee Harbour Commission was replaced by an Act of 1830, in accordance with its own advice and against that of the council, by the Dundee Harbour Trust. The new body was to control Dundee harbour in perpetuity and the trustees represented roughly the same interests as the commissioners.[26]

The town council renounced, at a price, its claims to the harbour property, while retaining a small share in the harbour dues. The first fruits of the new regime took the shape of a remodelling of the tidal harbour between 1832 and November 1834. Most of the harbour was converted into a wet dock, smaller than the King William Dock but with a deeper entrance to cater for new and larger steamers due to be introduced on the Dundee–London run. Significantly, the new dock was christened the Earl Grey Dock, after the statesman who had carried through the first great instalment of political reform in 1832. A small part of the tidal harbour, now called the West Tidal Harbour, was left to act as a receiving basin for both wet docks. Two features of the new arrangement were unsatisfactory. One was that the new dock was to the west of the King William Dock, and therefore rather exposed to silting problems. The other was that the textile boom rendered the facilities inadequate almost as soon as the Earl Grey Dock opened. By 1835 Dundee Harbour Trustees agreed on the need for two more wet docks. By 1836, after fresh enabling legislation, work started on the first (later named the Victoria Dock). In 1839 it was still unfinished and acting only as a tidal basin.

By then, however, the railway era had reached Tayside. The Dundee and Newtyle Railway had been incorporated by an act of 1826. It opened in 1831. Newtyle was a small village in Strathmore, north of Dundee, and the line only abandoned horses and stationary engines for locomotives in 1833.[27] Still, it was a harbinger of future developments which began to occur when the Dundee and Arbroath Railway was incorporated in 1836, and opened in 1840. The range of transport options, at least for medium-distance haulage, was widening significantly.

Fortunately for Dundee's pre-eminence amongst Tayside ports, Dundee was unique both in the scale of harbour improvement there, and in the early date of the decisive break between town council and port interests. Arbroath's harbour was denounced as grossly inadequate in a memorial presented by local seamen, shipowners, and merchants to the town council as early as 1786. Despite the memorial's insistence that the trade of the town would go into relative decline unless harbour facilities were improved, little was done before 1827. Gates were placed on the entrance to the harbour, a small lighthouse was built, and positively ruinous piers were rebuilt or protected by new breastworks. In 1827 a patent slip for raising ships clear of the water for repair was built at the east end of the harbour. By 1807 the shipowners and shipmasters again petitioned for improvement, and in 1822 the town council took the unprecedented step of consulting an engineer called Buchanan after extensive storm damage to the existing works.

Buchanan not only urged repairs. He also insisted that large-scale improvement was desirable. The council accepted both conclusions, securing in 1826 reports from Robert Stevenson and Buchanan as to possible plans for improvement. Buchanan's plans, estimated as likely to cost over £42,000 were preferred. It was proposed to constitute an Arbroath Harbour Trust, composed of the representatives of various public bodies. The trust was expected to cover its expenses both by an increase in shore dues and by borrowing £20,000 from the government. Mr Hume, the local Member of Parliament, after suggesting procedures for approaching the government for a loan, counselled delay, and his advice was taken with a vengeance. The whole scheme hung fire until 1832, when there was a fresh protest by interested parties about the dilapidated state of the harbour. Even so, it was only in 1836 that matters came to a head.

As usual, the heart of the trouble was the financial embarrassment of the town council. The finances of that body had been hovering on the brink of disaster since 1790. To avoid ruin, the town simply had to use a large part of the revenues generated by shore dues to cover the cost of lighting, paving, and policing the town, which left little enough for the upkeep, let alone the improvement of the harbour. The few years before 1836 were marked by severe business

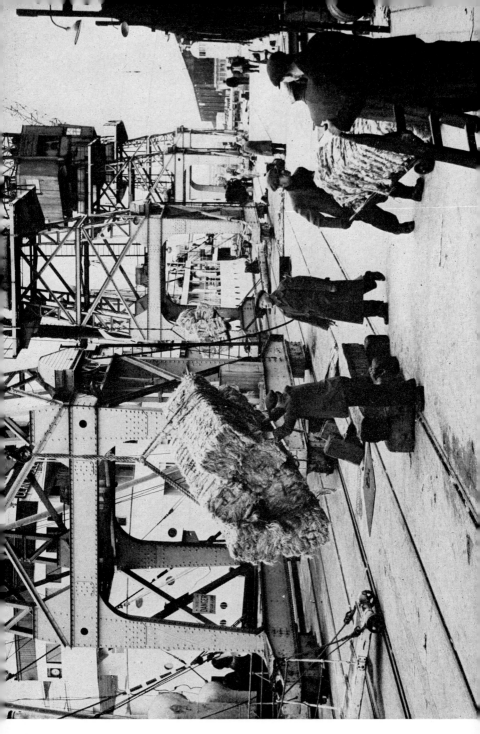

Unloading jute at Dundee Docks in the early 1950s

Grain elevator, ship and suction equipment in Kirkcaldy harbour in the 1970s recession in the town, so business pressure for improvement in transport facilities was running high. Public-spirited local landed proprietors like William Fullerton Lindsay Carnegie of Boysack and Spynie gave full support to a compromise whereby the town council surrendered control over the harbour and harbour dues for £10,000 and a promise that the inhabitants would adopt the Police Act, under which they would administer and pay for the paving, lighting, and policing of the town themselves. In 1839 parliamentary legislation set up an Arbroath Harbour Trust composed of representatives of the town council, the business community, the landed interest of the hinterland, and the inland burgh of Forfar.

This last provision is a reminder that harbour improvement was seen as simply a part of a general improvement in Arbroath's transport facilities. To enable Arbroath to tap the trade of central Strathmore men like William Fullerton Lindsay Carnegie were ardently promoting schemes to link Arbroath and Forfar by railway. Indeed, in 1836 the Arbroath and Forfar railway was incorporated by law. The sheer cost of all these enterprises was too much for the restricted capital resources of Arbroath, and despite the fact that the new harbour authority raised £58,000 (£8,000 more than was authorised by the legislation of 1839) Arbroath harbour, if no longer ruinous, was still tidal in 1846.[28]

Montrose was in an even weaker position for mobilising very large sums of money than Arbroath, nor did there seem to be much point in massive harbour improvements in Montrose. The town was quietly prosperous in 1845 with five flax-spinning mills, four of them driven by steam. Apart from this the town was a processing centre for an agricultural hinterland, with breweries, tanneries, and milling. Since the late eighteenth century the tonnage of shipping belonging to the port had nearly trebled and imports and exports had more than trebled. However, all the ships were small, for they were nearly all coastal vessels, Montrose having by 1845 very little overseas trade. A patent slip to facilitate ship repair was about the most sophisticated equipment needed in its convenient, tidal harbour.[29]

Apart from Dundee, Perth was perhaps the Tayside port most likely to make strenuous efforts to improve itself in the first decades of the nineteenth century. The whole position of Perth as the natural outlet for Strathmore was dependent on Perth harbour. On the other hand, Perth faced unique difficulties because of its geographical position, and these difficulties could only become graver as ship sizes increased. Deepening the Tay, however, was not at all a straightforward problem, for the stretch below Perth included very valuable salmon fishings to whom the shoals and banks obstructing navigation were a major asset, attracting fish. Nevertheless, something had to be done, for as a pamphlet of 1828 remarked, the shipping interest at Perth was large and increasing.[30]

Reports were duly obtained from Smeaton and Stevenson on the desirability and feasibility of substantial river and harbour improvement. By this time Dundee was already improving its harbour, and the incorporation of the Dundee and Newtyle Railway was seen at Perth, quite correctly, as an attempt by Dundee to cut across Perth's traditional communications with Strathmore.[31] Perth could no longer accept a situation which limited access to her quays to ships of under a hundred tons. Old palliatives like using Newburgh as an out-port for Perth had become anachronisms. In the eighteenth century it had been very profitable for Perth merchants to rent the harbour facilities and dues at Newburgh and to trade through that port.[32] In the more competitive nineteenth century an out-port spelled inefficiency and additional cost.

The proposals for improvement fell into two groups. One envisaged the repair and expansion of the existing quays on the river, allied to a deepening of the navigation channel in the river. A more ambitious scheme envisaged the creation of a dock linked by a short canal to the existing quays. Under legislation passed in 1830 thirty harbour commissioners were given power to execute the more modest programme. These commissioners represented town council, landed, mercantile and shipping interests. They had the right to levy additional dues and raise loans, but the town council retained its control over existing shore dues. After a further report by Robert Stevenson, legislation in 1834 authorised the commissioners to tackle the task of creating a dock system, and also gave them complete control of port revenues. Between 1834 and 1844 £53,000 was spent on river improvement, a new tidal dock at Perth, and a road from Perth to the new dock.[33]

Fords were dredged away. Boulders, often of vast size, were removed. The channel was deepened. Islands were connected to the mainland in order to narrow the river and increase the scour. Elsewhere the river was widened. The effect on the salmon fishing was simply to re-distribute the catch amongst the various proprietors. Though losers had to be compensated, the total catch if anything increased.[34] In 1833 the largest vessel registered at Perth was 144 tons. By 1848 not only had the registered tonnage increased by over a half but there were three vessels on the register over 400 tons. Perth had at least secured itself against the sort of eclipse as a port which had long before overtaken Stirling. On the other hand, her improvements were relatively slow in coming and very modest in terms of concrete harbour facilities. By 1845 or so Dundee was clearly in a class of its own amongst Tayside ports.

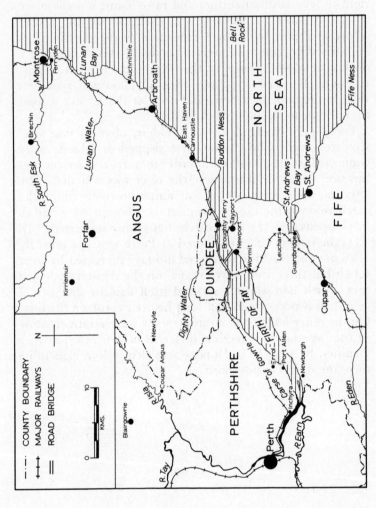

The Firth of Tay Ports

Legend:
COUNTY BOUNDARY
MAJOR RAILWAYS
ROAD BRIDGE

CHAPTER III

The Ports of the Forth and Tay and the Coming of the Railways

THE CREATION OF A RAILWAY NETWORK ON THE EAST COAST

The first efficient railways making use of steam locomotives as their principal source of power date from the third decade of the nineteenth century. In 1825 there opened the Stockton and Darlington Railway, part of whose line was still horse-operated, but which made an unprecedented use of locomotives. By 1826 the Monkland and Kirkintilloch Railway had opened near Glasgow. Part of its line was horse-operated, part was worked by locomotives. With the opening of the Liverpool and Manchester Railway in 1830 the first modern, locomotive-operated steam railway had been created. Long before 1830, however, there had been substantial railway systems in Britain using horses to pull waggons along rails made first of wood, then of cast iron, and then of malleable iron. These lines were usually connected with the exploitation of minerals, and most of them were built as feeders to water transport, the principal means of carrying heavy goods before the era of the steam locomotive.

This generalisation is notably true of the pre-locomotive railways of the east coast of Scotland. Of these there were a substantial number. They were all connected with coal pits, limeworks, or iron works, and their prime function was to render access to the great water highways of the Firths of

Forth and Tay easier. Perhaps the best-known example on the northern shore of the Forth was the Alloa waggonway which enabled coal from the Alloa pits belonging to the Erskines of Mar to be conveyed, originally on wooden rails, to the port of Alloa. This line was opened in 1768. Prior to that date the coal had had to be transported by Erskine tenants using small carts on poor roads. The increase in efficiency was spectacular. On the new line, which ran under the main streets of Alloa by means of two short tunnels, one horse could successfully pull three waggons, each of which when fully loaded weighed more than thirty hundredweights. Another line in the same county of Clackmannan ran for over five miles between Clackmannan Pow (or Creek) on the Forth and coal and iron works at Devonside and Tillicoultry.

Predictably, the early horse-operated railroads in the southern part of Fife were designed to link coal pits and limeworks with the Forth. Such was the line between the Wemyss collieries and the harbour of Methil, built by the Earl of Wemyss before 1795. Another noble proprietor, the Earl of Elgin, owned an early railroad between the harbour of Limekilns and his Berry Law Pits, four miles to the north. In 1812 this line was superseded by a new one built by Lord Elgin from Charleston harbour on the Forth to his collieries north-west of Dunfermline. Another early railway linked Inverkeithing with the Halbeath and Townhill Collieries situated some four miles away. All these lines were at least several miles long, but there were shorter ones like Newbigging Railway, which serviced a limeworks not far from Burntisland, and the Fordell Railway, which linked quarries a short distance inland with the harbour of Saint Davids, just east of Inverkeithing.

The scale of these enterprises can be judged by the fact that several of their terminal harbours are rather difficult to find on a modern map. On the southern shore of the Forth the early horse-operated railways also tended to run between collieries and small harbours. There was an eighteenth-century railway in East Lothian between

Tranent Coalmine and the harbour of Cockenzie. In Midlothian a line was opened in 1814 between Pinkie Hill Colliery and the harbour of Fisher Row outside Musselburgh, which lay a couple of miles from the mine.

All these lines were essentially feeders for water transport. They were relatively cheap to construct and the simple bulk commodities they dealt in could be conveniently shipped from very small harbours, some little better than a wooden pier projecting from a muddy bank. Nevertheless, the potential of the horse-operated waggonway when it was linked to the small coastal ship, was considerable. The great civil engineer Robert Stevenson, was excited by the possibility of developing this combination into a major transport system. A Glaswegian by birth, Stevenson did a great deal of work in Edinburgh and along the east coast of Scotland where he became familiar with horse-operated waggonways, which he thought eight to ten times as efficient for goods traffic as contemporary roads. He even considered that, under certain circumstances, such a railroad was more efficient than a canal. Of course, a horse-drawn waggon could not carry as heavy a single load as a canal barge, but then the construction costs of a railway were far below those of a canal. It is significant that Stevenson, who in 1812 had been engaged in surveying a route for what proved to be an abortive canal project up the valley of Strathmore, was by 1819 suggesting the creation of a horse-drawn railway in Strathmore which would link Perth with Forfar, Brechin, and ultimately Montrose. This scheme was part of a more ambitious design for a whole series of horse-operated railways linking Glasgow and Edinburgh and running up the east coast of Scotland from Berwick to Aberdeen. Stevenson did a great deal of surveying for this scheme between 1819 and 1826. At this time he seriously envisaged horse-operated railways replacing roads as the principal form of land transport. He repeatedly referred to these railroads as the 'British Roadway' or 'Iron Rail'.[1]

Stevenson's vision was therefore one in which a system of

horse-operated railways acted primarily as a feeder to and only marginally as a competitor to harbours and canals. This was a development of an existing situation in which most railroads fed harbours. Few railroads on the east coast fed canals because, the Forth and Clyde apart, there were few canals. An exception may be made for the two miles of track opened in 1810 by the Carron Company between the Forth and Clyde Canal at Bainsford Basin, and Carron Ironworks. This particular line was operated simultaneously with the 'cut' or short canal which gave Carron Company access to its own harbour facilities at Carron shore further down the River Carron.

In fact, by the time the Edinburgh and Dalkeith Railway, and the Dundee and Newtyle Railway opened, which they both did in 1831, Stevenson's vision was out of date. Steam power applied to railroads in the shape of locomotives, or even in the shape of stationary engines, marked the beginning of a revolution in transport economics. As early as 1821 the pioneer locomotive engineer George Stephenson had written to Robert Stevenson, making what turned out to be very modest claims for the potential of an efficient steam locomotive. Stephenson hoped that he would eventually be able to produce a locomotive capable of moving goods for a fourth of the cost involved in moving the same goods by canal.[2]

There was, however, more to the steam engine than economy. It also spelled power. Thus, while the Dundee and Newtyle Railway was originally dependent on horses for most of its work, it had from the start to make use of stationary engines to enable its waggons to climb the three very steep gradients at the Law Hill, Balbeuchly, and Hatton, which its obsession with ruler-straight lines imposed on it. As Joseph Priestley remarked, in his classic contemporary study, the ability of the Dundee and Newtyle Railway to bring the hilly areas behind Dundee into direct contact with the port of Dundee was something which previous generations would have regarded as 'quite impracticable'.[3] The Edinburgh and Dalkeith Railway showed no comparable zest for defying topography. On the contrary, a good part of its line simply superseded an existing, and very conventional railway. This was the Edmonston (or Newton) Railway which had been opened in 1818 to bring coal into Edinburgh from Newton Colliery, which lay a little under four miles south-east of the city in the direction of Dalkeith. The Edinburgh and Dalkeith Railway, however, also had branches to the harbour of Fisher Row and to the Cowpit Collieries which lay between Dalkeith and Fisher Row. Like the Dundee and Newtyle, the Edinburgh and Dalkeith started carrying passengers in 1833. Prior to that date both were purely goods lines. A return of 1838, when the Edinburgh and Dalkeith was still using horse-drawn passenger vehicles, showed that the company was carrying on its twelve and a quarter miles of line the astonishing number of 5,754 passengers weekly.[4] With the coming of the locomotive, railways were to become by far the speediest and most convenient mode of passenger travel.

Of course, as long as railways remained purely local systems they could only act as feeders to water transport. Their full potential as carriers of passengers and freight could not be developed. Thus, when the Edinburgh and Dalkeith Railway began to consider building an extension to the port of Leith a contemporary observer could remark that:

> The principal object of this railway and branches, is to open more effectually, a better and cheaper communication between the City of Edinburgh and the port of Leith, with the valuable collieries and limestone quarries that abound in the rich mineral district to which they extend.[5]

However, in 1842 Scotland's first real trunk-line railway opened between Edinburgh and Glasgow. It was a time of much reckless investment in the railways which were clearly destined to supersede canals like the Forth and Clyde. Eventually this 'Railway Mania' culminated in a frenetic boom followed by a devastating slump. Nevertheless, it ensured that the main urban centres on the east coast of

89

Scotland would be linked in a finite time not only with one another, but also with the expanding English railway network.

If the vital link between Edinburgh and England via an east-coast route came quickly, its subsequent history was far from smooth. John Learmonth, chairman of the Edinburgh and Glasgow Railway, was instrumental in creating in 1843 the North British Railway Company. In 1846 that company opened a hastily and badly built line which ran from Edinburgh via Dunbar to a terminus at Berwick Castle, where it was stopped, admittedly on English ground, by the unbridged valley of the Tweed. The new railway had close ties with the Edinburgh and Glasgow. Indeed their main Edinburgh stations were adjacent to one another, and were eventually to be united into the present day Waverley Station. A permanent through-route to England from Glasgow and Edinburgh via the east coast was finally established with the bridging of the last two major river barriers. The Tyne was permanently bridged in 1849, and the Tweed in 1850.

Although the North British managed to escape control by George Hudson, the English railway speculator whose great empire of east-coast lines crashed round his ears in 1849, Learmonth and his successors had a strong dose of reckless expansionism in their own right. By 1855 the North British was on the verge of financial ruin and mechanical paralysis. Richard Hodgson, who was called in to redeem the situation, soon embarked on a titanic struggle, with the rival Caledonian Railway. By 1866 Hodgson's megalomaniac pursuit of expansion to spite the Caledonian had again brought the North British to the verge of bankruptcy. John Stirling of Kippendavie, a Caledonian director, replaced him on a platform of peace, retrenchment, and reform. On the road to 1866 the North British, perpetually short of working capital, had left a trail of collapsed bridges, disintegrating track, scarce and sub-standard rolling stock, and defective locomotives.

Understandably, the impact of the new Edinburgh to

London east-coast route and its branches was limited by its relative inefficiency. In 1849, for example, the North British booked only 5,792 passengers from Edinburgh to London, whereas steamships sailing from Leith and Granton to London carried 11,584 passengers. Only with the Great Exhibition of 1851 in London did the volume of passengers from Edinburgh to London by rail reach adequate proportions. After that date steamship services could still offer effective competition to both the east and the west coast lines from Scotland. The Caledonian and North British were so worried about this that at one stage they even turned from their chief business of doing one another down to try to reach a joint agreement on fares with the General Steam Navigation Company of Leith. Minerals were a slightly happier story, providing from the start the backbone of North British revenue. Coal was moved from Lothian pits into Edinburgh for consumption, and to Leith for export. The first sign of competition for coastal shipping came when Newcastle coalowners found that it paid to send coal from Northumberland to Edinburgh via the North British. Nevertheless, between 1852 and 1854 North British mineral revenues slumped while despairing coalowners wept at the thought that they could produce twice as much coal as the North British seemed capable of carrying.[6]

The creation of an effective coastal rail network northwards from Edinburgh was technically a much more difficult exercise than the building of the east-coast route to England from Edinburgh. This was because the Forth and Tay were much more formidable barriers than the Tweed and Tyne. At first, therefore, railways were links between existing ferry harbours. On the southern shore of the Forth there were only three ferry harbours of real consequence—Queensferry, Granton, and Newhaven. Of these, Queensferry was in decline throughout much of the nineteenth century. Its rivals enjoyed more capital investment and usually managed to introduce new techniques well ahead of Queensferry. Thus Granton, a small harbour a little over two miles west of Leith, was the scene of heavy investment by its feudal superior the Duke of Buccleuch. Starting in 1835, the Duke created a complex of piers, jetties, and breakwaters of which the most striking feature was the 1,700 foot long pier. By 1844 that pier could furnish berths for ten steamers of up to 1,000 tons. Newhaven, even closer to Leith, made an even earlier start with the improvement of its ferry harbour. By the 1820s its new Chain Pier was fit to receive the august personnage of George IV, on his way to Edinburgh. Steamers were introduced into Leith, Granton and Newhaven about 1815. Competition for the sailing ships of Queensferry included not only Granton and Newhaven sailings to Burntisland, Kinghorn and Aberdour, but also sailings from Leith to Kirkcaldy. This Kirkcaldy service was in fact an intermediate stop on a service up the Forth from Leith to Grangemouth. By 1820 Queensferry had entered the age of the steam ferry, but it continued to lag in the race for traffic.

Understandably, the first railway line projected between Edinburgh and a Forth ferry port was the Edinburgh Leith and Newhaven Railway. By 1836 the line had been authorised by legislation and the company's shares stood at a very high premium. Those directors wise enough to sell out at this point must have later congratulated themselves, for the subsequent history of the line was a quagmire of financial miscalculation, rascality, and vituperation. By 1844 the line had decided on the need for an extension to Granton, mainly because of the Duke of Buccleuch's investment there, so it changed its name to the Edinburgh Leith and Granton Railway before it finally opened in 1846. By then it was only likely to make sense as a property which another and larger railway might buy as a strategic investment, at a premium.[7]

Fortunately for the Edinburgh Leith and Granton, this was quite likely, because it had become a vital link between the developing railway system of Fife, and the North British. In 1845 Fife experienced a railway mania of its own, with over sixteen projects for railways lodged with the county authorities.[8] After a great deal of the usual unscrupulous jockeying for funds and parliamentary sanction, the Edinburgh and Northern Railway emerged triumphant from the scramble. Its line ran from Burntisland across Fife. Dundee was ever its real objective, and it originally proposed to reach it by bridging the Tay well west of Dundee at Mugdrum Island. Opposition from the Admiralty destroyed this scheme, while attempts to secure control of the ferry between Dundee and Newport proved abortive. Finally the Edinburgh and Northern gained control of an old-established ferry downstream from Dundee. This was the one between Broughty Ferry and Ferryport-on-Craig (now Tayport). The company, whose main line from Burntisland to Ladybank with branches to Cupar and Lindores opened in 1847, completed linkages to Ferryport-on-Craig and Perth in 1848, the year it also opened a Dunfermline branch. Under an act of 1842 the harbour of Burntisland had been much improved by the Duke of Buccleuch and Sir John Gladstone, father of the future premier William Ewart Gladstone. Sir John was a substantial shareholder in the Edinburgh and Northern, which unlike most contemporary Scottish lines was largely financed by Scottish, mainly Edinburgh and Fife, money. Most other Scottish lines, like the North British, were in fact financed from England.

The Edinburgh and Northern bought Burntisland harbour in due course, along with ferry rights belonging to the Duke. When the railway changed its name to the Edinburgh, Perth and Dundee Railway in 1849, it effectively dominated transport in Fife. In 1847 it had amalgamated with the Edinburgh Leith and Granton Railway. The Edinburgh, Perth and Dundee Railway was therefore a most valuable component in any unified east-coast route. At the height of the rivalry between the North British and Caledonian in the early 1860s, a spate of amalgamations occurred. The North British, girding its loins for battle, not only secured the Edinburgh and Glasgow, but also the Edinburgh, Perth and Dundee.

From the Tyne to the Tay, the North British was supreme. North of the Tay railways had begun to link the major east-coast towns at an early date. The Dundee and Arbroath Railway opened in 1840 and the Dundee and Perth in 1847. It was soon feasible to establish a through-connection from Perth or Dundee to Aberdeen via Arbroath. Only at Aberdeen did serious trouble set in, mainly because of the insanely despotic and uncooperative attitude of the Great North of Scotland Railway which held a key position north of Aberdeen. As was the case south of the Tay, a fantastic sequence of intrigues, alliances, and diplomatic revolutions ensued between the railways of the region. In the long run, the Caledonian emerged as the great amalgamator, using the Scottish Central Railway as its stalking horse. The Caledonian never abandoned its epic struggle with the North British. It even maintained a presence in Edinburgh and built branches to Granton and Leith. In 1863 the Dundee and Perth and Aberdeen Junction Railway was absorbed by the Scottish Central, which in turn amalgamated with the Caledonian in 1865. In 1866 the Caledonian acquired control of the Scottish North Eastern Railway, which owned a complex of lines in Strathmore. Between 1865 and 1867 the Caledonian more than doubled its mileage by amalgamation. It had, however, to cede running rights to the North British north of Dundee, as part of the price of parliamentary sanction.[9]

By 1862 the forerunner of the modern *Flying Scotsman* was running between London King's Cross and Edinburgh in a little under eleven hours.[10] It was only a logical development to push this fast passenger service from London at least as far as Aberdeen. Before this could be done, however, the Tay and Forth had to be conquered. As early as 1850 the Edinburgh, Perth and Dundee had started running a train ferry between Granton and Burntisland. Its Manager and Engineer, Thomas Bouch, combined a sliding platform on an inclined plane, which lowered waggons to the ferry regardless of the state of the tide, and a paddle ferry *Leviathian* which carried them across the Forth. From

Ferryport-on-Craig the railway ran a huge iron paddle ferry, 170 feet long and 34 feet broad within the paddles, across to Broughty Ferry with whole waggon trains aboard.[11] For the ambitious mind of Thomas Bouch, however, this was not enough. In 1854 he conceived the idea of bridging the Tay at Dundee.

He had to wait, for it was not until 1863 that a Dundee pressure group largely inspired by a local solicitor Thomas Thornton (later Sir Thomas) began to agitate for a rail bridge. By 1864 the North British was a firm convert. It gradually wore down opposition. Perth's fears for her harbour were quietened by a promise in 1870 that the bridge would be designed with eighty-eight feet high navigation spans in the centre. In 1871 the foundation-stone was laid. In 1877 the first train crossed from Wormit, on the Fife shore, to Dundee. In December 1879 the navigation spans collapsed in a great gale, taking a train and seventy-five lives with them. Lack of allowance for wind-pressure, and shocking workmanship had destroyed the bridge, those lives and the career of Thomas Bouch, who was stopped as he began work on a bridge over the Forth. It would almost certainly have fallen down too.

Such was the vitality of Victorian society in Scotland that by 1887 a new and substantial rail bridge across the Tay, on the site of the old one, was open for traffic. William Barlow's design was neither beautiful nor original, but it was the longest bridge in the British Isles, and it proved functionally most efficient. To crown this great struggle of railways against water, the Forth itself was to be bridged three years later. The neglected Queensferry became the site of a spectacular cantilever bridge designed by John Fowler and Benjamin Baker. It opened for traffic in 1890. Soon rival railway companies were racing one another to Aberdeen.[12]

By 1890 the east-coast railway system was a serious contender for medium-distance haulage of passengers and freight. The impact of railways on ports and harbours was therefore bound to involve harm as well as gain. For some there was no conflict of interest. James Cox, jute baron, Provost of Dundee, and member of Dundee Harbour Trust, invested enough in the Tay Rail Bridge to be immortalised in the celebratory verse of William McGonagall:

> Beautiful Railway Bridge of the Silvery Tay!
> And prosperity to Provost Cox, who has given
> Thirty thousand pounds and upwards away
> In helping to erect the Bridge of the Tay,
> Most handsome to be seen,
> Near by Dundee and the Magdalene Green.

Cox did in fact have shipping interests. In his diary he recounts how he started in 1865 by buying a Baltimore clipper of 1800 tons which had taken refuge in London docks. This was the era of the American Civil War, when Confederate privateers were roving the seas. Renamed in honour of the Cox suburb of Lochee, that clipper was promptly despatched on a voyage to Calcutta for jute.[13] Such long hauls were not likely to be much affected by North British competition.

The only point at which coastal shipping seriously impinged on Cox's activities after 1879 was in connection with the rebuilding of the railway bridge. As it was the navigation spans which had collapsed, there was strong feeling on Tayside against the height of the central portions of the bridge which failed in 1879. Dundee textile lords like James Cox and A. B. Gilroy rather inclined to a low-level bridge, possibly with a central swing-bridge arrangement on the lines of Newcastle Swing Bridge. However, the North British rightly judged that Perth would obstruct any proposal which did not contain the high navigation spans which the city had been promised in 1870. They therefore offered to adopt the low-level proposals only if they were backed unanimously by the Tay cities. The bridge which opened in 1887 had navigation spans only a little lower than its predecessor.[14]

If Perth could protect its shipping interests, the small

ferry harbour of Newport found that it was not so strongly placed. Shortly after the first railway bridge over the Tay opened, a commuter line was built to link it with the communities on the north shore of Fife whose traditional link with Dundee was via the Newport or Woodhaven ferry. McGonagall was in attendance:

> Success to the Newport Railway,
> Along the braes of the Silvery Tay,
> And to Dundee straightway,
> Across the Railway Bridge o' the Silvery Tay,
> Which was opened on the 12th of May,
> In the year of our Lord 1879,
> Which will clear all expenses in a very short time
> Because the thrifty housewives of Newport
> To Dundee will often resort,
> Which will be to them profit and sport,
> By bringing cheap tea, bread, and jam,
> And also some of Lipton's ham, . . .[15]

The ferry proprietors had more than the verse to wince at.

The Smaller Ports and the Coming of the Railways

Within the category of 'smaller ports' it is not unreasonable to include all Forth and Tay ports except Dundee and Leith. Needless to say, the 'smaller ports' so defined are not a homogenous group. For the purpose of analysing the effect of the creation of an east-coast rail network, they may be crudely divided into two. First there were those ports which, either by way of export, or of import, continued to deal in a broad range of commodities. Secondly, there were the very specialised ports, of which the coal and ferry ports are the best examples. Taking the former group first, Arbroath's experience well sums up the problems they faced in an age of railways.

The harbour of Arbroath was financially sound by 1874. The revenue of Arbroath Harbour Trust in the year ending

D

14 October 1874 was nearly £5,000. After maintenance and salary charges were met, there was a surplus of just under £1,000. Customs receipts at the port had doubled since 1846, but shore dues, despite higher rates, had only gone up by a fourth between 1846 and 1874. This was because of a sharp fall in the total number of ships using the harbour. This fall was entirely concentrated in the coastal shipping figures. The number of vessels arriving from foreign ports had increased from fifty-two in 1846 to ninety-six in 1874. On the other hand, in the coasting trade arrivals had decreased from 731 in 1846 to 432 in 1874, and the tonnage from 46,080 to 38,421. Contemporaries were in no doubt that it was the railways which had taken away from the harbour a good deal of its former traffic.[16]

On top of the recorded decline in arrivals and tonnage, it is clear that the railways deprived the harbour of Arbroath of opportunities for growth, especially in the field of imported textile fibres. The textile industry of Arbroath grew steadily between 1847 and 1876. By 1864 Arbroath ranked as the second most important linen textile centre in Scotland. By 1876 there were thirty-four mills and factories, 40,000 spindles and 1,100 power looms at work in the town. Sailcloth was by far the most important product, but jute working spread from Dundee between 1855 and 1859. The only record of the importation of jute into Arbroath harbour is in 1861, when 149 tons were imported. After 1863 it is clear that all the jute used in Arbroath's coarser textile manufacture came by rail from Dundee. It was cheaper to take jute boats into Dundee and distribute the fibre by rail, than to run a separate sea service to Arbroath. Even in the case of Baltic flax, it became normal for Arbroath to take a high percentage of its supply from Dundee, by rail. Between 1859 and 1863, Arbroath's average annual import of textile fibres by rail and sea was 14,375 tons, of which sixty-eight per cent came by rail from Dundee. This percentage had been steady for over a decade. How much more prosperous Arbroath's harbour would have been without the railway may be gauged from the fact that of the eighty-four cargo vessels which called at the port in 1882 from overseas, seventy-two brought flax.[17] Arbroath's major harbour improvements only reached fruition as late as 1877 when the wet dock was completed. Thereafter, the lack of dynamism in the port was reflected in the fact that when the dock entrance collapsed in 1882, it was not until 1887 that it was fully restored.[18] On the other hand, Arbroath did have a very steady volume of imports and exports, which guaranteed the survival, if not the expansion, of the port. In addition to textile fibres, the harbour imported large quantities of timber, and of lime. The latter was clearly destined for the agricultural hinterland. Coal also came in bulk. Exports not only included textiles, but also wheat, barley, oats, peas, beans, and potatoes, and very large quantities of paving stones from the great flagstone quarries behind Arbroath. A steady 3–400,000 cubic feet of paving stones left the port each year. In a good year for the quarries, the figure was nearer 500,000.[19]

The experience of Perth harbour in the age of the coming of the railways was more traumatic than that of Arbroath. Perth had embarked on the great enterprise of improving both the harbour and the channel of the Tay just before the east coast began to acquire an effective railway network linked to the English railway system. By 1845, admittedly during a period of frenzied speculation in railways, there were plans for turning Perth into a great railway junction, where four major lines would meet. In practice it was the opening of the Dundee and Perth Railway in 1847 which marked the first serious impact of railways on Perth. This line subsequently became part of the Caledonian railway, forming an important link in its network, which eventually stretched from Carlisle to Aberdeen. Some idea of the implications of this growth of railways for Perth harbour may be gathered by examining the response of a major local shipping firm, the Dundee, Perth and London. The year after the Dundee and Perth line opened this firm withdrew its lighter service on the Tay between Perth and Dundee.

It was more economic to unload cargoes for Perth at Dundee and send them to Perth by rail. In 1844 the Dundee, Perth and London had been able to come to terms with the Edinburgh and Glasgow Railway, so that goods shipped from Dundee to Leith could be taken by rail at favourable rates to Glasgow. Direct rail links between Perth and Glasgow soon scuppered this route. After 1848 it was obsolete.[20]

The commissioners who were originally scheduled to complete great improvements to Perth harbour and the Tay in 1854, were hard hit by shortage of funds, and by diversion of trade from the harbour to the railways. The year 1854 turned out to be the year of their bankruptcy rather than the year of the fulfilment of their mission. An Act of Parliament transferred the harbour and its £86,000 or so of debt to the city of Perth, which acquired an expensive liability by the transaction. Harbour income declined steadily, while expenditure rose. The sad tale is at its most expressive in figures:

Date	Income (£)	Expenditure (£)	Loss (£)	Debt Due to City (£)
1857–8	1,874	3,556	1,682	87,631
1867–8	1,310	4,307	2,997	110,194
1877–8	892	5,374	4,481	148,796
1882–3	1,300	6,189	4,888	171,296

In effect, the harbour was borrowing large sums from the city to keep itself going. Its 1,300 feet of quays were clearly under-used. Gone were the days when fifteen sailing ships would reach Perth on a single tide. Indeed, the shipping figures for Perth were not much more inspiring than the revenue account:

Date	Entered (Tonnage)	Cleared (Tonnage)
1853	21,689	19,092
1867	12,404	9,047
1873	8,189	8,816
1882	11,143	10,770
1883	9,767	9,731

Concealed by these totals is the fact that coastal shipping was disproportionately important for Perth. In 1883, for example, foreign tonnage entered at Perth amounted to 2,829 as against a British tonnage of 6,938, most of it coastal. Like Arbroath, Perth lost any chance of taking a major role in the expansion of textile fibre imports, because railways made it cheaper to import into Dundee and redistribute from there. Perth survived as an essentially agricultural port. It imported Baltic timber, coals, cement, slates, oil cake, and quarry products. The importance of the potato trade was great. The area around Perth became famous for high-quality seed potatoes which were exported all over the world, and several of the few Perth ship owners of the late nineteenth century were potato merchants who had gone into shipping.[21]

Montrose's experience after the coming of the railway had more in common with that of Arbroath than with that of Perth. Under an Act of 1837, the harbour had been acquired from the town council by a body of trustees representative of Montrose, the county landowners, and the landward burgh of Brechin. In exchange for an annual payment of £600 to the town, the trustees controlled the harbour, and opened a new wet dock in 1839. They were not, however, recklessly ambitious. The river quays were still more extensive than the dock quays in 1840. Trade at the harbour was extremely buoyant between 1840 and 1880, mainly because of the flourishing state of timber imports and re-exports. In the period 1860–80, Montrose ranked second in Scotland to Greenock as timber importing port. Nearly all the timber came from Scandinavia and the Baltic lands, but as Montrose had no Glasgow in its hinterland, much of it was sawn, planed, and grooved, mainly for re-export to London. Two firms, Robert Millar and Sons, and Charles Birnie, dominated the Montrose wood yards. Thanks to these firms, very few ships ever left Montrose in ballast. Most outgoing ships were loaded with deal flooring for London, and many returned from England with coal. At one stage Montrose was even exporting timber on a large scale to the Australian colonies. Montrose's splendid agricultural hinterland produced much barley, oats, and potatoes, and some wheat. Nearby rivers were and are famous for salmon. The port of Montrose did not, however, retain its virtual monopoly over the shipment of these commodities after the coming of the railway. The speed and predictability of rail transport enabled Montrose salmon packed in ice to reach the London market in good condition in under twenty-four hours from Montrose. This compared with several days and much damage in the old sailing packets. It is clear that the railways also bit into the grain traffic. Only the peculiar vigour of the timber trade sustained overall port expansion, which even so was levelling off by 1880, as the following figures for the tonnage of ships using the harbour show:[22]

Year	Entered (Tonnage)	Cleared (Tonnage)
1860	66,520	50,856
1874	92,329	89,381
1881	92,745	89,069
1882	94,039	93,664

The experience of these modest Tayside ports, dealing as they did in a fair range of commodities, was that, at the best, the coming of the railways could take away nearly all the significance of an unlucky port. Not surprisingly, the experience of the similar ports of the Firth of Forth was very much the same, with one blazing exception. This exception was Grangemouth, and it was an exception almost entirely because of its special relationship with Glasgow and the west coast of Scotland. It is, however, more convenient to look first at a few more normal Forth ports.

On the north shore of the Forth Kirkcaldy had, on the whole, a disappointing experience as far as its port was concerned. Improvement came late to the harbour, which was still tidal in 1843. Thereafter over £40,000 were spent on substantial reconstruction which gave the town a wet dock of nearly three acres area, as well as tidal inner and outer harbours. By the time these improvements were nearing completion, the railway age had reached Fife. Kirkcaldy, with most of Fife, soon found itself within the sphere of influence of the North British Railway. However, the Caledonian Railway was always anxious to poach on its rival's territory, and it found a good excuse for doing so when it undertook to build a new dock at Seafield, on the west side of Kirkcaldy. Once the dock was built, it would have been difficult to refuse the Caledonian permission to construct a line linking the new port facilities with its existing rail network. The Caledonian therefore started work on the docks before it had secured essential parliamentary legislation approving the project, while the North British fought hard to prevent the Caledonian from obtaining this vital parliamentary sanction. The North British lobbying proved successful. At a cost of £90,000 in compensation, the North British not only secured the abandonment of the enabling legislation, but also forced the abandonment of the partially-built docks. As a sop to local opinion, the North British undertook to provide £150,000 towards the cost of a new deep-water harbour near Ravenscraig, at the east end of Kirkcaldy, provided local capitalists put up another £150,000. The railway's generosity was as frugal as it was shrewd, for local capitalists did no such thing.[23]

Truth to tell, without a special connection with the west coast through the Caledonian network, Kirkcaldy did not need a great expansion in port facilities. The local economy was reasonably buoyant, mainly because of the rapid growth of the local floorcloth and linoleum industries. Michael Nairn produced the first floorcloth in Kirkcaldy in 1847, in a factory at Pathhead known locally as 'Nairn's folly'. By 1876 the great firm of Nairns of Kirkcaldy had begun to manufacture linoleum. Other great firms, like Barry Ostler and Shepherd, were to rise to prominence in the Kirkcaldy linoleum industry, which grew out of coarse linen, especially sailcloth, via the floorcloth trade. The linen trade itself was modestly prosperous in Kirkcaldy in the

1880s, employing over 2,000 people. There was also a local engineering industry, and a small pottery industry. To some extent all these industries generated port business by importing raw materials. Flax is an obvious example, and the linoleum trade required linseed and cork in substantial quantities. However, a fair amount of material came in by rail. Here the best example is perhaps the jute backing for linoleum, which usually came from Dundee factories. Equally, many of the products of Kirkcaldy firms could be conveniently despatched by rail. Specialised engineering firms like the Fife Forge Company would have their own sidings to link them to the rail network, and much of their production, which was mainly marine shafting, went to Clydeside shipbuilding firms. The slump in vessels registered in Kirkcaldy from ninety-five with a tonnage of 10,610 in 1831 to eighteen with a tonnage of 1,565 in 1883, did not reflect a comparable decline in port facilities, but it did show that port expansion was too slow to generate enough wealth in local shipping circles to enable them to cope with the increasing size and cost of ships.[24]

Bo'ness on the southern shore of the Forth also experienced a substantial fall in shipowning, from a tonnage of 13,888 in 1790 to a mere 3,349 in 1874. As late as the 1880s this

Date	Entered (Tonnage)	Cleared (Tonnage)
1854	13,876	96,045
1862	31,287	157,758
1873	191,783	190,483
1879	250,230	244,426
1880	272,200	268,210

port was still feeling the effects of the opening of the Forth and Clyde Canal and of the erection of Grangemouth into a separate port. It never recovered its old status as a port dealing in a very wide variety of commodities, being forced more and more into the role of a coal exporting port. A great many of the ships which came to Bo'ness came in ballast in order to take away coal. In the 1880s Bo'ness exported coal on a scale which made her rank second in amount and fourth in value amongst Scottish coal ports, and as can be seen from the table opposite the tonnage figures for shipping using the harbour were very healthy.

It was fortunate for Bo'ness that most of this coal went abroad, and was therefore obliged to use sea rather than rail transport. In reverse, the fact that the six saw mills in the town in 1885 used mainly Baltic timber helped to sustain a fair importation of timber, but Grangemouth's rivalry prevented Bo'ness from becoming a great centre for re-distribution of exports to the west. It was only in 1881 that Bo'ness was able to open a major wet dock of seven and a half acres.

Forced specialisation was quite a common feature amongst east coast ports in the railway age. While port development in Bo'ness was obiously hampered by the failure of the port to retain a vigorous general import-export trade, coal did enable the harbour to expand, albeit slowly. Dunbar suffered from a much more radical form of compulsory specialisation after the opening of the North British Railway. The burgh had secured government assistance for substantial harbour improvement in 1844. One result of this was the creation of a handsome New or Victoria Harbour covering five acres, but the coming of the railway virtually destroyed the local import-export trade, and left Dunbar little more than a haven of refuge mainly used by coastal shipping caught by bad weather when plying between Leith and Tyneside.[25]

Grangemouth, the great exception amongst the smaller ports of the Forth and Tay, owed its peculiar vitality entirely to its relationship with Scotland's internal transport system. It was the Forth and Clyde Navigation Company, which constructed the Forth and Clyde Canal, which presided over the birth and early expansion of the port of Grangemouth. Under the aegis of the Navigation Company Grangemouth grew into the chief port for Stirlingshire as well as Glasgow's window on the North Sea. The Navigation Company itself constructed two small docks known as the Old and the Junction Docks which were opened in 1843 and 1859 respectively. Another very significant development came in 1848, when the Navigation Company obtained powers to construct a short length of railway. Railway development could only enhance Grangemouth's special relationship with the Glasgow area.

After 1860 there was in fact a very sharp increase in the rate of expansion of trade through Grangemouth harbour. Both the North British and the Caledonian Railways had very substantial interests in the port.[26] Indeed as early as 1857 a joint committee had been formed by the Caledonian, Edinburgh and Glasgow, and Scottish Central Railways and the Forth and Clyde Canal, in order to adjust their rival interests in traffic to and from Grangemouth. After a great deal of negotiation, it was agreed that the railways should take sixty per cent of the traffic, and the canal forty per cent. Rates were controlled by the committee to ensure that agreements were honoured.[27] All these adjustments broke down, however, in the frenzied bout of competitive take-over bids in which both the Caledonian and the North British indulged in the 1860s. The Edinburgh and Glasgow Railway vanished into the North British, but the Caledonian, fighting for eastern outlets bought the Forth and Clyde Canal. Naturally, the Caledonian also secured the two small docks and the length of railway which the canal company had built at Grangemouth. In short, the Caledonian bought Grangemouth harbour.

The tonnage of shipping using the harbour soared. In the early 1850s it had nearly all been coastal, but by the next decade a very vigorous foreign trade existed, as the figures in the table opposite show.

As on top of this the total tonnage registered at the port was also rising, from 9,080 in 1853 to 12,649 in 1869, the need for more extensive docks was clamant. It is true that tonnage registered at the port declined to 10,499 in 1881, but of this tonnage 8,624 was accounted for by thirty-two steamers, whereas in 1853 steamers had accounted for a mere 828 tons.[28] Steamers were on average much larger vessels than the sailing craft frequenting Grangemouth, so

Date	Entered (Tonnage)			Cleared (Tonnage)		
	British	Foreign	Total	British	Foreign	Total
1867	153,378	78,422	231,800	136,613	74,375	210,988
1873	194,899	144,337	339,236	199,143	149,122	348,265
1877	314,278	121,068	435,346	315,293	117,837	433,130
1881	302,899	79,826	382,725	306,164	79,916	383,080

technological change reinforced the pressures created by sheer increase in total tonnage. By 1875 eighty ships at a time occasionally lay in the roads waiting for admission to the harbour.

It was logical enough that the Caledonian Railway, the proprietor of the existing harbour, should build the new docks which were obviously required. On the other hand, this would clearly confirm the Caledonian stranglehold on Grangemouth. The select committee of the House of Commons which considered the Caledonian's request for powers to build docks at Grangemouth therefore witnessed the last bid by the North British to challenge the Caledonian grip on the port. The challenge proved vain, for the Caledonian secured the necessary powers and went on to build a new dock of ten and a half acres, as well as a slightly smaller area of timber basin. The quays of the new dock were generously equipped with hydraulic coal-hoists and Armstrong cranes. The whole complex of improvements cost £300,000, and it was opened, with much jubilation, in 1882.[29]

The trade of Grangemouth remained of a very general character. The principal imports were timber, metals, flax, grain, sugar, fruit, chemicals, paper, and provisions. In

1881 the port imported 92,940 tons of timber and was just
beginning to import substantial quantities of English pig
iron from Middlesbrough. This new import reflected the
rise of a steel industry in Motherwell in Lanarkshire. The
earlier-established wrought iron industry of Coatbridge,
another Lanarkshire town not far from Glasgow, was slow
to adapt to the arrival of the age of steel. Motherwell
seized its opportunity to become the home of a new industry
which from the start relied on imported, rather than
Scottish, pig-iron. Grangemouth's exports were dominated
by coal, of which the port exported 101,359 tons in 1881.
Other exports were largely in the hands of the Carron Iron
Company, which virtually monopolised trade between
Grangemouth and London. Even so, many ships left
Grangemouth in ballast because exports through the
harbour did not match imports.[30]

If the impact of the railways on the ports of the east coast
dealing in a fair spread of commodities was profound, their
impact on the more specialist ferry and coal ports was no
less dramatic. As has already been shown, some traditional
ferry ports were crucial to the early railway network. They
were not, however, necessarily the same ferry ports that had
been assiduously built up by private and public effort in the
first three or four decades of the nineteenth century. There
were, for example, a great many ferries linking Dundee and
Angus with the northern shore of Fife. Of these, the most
important in the early nineteenth century were the ones
between Dundee and Newport and Woodhaven, small
villages on the Fife shore south of Dundee. In May 1815
one of the sailing pinnaces used on these services overturned
in the Tay, with the loss of nineteen lives. Under the stimulus
of this tragedy, there arose a strong agitation for improvement of the ferry service. By 1819 local pressure groups were
appealing to the government for financial support for
improvements to the ferry, which was described as being in
'a wretched state', despite the fact that it was of immense
importance as a major link in the chain of communication
between Edinburgh and the northern parts of Scotland.[31]

In 1819 parliamentary legislation appointed a board of trustees to administer these services, and the trustees elected to replace sail by steam to make the service less dependent on favourable weather and tides. By 1821 the first ferry steamer, the *Union*, was in service, with the result that nearby ferries lost nearly all their custom to the modernised service between Dundee and Newport. The ancient ferry between Broughty Ferry, which lies a few miles east of Dundee, and Ferryport-on-Craig (or Tayport) in Fife, lost nearly all its once substantial trade in passengers and animals, being reduced to two small boats, one propelled by sail, the other by oars. When, however, the railway interest bought the ferry in 1846, something of a financial revolution ensued. The railway changed the name of the southern terminus to Tayport, improved facilities there, and eventually built a substantial new harbour at Broughty Ferry, to accommodate its great steam ferries. The ferry between Dundee and Newport lost enough trade to become a liability to a succession of owners, eventually passing into the hands of Dundee Harbour Trustees in 1873 in exchange for a payment of £20,000 to the then owners, the Caledonian Railway Company. From the point of view of the trustees, it was a bad bargain. They can have derived little comfort from the thought that after the creation of a permanent railway bridge over the Tay at Dundee, the Tayport ferry also lost enough trade to become a financial liability. In 1892 the North British Railway, in a Bill it was sponsoring in parliament, tried to secure the right to abandon the ferry. The Commissioners of Police of Broughty Ferry, however, successfully petitioned against this part of the proposed legislation.[32]

Widespread public concern about ferry services was as common on the Forth in the early nineteenth century as it was on the Tay. The ferries between Fife and Midlothian were in the hands of trustees by the third decade of the century, but both in Edinburgh and in Dundee, it was felt that the trustees were spreading their effort and money too thinly over too many harbours. Edinburgh merchants preferred the concept of concentrating on what they called 'a great national ferry' between Newhaven and Burntisland. Dundee opinion also favoured concentration, but with Kinghorn rather than Burntisland as the Fife terminal.[33] The arguments became rather obsolete when ducal and railway capital developed Granton harbour as the most important ferry terminus on the southern shore of the Forth. There was an element of the capricious in the impact of Victorian technology and Victorian capitalism on the east-coast ferry ports. For the ferry ports of the Forth, the supreme symbol of that element was what was known locally as The Great Bridge, with which the railways spanned the Forth at Queensferry in 1890. Only with the coming of the motor car were ferries as such revitalised.

The ports of the Forth and Tay which concentrated on coal exports were, in the long run, peculiarly susceptible to drastic economic and technological change. Bulk shipment of coal had called forth exceptional loading arrangements from the late eighteenth century. By that period the river bed at the Old Landing Place at Clackmannan Pow, at the mouth of the River Black Devon just east of Alloa, was entirely artificial. The bed of the river was lined with hewn sandstone blocks, and lateral blocks of timber. When the river bed was completely uncovered at low tide, the smooth stonework allowed the flat-bottomed coal barques to settle down without damage to keel or hull. This meant that they could be loaded at any point of the tide without fear of breaking their backs or being stuck in the mud.[34]

As we have seen, Bo'ness was increasingly becoming a coal-exporting port between 1840 and 1870. There was nothing unique in this experience, for Alloa was also becoming increasingly dependent on coal exports after 1840. Indeed in 1879 Alloa exported 159,780 tons of coal to foreign countries, as well as 15,236 tons coastwise. In value, this was well over ninety per cent of Alloa's total exports. Like Bo'ness, Alloa was developing special handling facilities for bulk coal shipment.[35] Both ports, however, retained a fairly broad range of imports, and the great age of the highly-specialised coal ports, most of which were in Fife, really dates from after 1870.

It would therefore be wrong to see the impact of the railways on the smaller ports of the Tay and Forth as other than a complex and protracted phenomenon. At the height of the first great railway boom in 1845 rails from England and Wales were being shipped by sea to ports like Perth for distribution to Scottish railway construction sites, because there were no through railway routes along which the rails could have been delivered. Once, however, there were efficient through rail routes along the east coast of Great Britain, certain ports, such as Perth, suffered very badly. Nearly all ports experienced a falling off in the rate of traffic growth they had come to take for granted. Many were over-extended financially when the impact of railway development began to hit them. On the whole, the bigger the port the better it weathered the crisis. In any port, it was primarily coastal traffic that declined. There were exceptions even to this, notably in the case of iron ore imports, and pig-iron exports.[36] However, it is still true that imports from abroad, like jute from Calcutta, and exports to foreign parts, like coal to Europe, stood up to the pressures of the railway age best of all.

DUNDEE AND LEITH AND THE COMING OF THE RAILWAYS

The prosperity of the harbour of Dundee was closely linked to the fortunes of the local textile industry. When that industry went into depression in 1839, due to competition from cheap cottons for some of Dundee's coarse linen lines, the harbour was at once affected. By 1840 just under half the town's power-spinning capacity was idle. Between 1839 and 1840 there was a substantial fall in harbour traffic, which only began to pick up again when the textile industry fought back against cotton by using more and more of the even cheaper jute. By 1846 a partial recovery had occurred in the Dundee textile trade, carrying with it renewed activity in the harbour, where there were 672 more arrivals and departures of ships in 1847 than in 1840. However, the ability of the harbour to take continuing advantage of the textile boom in Dundee after 1848 was deeply affected by the fact that from early in that year Dundee was effectively integrated into a national railway network.

The opening of direct rail links with Arbroath in 1840 and Perth in 1847 had been beneficial to the trade of the port of Dundee, for it led to a diversion of maritime trade from Arbroath and Perth to Dundee. Dundee itself, however, was deprived of trade when in 1848 a through route by rail from Dundee to the Glasgow area, via Stirling, was opened. This followed the creation of a connection between Stirling and Perth by the Scottish Central Railway. It followed from this development that there was soon rail communication between Dundee and the western coast of England, via the Caledonian link with the English railway network. Liverpool was consequently linked by rail to Dundee. On the east coast equally dramatic developments occurred when in 1848 the Edinburgh and Northern Railway completed a line across Fife, which crossed the Tay by means of a rail ferry between Ferryport-on-Craig (or Tayport) and Broughty Ferry. This linked Dundee by rail and ferry with the North British Railway and thence with the railway network on the eastern coast of England. Once rail connections existed between Dundee and other major ports like Leith, Glasgow, Liverpool, and London, it was inevitable that the railways would take away some of the trade on the longer coasting routes, such as those between Dundee and these ports.

The railways were speedy and regular. Their routes to Glasgow and Liverpool were short compared with any possible coastal route. Naturally enough, they creamed off a great deal of traffic from the port of Dundee. Between 1840 and 1855 port facilities were stagnant, and traffic in decline, despite prosperity in the local textile trade. In 1855 arrivals and departures with cargo were 2,072 fewer than in 1847. Textile fibre imports were still dominated by flax. It was not until the Crimean War that jute loomed very large in Dundee's imports. Indeed as late as 1855 only 19,143 tons of jute reached Dundee by both sea and rail. Most of the jute was forwarded from big ports like Liverpool and Calcutta which themselves supported a large Indian trade. Jute would come into these ports as a fraction of the cargo carried in a large ship. Before 1848 it would then be sent to Dundee by coastal shipping. After that date it was much more likely to be despatched by rail. Flax imports from the Baltic, mostly from Russian ports, usually reached Dundee direct by sea, but some flax did come in by rail from other ports. The percentage of Dundee's intake of textile fibres which arrived by sea fell from 100 in 1847 to 87.6 in 1853.

Other trades proved more buoyant, from the point of view of Dundee harbour. Timber, for example, came largely from the Baltic. There was no alternative to sea transport, and demand for timber was governed almost entirely by the state of the local building trade. This in turn depended on the prosperity of the local textile industry, because most incomes in Dundee were connected, directly or indirectly, with textiles. After a slump in 1839–40, due to the depression, timber imports recovered and increased as textile fibre imports declined. Whereas timber and tar boats had been 2.4 per cent of all cargo-carrying arrivals in 1840, they were 4.1 per cent of such arrivals in 1855, and as they were on average twice the size of other cargo ships, their real significance was double the stated figure.

The coal trade was another important one for Dundee harbour. Dundee imported a great deal of coal for industrial and domestic use, from two main sources. One was the Forth, with its many coalfields, and the other was the north of England around Newcastle. After 1848 imports from the Forth were much restricted by railway competition, especially after 1851 when the new giant ferry steamer service from Ferryport-on-Craig to Broughty Ferry became capable of carrying whole waggon trains across the river, thus eliminating any need to unload and reload waggons. The importation of coal from Northumberland and Durham via

Dundee harbour was much less affected, though between 1840 and 1855 Newcastle was displaced as the main port trading in coal with Dundee. Seaham and Sunderland took its place.

In general, the railways cut heavily into the trade of the port with nearby areas, like the Forth, and with western ports like Glasgow and Liverpool. This was a matter of elementary economics. When the Edinburgh and Dundee Steamship Company tried to retain Forth trade by cutting rates in competition with the railway, it promptly bankrupted itself. On the other hand, longer hauls to Sunderland, Hull and London remained an economic proposition for coastal shipping carrying general cargo and passengers. Though slower, sea transport was cheaper. This sort of trade carried a disproportionate percentage of the export trade from Dundee harbour, for exports, mainly textiles, were much smaller than imports. In 1855 69.3 per cent of all ships leaving Dundee harbour left in ballast, and these were mainly coal or flax ships from England and the Baltic respectively.

In the short run, the freezing of improvement schemes at Dundee harbour was a sensible adjustment to falling revenue, but it could not continue indefinitely, if only because changes in the design of ships made a higher standard of facilities in the harbour essential. There was a noticeable increase in the size of ships using the harbour. By 1854 the largest ships visiting the port could not use the King William Dock at all, and even had difficulties over the Earl Grey Dock, except at very high tides. On top of this, the local textile industry entered in 1854 the first of its two most spectacular nineteenth-century booms. This particular boom was associated with the outbreak of the Crimean War between Britain, France, and Turkey, and Russia.[37]

War was a great consumer of heavy textiles. The fact that Britain was at war with Dundee's principal source of flax was embarrassing, but not fatal. Indirect trade with Russia through the ports of neutral Prussia or through Hamburg, was quickly organised. Even so, the demand for coarse cloth was so heavy that it could only be met by a massive increase in the consumption of Indian jute in Dundee. In 1852 Dundee imported 20,379 tons of flax, tow, and codilla. Tow and codilla were simply inferior varieties of flax. By 1856 the figure was 27,561. With jute, the jump in imports was much more spectacular. In 1852 Dundee imported a total of 16,983 tons of jute by sea and rail. By 1856 the figure was 31,031. Nearly all the flax, and more than half the jute came by sea, so harbour revenues soared.[38]

By 1857 post-war depression had set in, but by April 1861 the American Civil War had broken out, and the textile trade of Dundee and district was on the verge of the dizziest boom in its history. Expansion was on a scale never matched before or since. Between 1861 and 1871 the population of Dundee increased from 91,664 to 120,724. Imports of flax did not increase spectacularly, but imports of jute soared from 35,716 tons in 1861 to 94,608 tons in 1871.[39] It was not just that the American war was a great consumer of textiles, like all wars. There was also the very important fact that in America cottons were used for purposes which in Europe would have been served by fabrics made from flax or coarser fibres.[40] When therefore the cotton South was cut off from the North by civil war, there was a glorious opportunity for British textile manufacturers to step into the gap. The North did, of course, search around for alternative sources of raw material, but it is significant that one of the first prizes captured by the Southern sea-raider *Alabama* was the *T. B. Wales* of Boston returning home from Calcutta with a cargo of jute, linseed, and saltpeter.[41]

Dundee actually had two major harbour projects in a state of suspended animation. Both had been left unfinished when the previously boyant harbour revenues had begun to sag around 1840. One was the Victoria wet dock, which lay to the east of existing facilities, and the other was a proposed eastern tidal harbour outside it. Soaring jute imports revived both. The tidal harbour was turned into a wet dock, named Camperdown Dock. It covered over eight acres and was complete by 1865. Victoria Dock, whose water area was not far short of eleven acres, was a more formidable undertaking, but it in turn was complete by 1875. Both these docks were deeper than any previous Dundee wet dock, and both were very much better endowed with warehouses. The volume of the jute trade made this essential. Equally significant was the fact that the Dundee and Arbroath Railway's station was immediately adjacent to the north quay of Victoria Dock. Jute and railways in combination had given new life to the port of Dundee by 1875.[42]

Unlike Dundee, Leith faced the coming of the railway age without normal freedom of manoeuvre. The elaborate settlement which had freed Leith harbour from the overlordship of Edinburgh, and which had handed the port over to the control of an autonomous body, was meant to be liberating in its effects, but its financial provisions soon proved something of a straight jacket. On top of this, the peculiar engineering difficulties posed by a major port situated on half a mile of flat foreshore much exposed to drifting sand ensured that engineering opinion was seldom unanimous about the most desirable course of improvement. Surveys by Walker and Cubbitt, two eminent London civil engineers, were conducted in 1838–9, with contradictory results. By 1846 another survey and set of proposals had been produced by a Mr A. M. Rendel. It was generally agreed that what was desperately needed, apart from increased accommodation, was an improved deep-water entrance to the harbour.

The impasse was broken when in 1848 a government commission on Tidal Harbours reported. It devoted a great deal of space to Leith, arguing that despite the large sums spent on the port, it was still scandalously devoid of facilities for large steamships. There were, for example, no adequate patent ship or graving dock facilities for repairing the steamers using the port, with the result that they were normally repaired in Dundee or London. The income of the port had latterly exceeded £25,000 per annum, yet the entrance was restricted, and dock accommodation scarce. The commissioners reckoned that diversion of shipping to other Forth ports was depriving Leith of harbour revenues to the tune of

£5,000 per annum. It was no help at all that the immensely complex Leith harbour dues were levied in obsolete Scots currency.

Acts were quickly passed to improve this intolerable situation. The previous financial limit of £125,000, which the government had regarded as the maximum possible expenditure on Leith harbour improvements in the days of Walker and Cubbitt, was ignored. The schedule of harbour dues was rationalised. Rendel's scheme for improving the entrance was adopted. It involved the extension of the pier on the east of the entrance by 1,000 feet, and the conversion of the western breakwater into a pier, which was then extended by 1,750 feet. This latter pier was constructed strong enough to bear the weight of a railway. Provision was also made for a low-water landing place at the end of the West Pier. All these developments were strongly'reminiscent of works which had already been executed at Granton. At Leith, however, a new dock of just under five acres water area was opened in 1851. It had a minimum depth of twenty-one feet at the very lowest tides, and was used mainly by shipping moving between Leith and London, or Leith and Hamburg. This new dock was christened the Victoria Dock.[43]

The immediate financial consequences of a renewed development programme were uncomfortable. Leith docks, which already carried nearly £300,000 of debt, ran at a deficit of over £34,000 in the financial year 1850–1. Nevertheless, there was a fundamental buoyancy in the trade of the port which enabled it to run at a profit by the end of the 1850s. In 1862–3 there was a profit of over £5,000 in the harbour accounts, and the accumulated debt was down to a little over £100,000.[44] In the last analysis, the growth of the Leith–Edinburgh urban complex guaranteed growth for the port. Industrialisation in the area was less extensive than in Glasgow, which had a more spectacular growth of population in the Victorian period, but population growth in Edinburgh and Leith was still impressive. Their combined population of 200,000 on 1861 rose to 240,000 by 1871.

Heavy industry was not prominent in Edinburgh and Leith, apart from the Lothian coalfields around them. Their prosperity was based on a range of industries including a very large construction industry, substantial paper and printing industries, and many other trades like brewing, distilling, and leather, glass, brass, and rubber manufacture. Allied to the traditionally large middle-class professional sector in the Edinburgh economy, this range of economic activity was enough to ensure a steady growth of production, population, and purchasing power.[45]

Inevitably, there were demands for increased dock accommodation at Leith almost as soon as the Victoria Dock was opened. It was, however, a good ten years before preliminary surveys were made for what was to become the Albert Dock. This great dock was sited east of the existing dock complex on an area known as the East Sands. Its construction involved the reclamation of over eighty acres of sand on which Leith Races had been held for a very long time. The races had been discontinued in 1856 as a result of bitter protests from Leith householders about the scale of the drunkenness and profligacy which accompanied the horse racing.[46] No doubt the worthy citizens of Leith considered the Albert Dock a very fair exchange for an obsolete race course. It cost nearly quarter of a million pounds, covered nearly eleven acres, and was 1,100 feet long and 450 broad.

The Albert Dock was formally opened in August 1869, when it became at once the home of Messrs Gibson's fleet of ships engaged in trade with Europe. Significantly, roughly a sixth of the total cost of the dock represented expenditure on cranes and warehouses. The cost of equipping a major dock in order to secure rapid loading and unloading, and therefore a rapid turn-round of shipping was soaring in the late nineteenth century. The Albert Dock was equipped with the first hydraulic cranes installed in any Scottish port, and Leith was proud of the rapid turn-round in shipping which they made possible. Leith was fortunate, both in the size of the population in its immediate hinterland,

and in the fact that its harbour was linked with the national rail network which covered most of Great Britain by 1870. As compared with Dundee, Leith not only enjoyed a larger trade, but it also had a much more complex pattern of trade, especially with regard to exports. Dundee's imports around 1870 consisted of textile fibres, timber, coal, fertiliser, and grain. There were no other significant categories apart from the products of the local whaling industry. Leith's imports about the same time consisted mainly of corn and timber, flax and hemp, hides, fertiliser, foodstuffs, sugar and other colonial produce, wool, wine, spirits and dyestuffs. This was a broader range of items than entered Dundee, partly because Leith had more sophisticated processing industries than Dundee. Dundee, for example, had no sugar refineries, and imported most of the sugar it consumed by rail. It was, however, in the field of exports that the differences between the two ports became most striking. Over ninety per cent, by value, of Dundee's exports around 1870 consisted of cloth or yarn. Leith had a far wider range of export commodities. It exported in 1866 a fair amount of linen and yarn, mostly brought from Dundee and the county of Fife. Leith also exported cottons and cotton yarn from Lanarkshire in the west, and it acted as an eastern outlet for iron from the same county. Coal was exported from Leith in quantity, as were woollens and worsteds from the Border area of Scotland. Industrial chemicals, wines and spirits, leather and paper, and a score of other products flowed out of Leith. Salt fish were still a very significant export from the port in 1866.[47]

Leith and Dundee were clearly in a class by themselves amongst the ports of the Forth and Tay by 1870. The coming of the railways, the growth of steamship sizes, and the evolution of elaborate mechanical loading and unloading devices had all favoured the larger port, with its capacity to mobilise large quantities of capital. By 1876 not far under a million tons of shipping was being entered and cleared from Leith within a year. Yet in so far as any port of the Forth and Tay shared Leith's extraordinary range of commodities handled, that port was Grangemouth rather than Dundee.

It was Dundee's misfortune to have expanded as a major port in the railway age almost entirely on the strength of bulk imports of textile fibres. If Dundee was 'a one-industry town', her port was 'a one-commodity port'.

CHAPTER IV

The Last Age of Massive
Dock Development, 1870–1914

INTRODUCTION

By about 1870 the ports of the Firths of Tay and Forth had more or less digested the economic consequences of railway development. They were part of an integrated transport system whose hard core was a division of labour between the steam-driven locomotive and the steamship. There was a continuing process of adjustment between different components of the overall transport network, but as far as the ports were concerned the most traumatic period of adjustment was over. In the two biggest ports another milestone had been passed. After 1869 in Leith, and after 1875 in Dundee, it was impossible to create further dock facilities without extensive land reclamation, which added greatly to the expense of such operations.

Nevertheless, there was substantial investment in improved port facilities in many harbours of the Forth and Tay between 1870 and 1914, and this investment was by no means confined to the two largest ones. Continuing economic growth made selective investment in port facilities inevitable. The textile industry of east-central Scotland had passed through its two greatest booms, but it continued to expand, albeit much more slowly, between 1870 and 1914. Within these same years there was considerable growth in coal exports from the southern parts of Fife. Edinburgh remained a great and growing consumer and therefore importer of commodities. Finally Glasgow and the western coast of Scotland experienced vigorous growth based on shipbuilding and the allied steel industry. A port like Grangemouth which was closely identified with the economic fate of Glasgow could not fail to benefit from this.

LEITH AND DOCK EXTENSION TO 1914

By 1870 Leith had reached a stage where any further extension of its dock facilities would clearly involve land reclamation on a substantial scale. Nevertheless, no sooner had the Albert Dock been opened in 1869, than plans were laid for an even larger dock to the east of it, which was to be christened the Edinburgh Dock. In 1874 an essential preliminary operation began with the construction of a great sea wall from the east end of the Albert Dock to a point not far from where the Seafield toll-gate had once stood. The massive embankment was completed early in 1877, and it served to make 108 acres of land available for reclamation. Soon an army of navvies were at work on the excavation of the dock proper, assisted by two steam-driven excavating machines which were deemed capable of doing the work of eighty men, and of shifting together 1100 tons of earth a day. By 1881 the new dock was ready. It was opened in July of that year by the Duke of Edinburgh, after whom it was named.

It was indeed a formidable undertaking. The dock itself was nearly seventeen acres in extent. It was lined with masonry from Craigmillar quarry near Edinburgh, and it was linked to the Albert Dock by a channel 270 feet in length and 65 in breadth. A hydraulic swing-bridge weighing over 400 tons spanned the channel. In the east end of the dock an artificial peninsula surrounded a fine new graving dock itself 350 feet long and 48 wide. On the south side of the dock there were extensive sheds, while the coal trade was catered for by a hydraulic coal hoist capable of

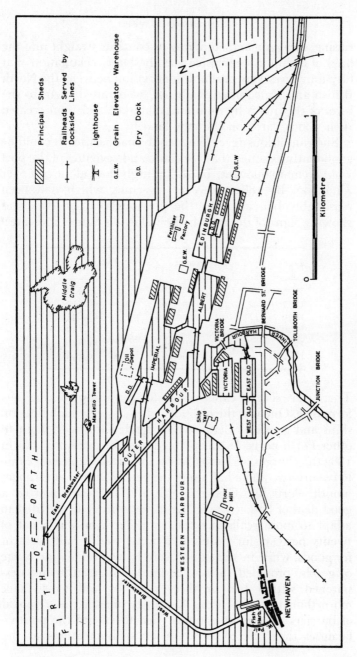

The Port of Leith 1956

Legend:
- Principal Sheds
- Railheads Served by Dockside Lines
- Lighthouse
- G.E.W. Grain Elevator Warehouse
- D.D. Dry Dock

FIRTH OF FORTH

Middle Craig

Martello Tower

East Breakwater

West Breakwater

OUTER HARBOUR

WESTERN HARBOUR

Oil Depot

D.D.

IMPERIAL

ALBERT

EDINBURGH

G.E.W.

Fertiliser Factory

G.E.W.

Ship Yard

Flour Mill

VICTORIA

WEST OLD

EAST OLD

Victoria Bridge

INNER HARBOUR

Bernard St. Bridge

Tollbooth Bridge

Junction Bridge

Fish Harb.

NEWHAVEN

Kilometre

raising a waggon and emptying its contents straight into the hold of a ship. So extensive was the land reclamation that fifty-four acres were available for division between the North British and Caledonian Railways, who raised them to the level of the quays by dumping material, and then created their goods yards on the new land.[1]

Such ambitious development only made sense if it could be confidently assumed that the trade and revenues of the port would remain buoyant. The Edinburgh Dock alone cost over £400,000. By 1882, however, revenue, which had been reasonably buoyant over the previous year or two, was showing signs of decline, as the following figures indicate:[2]

Year	Revenue (£)	Expenditure (£)
1975	74,484	79,449
1877	207,387	198,716
1879	100,553	125,865
1880	135,910	121,156
1881	107,491	89,865
1882	96,264	99,399

There were several explanations for this disappointing performance. One was the old story of excessively high dues on ships and goods at Leith, which tended to divert both to other Forth ports. It was pointed out, for example, that in 1883 the charges on basket wares imported into Leith came to twenty-two and a half times the rates charged at Grangemouth. Ports like Grangemouth and Bo'ness imported a good deal of basket wares: Leith very little. Leith tried to adapt to more realistic rates. In 1882 there was a cut of twenty per cent for vessels and twelve and a half per cent for goods, while in 1883 dues were halved on a wide range of goods, provided they were landed in transit and despatched within two or three days by rail to a place more than ten miles from Leith. To match this removal of barriers, the commissioners tried to extend the positive facilities they offered at Leith by such measures as the building of special sheds on the north side of Edinburgh Dock for the storage of the esparto grass which by 1885 had become an important raw material for the Lothian paper industry.

None of these measures were wholly successful, partly because in some vital areas like the coal trade Leith suffered from discrimination by the railways. The railways had a direct financial stake in the docks at Burntisland, Bo'ness, and Grangemouth, so they deliberately charged high rates for the transport of coal from the colliery areas to Leith. This made it very difficult for Leith to compete for coal traffic, and, incidentally helps to explain why state control over railway rates was a burning political issue on a national scale in the 1880s. It was often best for an owner to shift his ship in ballast from Leith to some other Forth port to load coal. It was estimated that in one twelve month period 400,000 tons carrying capacity left Leith in ballast, but when, as in the winter of 1883, profit margins on coal ranged between one and two pennies a ton, owners could not ignore the fact that shipment at Bo'ness or Grangemouth cost six pence per ton less than shipment at Leith.

On top of these factors, there was a general recession in trade in 1885, with an attendant decline in the import of foodstuffs and building materials like timber. The Leith Dock Commission was left to console itself with the thought that the problem of the discharge of Edinburgh's sewage into the Water of Leith and therefore Leith docks was primarily a matter of concern to the Corporations of Leith and Edinburgh. While these two bodies quarrelled bitterly over a piece of local legislation involving new sewage outlets, and while alarmists complained of the smell at Leith docks and insisted it would lead to a cholera outbreak, the commissioners solemnly denied all responsibility. They had other matters to worry about. The railways were still obstructing Leith's coal trade, with the result that in 1885 the revenue of the port of Leith fell to £80,376. As no major construction projects were in progress, expenditure was only £37,102, but the overall trend was not healthy.[3]

The year 1886-7 was a crucial one for Leith docks. Another substantial reduction in rates and charges was put into effect, in the hope of attracting more custom to the port. This object was attained, for the total number of vessels arriving at Leith in the year 1886-7 was 4,114, of a total tonnage of 1,101,530—an increase of 43 vessels and 4,714 tons over the previous year. Sailings from Leith numbered 4,119, of 1,108,108 tons, being an increase of 64 vessels and 10,246 tons on the previous year. Revenue was not particularly good, having fallen to £73,062, £6,793 less than in the previous year. However, expenditure at £67,078 was a good £11,355 down on the previous twelve months, which pleased contemporary observers. The docks could not hope to avoid substantial expenditure from time to time, if only in order to cope with unsuspected defects in recent developments. Thus, because of water pressure building up behind it, the north wall of the Edinburgh dock began to subside in 1887, rendering remedial action imperative. This was nothing unusual by contemporary standards. The problems involved in the construction of very large sea walls and docks were far from fully understood by the engineering science of the period. Indeed such basic problems as the action of sea water on Portland Cement were only being tackled in the late 1880s, and that only because several substantial harbour works on the east coast suffered severe damage when the cement used in them disintegrated under physical and chemical attack from the sea.

Fortunately, by 1888 Leith was experiencing the benefits of a sharp upswing in economic activity. The condition of trade in the port was one of exceptional prosperity. Direct trade with America expanded. Continental trade was particularly brisk, with a high demand in Russian and other Baltic ports for Scottish coal. The provision trade was assisted by low prices for commodities like butter, which combined with prosperity in the hinterland to produce a large rise in consumption. Timber imports, always a good indicator of the general level of economic activity, were buoyant.[4]

By 1889 the level of business at Leith docks was being described as unprecedented, and powerful arguments were being advanced to the effect that the existing dock capacity was likely to become inadequate within a year or two unless there was further expansion. For the statistical year 1888–9 there was an increase in arrivals at the port of 262 vessels and 57,253 tons. Leith Dock Commission was not primarily a revenue-collecting body, so it reduced rates and charges on goods and shipping once again at the beginning of 1888–9, in the hope of attracting more shipping, at the cost of a stable, or even declining revenue. More shipping was attracted, but on a scale that ensured a substantial growth in revenue. The commissioners had for some time been holding at bay demands that they should construct a new fish market for Leith's own fishing village of Newhaven. Faced by demands for dock-extension in Leith itself they proved much less obdurate.

Certainly, pressure on quay space was very heavy by 1891. With up to thirty-six steamships arriving within the week, it was quite common to see vessels lying out in the middle of the Edinburgh and Albert Docks, waiting for their turn at the quays. In 1890–1 4,996 vessels with a registered tonnage of 1,369,000 entered Leith. None of this meant that shipowning as such was profitable in Leith; quite the reverse. The early 1890s were a period of very low profitability for Leith ship-owners, and of wage reductions for seamen in the teeth of bitter opposition by the seamen's union. It was as an import-export unit that Leith was booming. On top of the increased number of ships frequenting the port there was the problem of an increase in the size of the largest vessels, especially those involved in the important, and growing Canadian and American trades. Nor was this trade confined to people and cargo. For some years Glasgow monopolised the traffic in cattle between Canada and Scotland, but by 1891 1,000 head of Canadian cattle were being discharged at Leith within twelve months, and by 1892 the commissioners were building special cattle sheds at the Albert Dock to encourage this traffic. By 1893 the commissioners had completed parliamentary lobbying for enabling legislation and were accepting tenders for a new and ambitious scheme of dock-extension.[5]

There was no specific industry whose demands on shipping space provided the dynamic behind this pattern of expansion. The most rapidly-growing manufacturing industry in Edinburgh and Leith in the late nineteenth century was probably the rubber industry, but it merely contributed to growth rooted in the physical expansion of the conurbation. The combined populations of Edinburgh and Leith grew from 201,628 in 1862 to 328,921 in 1892. The green fields which separated Edinburgh and Leith in the early nineteenth century had disappeared under speculative building by 1892. With the creation of a tramway system, it had become common for Leith merchants to live in Edinburgh and to commute daily by tramway to their work in the less prestigious town. Practical considerations had already compelled Leith and Edinburgh to co-operate on such matters as gas and water supply, and water purification. Leith Dock Commissioners, whose territories lay outside the legal boundaries of the municipality of Leith, can have had little doubt as to the importance of the general trade of Edinburgh for their expanding dock complex in 1893, but it is significant that about the same time the city fathers of Leith were being wooed by Edinburgh Town Council with a view to reuniting the two communities under one authority.[6]

Leith Dock Commission, whose financial soundness was recognised by the removal of government nominees from their midst in 1875, had embarked upon a major piece of reclamation by their decisions in 1893. Another sea wall enabled some eighty acres of land on what was known as the East Sands to be consolidated, or made available for the great new dock. It was to be christened the Imperial Dock, and was designed to give five feet more of depth at all times than existing docks. Extensive dredging in the approach channel ensured that the normal class of coasting steamer could enter the new dock at all states of the tide.[7]

Originally the Imperial Dock was to have cost £500,000.

Grain elevator with suction equipment, Leith Docks 1971

Gantry crane for container traffic, Albert Dock, Leith 1971

Almost at once these plans ran into a storm of criticism from local merchants. These men were riding a major economic boom in the last years of the nineteenth century. 1898 was a good year, as was 1899, and 1900 was quite exceptional, partly due to the Boer War with its accompanying high level of government expenditure. The discriminatory rates charged by the railway companies were checked by parliamentary legislation, and with demand for Scots coal running at a high level in Western Europe, the main limitations on coal export through Leith were the strength of home demand, and the shortage of rolling stock suitable for taking coal from the pits to the docks. Leith Dock Commission, elected separately from Leith Town Council, with a bar against overlapping membership of the Commission and Edinburgh or Leith Town Councils, was denounced as a 'closed and conservative' body.

Under immense pressure, the Commission altered its plans. Local merchants and shipowners argued that both the volume of trade and the size of ships were increasing at an unprecedented pace, and that dock-extension should allow for this. As a result the original dimensions of the new dock—1,100 feet long by 550 feet wide—were altered to allow of an eastwards extension 600 feet long by 275 feet broad. Besides this, a new graving dock 500 feet long with an entrance 70 feet wide was decided on. Water was run into the Imperial Dock from the Albert Dock in 1902, and the new dock was formally opened in 1904, by which time its cost had risen to the sum of £750,000. Nor had the port neglected other improvements during this time, for in 1903 an 'America Silo' or 'Grain Elevator Warehouse' was opened at the east end of the Edinburgh Dock. It was built for Mr J. Saville Patmore of the North British Storage and Transit Company, Leith and Glasgow. This warehouse enabled Leith to exploit the mechanisation of unloading and storage by means of continuous, electrically-driven belts, with buckets attached to the moving belt. Such techniques were cutting down Dundee's markets for sacking, but they were a measure of the forward-looking mentality of the port of Leith.

129

E

To local observers the Imperial Dock seemed to mark only one more stage in an expansion of port facilities which had an indefinite future ahead of it in 1904. It was true that in 1904 there was a relative depression in the level of business activity, but it was felt that both population and trade could not but go on rising, however unevenly. Harbour revenue at nearly £90,000 was a record in 1904, and arrivals in that year, at 6,278 vessels of an aggregate tonnage of 1,959,080, showed an increase of 73 vessels and 42,274 tons over 1903. Coal was by far the most important of Leith's exports, and at 882,606 tons in 1904 it was 25,487 tons up on 1903. Leith Dock Commission, after inspecting their great rival Grangemouth Docks in 1905, reached the comforting conclusion that Leith's docks were as well, if not better equipped than Grangemouth's, and that Leith could well hold her own. This euphoric state was seldom disturbed by labour trouble at the docks of Leith, for dockers, once relatively scarce, were extremely abundant and poorly organised by 1905. Their energies went into desperate competition for work with one another, and the prosperity of the port ensured that most of them made a living, albeit a hard one, so that the militancy bred by total despair never appeared.

After a slight dip in the pace of expansion in 1908, Leith Docks went forward to fresh records in revenue and tonnage in 1910. When it was suggested that Leith Dock Commission buy the harbour of Granton from the Duke of Buccleuch, who owned it, there was little enthusiasm for the idea in Leith. Granton was not seen as a potential rival. The very idea of rivalry was regarded as absurd, and few tears were shed when negotiations fell through over the question of price. By 1911 Leith was more concerned with extending its own splendid facilities. Work was in hand to complete the dry dock which lay north of the eastern entrance to the Imperial Dock, while serious thought was being given to vastly improved facilities for the fishermen of Leith's own fishing village of Newhaven.[8] One jarring note warned of the approaching end of an era. In June 1911 Leith was affected by a national seamen's strike. No sooner had it begun to bite into the commercial life of the port than the local dockers' union, now 1,500 strong, struck for higher wages. The wave of social, communal, and economic strife which between 1910 and 1914 hurried the liberal capitalist society of the British Isles towards its deathbed was not to pass Leith by. Though the dockers' strike at Leith was settled without too traumatic a conflict, the age of cheap dock labour was passing. By 1912 there was talk of a 'dearth' of labour on the busy quays of Leith. Exaggeration apart, the days of over-supply had gone. In March 1912 Leith Dock Labour Employers' Association voluntarily came to terms with Leith Dockers' Union over several disputed points.

Undoubtedly one reason why the employers were willing to come to terms with men whose average wage lay between one and two pounds a week, was that the profits open to businessmen capable of exploiting a big working port like Leith were very attractive just before the First World War. Expansion was still in the air. The big new dry dock was finally opened in 1912. Trade was buoyant. Coal exporting in particular was going up by leaps and bounds, assisted by heavy investments in new handling equipment like hydraulic coal hoists. By the end of 1912 Leith Dock Commission had accepted a £250,000 project for further land reclamation to the east of the Imperial Dock, coupled with a new breakwater and enhanced facilities at Newhaven.

The year 1913 was a bitter one in Leith. Dockers and employers fought one another with no holds barred in a great strike. A Labour Member of Parliament deliberately blocked the enabling legislation for the new dock scheme in order to put pressure on the business interests of Leith. Settlement was followed in 1914 by further disputes until finally in August 1914 the whole fabric of Europe plunged into war. The next wage increase won by Leith dockers came in 1915 and the verbal flannel in which the package was wrapped included a reference to the need for solidarity in the national emergency of war. Like so many of the platitudes of industrial relations, this one was disturbingly true.

DUNDEE HARBOUR IN AN AGE OF RECLAMATION AND JUTE

The completion of the Victoria and Camperdown docks at Dundee was itself a tribute to the buoyancy of the local jute industry, for it was imports of raw jute that provided the vast bulk of business at the newly-expanded harbour. After 1875 the jute industry never quite recovered the dynamism it had known in the 1850s, 1860s, and early 1870s. Indeed by 1877 the jute trade in Dundee was in quite severe depression. It was prosperous again by 1882, but cyclical factors apart, certain long-term considerations were sobering. Dundee's traditional markets were being eroded by the growth of a rival jute industry in Calcutta. Between 1882 and 1885 the capacity of the Calcutta industry grew from 5,150 looms to 6,700. At the same time, the spread of a policy of high protective tariffs in Europe enabled several new jute industries, notably the German, to grow up behind them, and to deprive Dundee of more of her traditional outlets.

On the other hand, the main effect of these restrictions was simply to reduce the rate of growth of the Dundee jute industry. Fresh markets opened. A good example is the vast trade in sacks which sprang from the expansion of the Argentinian wheat belt in the early twentieth century.[10] Imports of jute through the port of Dundee expanded steadily in the late nineteenth century. The increasing volume of direct trade with India helped to ensure that by 1880 shipping from overseas exceeded coastal shipping in importance for the first time in the port's history. Imports of bulk jute through the port reached a peak in 1898 at 286,583 tons, but the figure was still as high as 238,412 tons in 1913.[11] Furthermore, although the textile industries of the east-central region of Scotland never again made the sort of profits they had made during the American Civil

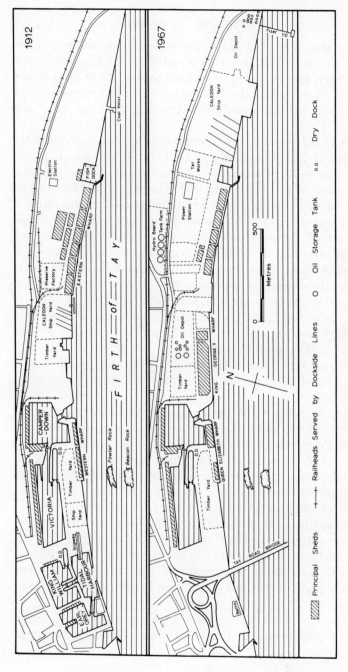

The Port of Dundee 1912 and 1967

Principal Sheds ▨ Railheads Served by Dockside Lines ┼ Oil Storage Tank ○ Dry Dock D.D.

War, they remained on the whole quietly profitable throughout the so-called 'Great Depression' of the late nineteenth
century, and persisted in relative prosperity to 1914. From
those profits came the large sums that the region invested
abroad, especially in North America, between 1870 and
1914.[12]

A Dundee Harbour Consolidation Act had been passed in
1875. It left control of the harbour in the hands of the
existing body of trustees, and transferred the lighting and
buoying of the river from the Fraternity of Masters and
Seamen in Dundee to the Harbour Trustees. One result of
this was the establishment of the lightship Abertay at the
mouth of the river in 1877. Another was a more efficient
buoy system in the shifting navigation channel. Substantial
improvement in harbour facilities, however, required more
dramatic changes in approach. Any major improvement was
bound to involve extensive land reclamation to the east of
Camperdown Dock. On the other hand, some improvement
in facilities was essential. Jute ships were growing in size.
In 1875 they were all quite small sailing ships. By 1890 they
were all quite big steamers. On top of this there was
unsatisfied demand for more space for storage and shipbuilding.

In the event a substantial bay between the east end of
Camperdown Dock and a rocky headland called Stannergate Point, which lay more than a mile to the east, was
reclaimed. It was sealed off from the river by a great sea
wall by 1893, and completely infilled by 1906. A blunder was
committed by letting between 1870 and 1884 a substantial
slice of reclaimed land just east of Camperdown Dock to
shipbuilders. This meant that until these yards closed any
future extension of river quays east of Camperdown Dock
would be separated from the town's centre and industrial
area by a shipbuilding complex. The decision was the more
unfortunate in that quay-extension became very important
in Dundee.[13]

There were several reasons why an extension of quays in
the shape of riverside wharves was the method chosen to cope

with the problem of Dundee's mounting jute imports. Existing docks were not capable of receiving the largest class of fully loaded jute ship by 1880, even at high tide. Ships had to be lightened in the river before admission to the docks, with attendant expense and delay. Quays were likely to be much less expensive than docks. They could not be built to the west of the harbour because a rocky river bed made construction difficult, and in any case quays in this position would interfere with shipyard interests. Unfortunately this last point was also true for a substantial area east of the docks. In 1881–4 a first stretch of wharf was built due west of Camperdown Dock entrance. This was, however, only big enough to berth one jute ship. The wharf was extended in 1885–6, and again in 1889–92, but even then it could only accommodate three ships. Furthermore, the free space behind this stretch of quay, known by 1898 as the Western Wharf, was very restricted, which meant that only limited shed accommodation could be erected for jute. The Western Wharf was an attempt to use the last space free for quays which did not involve going well east of Camperdown Dock. By 1890 this last step had become inevitable.

Meanwhile Dundee had built its only wharf never intended to carry jute traffic. In 1890 a cattle depot and wharf at the Stannergate were built. Canadian cattle were landed in significant numbers until parliamentary legislation in 1893 prohibited the importation of foreign cattle except for slaughter at the port of landing. The cattle traffic promptly ceased. However, the cattle depot provided the point of departure for the next substantial wharf.

In November 1890 a report from the Harbourmaster of Dundee complained that large jute steamers, nearly all of which drew about twenty-three feet of water, were experiencing grave delays in unloading. The Western Wharf was inadequate, and entry to the docks was only possible after extensive lightening. It was decided to construct a wharf and sheds to the west of the cattle depot. By 1898 nearly 1,300 feet of quay were available in what was known as the Eastern Wharf. Mr David Cunningham, the Harbour Engineer, supervised construction. The wharf was a timber-pile structure. Depth was secured by dredging. The shed space was far more generous than at the Western Wharf, but the Eastern Wharf's timbers showed a weakness which compelled the harbour authorities to reconstruct the downstream 1,000 feet of the Eastern Wharf in reinforced concrete between 1903 and 1911.

From the start jute was unloaded at the new wharves by means of hydraulic machines called jiggers. Before 1882 attempts to modernise jute-handling at the docks had hinged on the use of small steam engines. As raw jute is an extremely inflammable commodity, this proved a dangerous expedient, and hydraulic hoists were a great improvement. The Dundee Harbour Trust, which pioneered the use of reinforced concrete in harbour work in Scotland, could not be accused of technological backwardness. In 1912 it looked back on nearly a century of achievement. Its property covered 190 acres, all but five of which had been recovered from the river. The length of river frontage owned by the Dundee Harbour Trustees was two miles. In their own minds there was plenty of room for further improvement and expansion. More than a quarter of the land they controlled was undeveloped. Though jute imports were stabilising, bigger and much faster vessels were straining berth capacity, and concentrating jute imports into a shorter period than ever before. All the jute coming into Dundee in 1912 came within five or six months. Despite the new wharves, congestion still occurred.[14]

Partly because of this congestion, and partly because of the need for a quick turn-round for the new and larger jute steamers, there was further extension of wharves from 1913. By then the western 1,000 feet of reclaimed land east of Camperdown Dock had been cleared of shipyards by contraction in the shipbuilding industry. On this land was built the first section of the King George the Fifth Wharf. Between 1913 and 1915 630 feet of wharf were built, to be followed by later extensions completed only in the 1930s. It was, however, significant that bulk jute imports remained crushingly dominant in the business of Dundee's harbour. Attempts at diversification usually proved abortive. When, for example, in 1899 three Dundee steam trawler companies were formed, it seemed possible that Dundee, which had no fishing fleet in 1898, might develop as a fishing port. Dundee Harbour Trust in 1900 opened an East Tidal Basin specifically for the fish trade. It was under two acres in extent, and situated well to the east. So far from proving a growth-point, it remained permanently under-used.[15]

THE SPECIALIST COAL PORTS OF FIFE

Some of the most interesting examples of very heavy investment in new port facilities between 1870 and 1914 can be found on the southern shore of Fife. The explanation for this is simple. Between 1880 and 1914 there was enormous growth in the British coal industry. Total output rose from 147 million tons in 1880 to the all-time maximum of just over 287 million tons in 1913. Of this production a very large quantity was exported. British coal exports rose from under eighteen million tons in 1880 to the record figure of over ninety-eight million tons in 1913.[16] The mines of Fife shared fully in this expansion. Indeed they had entered a period of great prosperity in the early 1870s, just after the end of the Franco-Prussian war. Coal prices were high and many mining companies were being formed.

A good example of these was the Fife Coal Company, founded in 1872. Its directors included William Lindsay, the son of a Leith shipmaster who himself rose to be an important figure in Leith shipping circles, not to mention his spell as Provost of Leith. Side by side with him on the board sat James Cox, a former Provost of Dundee and one of the greatest of the jute barons. The company did not have an easy first decade, for between 1875 and 1883 it had to weather a spell of very poor trading results. Nevertheless, it survived and went on to further expansion in the course of

which it established a well-deserved reputation for technological innovation.[17] Fife was fortunate that sharp increases
in demand for coal at home and abroad coincided with improvements in mining techniques in the county. The introduction of water pumps operated by vertical-cylindered
beam engines driven by steam had occurred over a lengthy
period in the late eighteenth and early nineteenth century.
Steam engines were operating in the Dysart area in 1791, in
Kirkcaldy by 1818, Wemyss by 1838, and Kilmux and
Balbirnie by 1837 and 1840 respectively. In the 1860s and
1870s new and much more powerful steam-driven pumps
capable of draining pits at depths of 3,000 feet began to
invade the Fife landscape. Their improved engines, with a
horizontal cylinder, working on the reciprocal principle,
were much more efficient than the old beam engines.[18]

These long-term factors of technological progress and
buoyant demand ensured that the histories of most of the
bigger coal companies in the Fife coalfield closely resembled
one another. In Clackmannan, a county whose coal seams
are a continuation of the Fife ones, the Alloa Coal Company
showed much the same pattern of heavy investment and uneven but vigorous growth reaching a crescendo in the early
twentieth century on the strength of very large exports to
Europe.[19]

With a bulk commodity like coal, efficient transport is
vital, so Fife mining was closely connected both with rail and
with harbour facilities. Increasingly the railways of Fife came
to be dominated by the mighty North British. Suitable docks
were no less essential. When, for example, a company was
formed to develop the harbour of Leven, a small port about
eleven miles north east of Kirkcaldy, the news greatly
stimulated competition for rights on the nearby Durie coal-
field. Directors of the Fife Coal Company, among others,
bought shares in the harbour company. Prior to 1876 the
most sophisticated facility at Leven consisted of a small quay
built in 1833. In 1876, however, under enabling legislation
known as the Leven Harbour Act, a new wet dock, river wall,
protection wall, and railway siding were constructed at a cost

of £40,000 and opened in 1880. The dock, 500 feet long and 250 broad, could cope with vessels of 800 tons. Unfortunately £40,000 was not a big enough investment to give Leven a lasting advantage over nearby ports with better natural endowments and by 1885 the scheme was a financial failure and the promoting body had sold out, at a heavy loss.[20]

There were several reasons why the developments at Leven failed to come to fruition. One was purely physical. The shifting sands at the mouth of the River Leven had played havoc with the old tidal harbour at Leven, and they were no kinder to the new dock. Nevertheless, the decisive factor stunting growth at Leven was the rapid development of the rival port of Methil, largely because of the enterprise of the family of Wemyss of Castle Wemyss. David, second Earl of Wemyss, who held the title between 1649 and 1679, had not only been an innovator in mine-drainage techniques, but also the builder of tidal harbours at Methil and Wemyss, from which he exported his own coal and salt. The great developer of the late nineteenth and early twentieth century was to be Randolph Gordon Erskine Wemyss, who succeeded to the family estates in 1864 as a minor. The shape of things to come was clearly shown during the vigorous guardianship of his mother, who herself initiated the first dock development at Methil.

The times were propitious, for it was during the great coal boom that followed the Franco-Prussian war that the first steps were taken. At West Wemyss a tidal harbour had existed from the sixteenth century, and it was from here that the coal from the older Wemyss pits was shipped. When trade was slack great blocks of coal would be built up in the coal yard against the demand of the summer months, when small Danish, Dutch, German and French sailing ships would crowd the harbour, waiting their turn to be loaded. A tramway led directly from the nearest mine to the quay, where a crane had once been used to lift the detachable body of each coal waggon, or 'hutch', off its wheels before lowering it into the hold where its contents were emptied. By the 1870s the hutches were tipped directly into a chute leading to the hold, and this was deemed a great improvement.

In 1871 Mrs Wemyss concluded that if the minerals on her son's estate were to be properly developed, improved facilities at Methil were essential. She therefore resolved on a wet dock. Plans were drawn up by Messrs J. and A. Leslie of Edinburgh; work commenced in 1872; and all was complete by 1875 at a cost of £10,000. Before Randolph Wemyss attained his majority in 1879 he had learned from his remarkable mother that railways and docks were the keys to greater prosperity for the family mines.

The coal-bearing strata of Fife fall into two groups geographically. There is a coalfield which centres on Dunfermline and which stretches from Kirkcaldy to the southern parts of Clackmannan. This area possessed several ports, but the North British Railway increasingly came to favour Burntisland as the natural outlet for much of its coal. East of this coalfield lies what may be called the Wemyss field covering the parishes of Dysart, Wemyss, Markinch and Scoonie, and stretching out under the waters of the Forth. It was for the sake of this field, much of which he owned, that Randolph Wemyss resolved to develop Methil harbour on a larger scale. He was inspired by the example of his ancestor David, the second Earl of Wemyss. By 1883 Randolph Wemyss had taken two essential preliminary steps. He had brought the parish of Wemyss into contact with the national rail network by building on his own initiative a line between Thornton and the mining community of Buckhaven, which lay just south of Methil. Secondly, he eliminated possible opposition to his own enabling legislation for Methil docks by the elegant and simple device of buying the Leven Harbour Company for £12,000.

By the end of 1883 Randolph Wemyss had engaged Messrs Cunningham, Blyth and Westland as engineers for the new dock, and had secured the necessary parliamentary powers. In 1887 the new works were formally opened. They had cost £227,000, for which the proprietor secured a great new wet dock 600 feet by 350 feet. A new outer sea wall 1,820 feet long was built of concrete, with a Welsh granite coping. The dock had a minimum depth of over twenty feet at low water at an ordinary spring tide. The main contractors, Messrs Wedell and Gibson, were, like the engineers, an Edinburgh firm. Allied to a brief extension of the railway from Buckhaven to Methil, the new dock made Methil a much more effective coal port. Nor were loading techniques neglected, for the new dock was equipped with four hydraulic coalhoists, each costing £5,000.

In 1889 Randolph Wemyss deemed it wise to sell his railway, and the harbour of Leven, to the North British Railway, whose board of directors he joined. From this strategic position he hoped to ensure harmony between coalmining and railway interests. His Methil dock proved a great success. In its first year of operation it was used by 253 steamers and 257 sailing ships. Two hundred and twenty thousand tons of coal were exported and 11,570 tons of general cargo, much of it pit props, were imported. In 1900 1,682,000 tons of coal were exported, and 57,000 tons of goods were imported. At this point Randolph Wemyss began to agitate for further expansion of facilities at Methil, only to find that the North British was not amenable to persuasion.[21]

The fact that the laird of Wemyss was on its board did not affect the company's calculation that it had sunk too much of its financial resources into Burntisland to build up another rival coal port. Burntisland was a curious example of a good natural harbour which before the coming of the railway had no immediately productive hinterland. It had risen to importance as a railway port for the rail ferry from Granton, before the Forth Bridge was opened. It became an indispensable link in the North British system, with the result that the railway was willing to spend a lot of money to make Burntisland a viable coal-exporting port. The harbour, formerly a tidal one, was improved under Acts of 1870, 1875, and 1881, by the construction of a wet dock, a seawall, and other works at a cost of £150,000 advanced by the North British Company. By the Act of 1881 the management of the harbour was vested in eight commissioners, four appointed by the town council, and four by the railway company. The wet dock, opened in 1876, covered five and a half acres, and was equipped with rail connections and three hydraulic loading machines. Altogether, the North British had a very high stake in the Fife coalfields. In the early twentieth century the company stated that a third of its capital—£20 millions out of £60 millions—was invested in Fife. Burntisland harbour seemed a good investment, for between 1860 and 1880 its revenue rose from £197 to £14,785. However, this was before Methil developed, and the Forth Bridge opened.

Undoubtedly, the North British realised that the high ground of the Binn behind Burntisland, which forced the railway lines from the mines around Cowdenbeath to take big detours as they approached the port, placed Burntisland in a weak position compared with a developed Methil, which would be likely to tap the north-east part of the coalfield from Wemyss to Lochore and Lochgelly. Burntisland remained a great coal port after Methil was further developed, but it is significant that Burntisland was one of the three Fife burghs to show a decline in population between 1901 and 1911.[22] The irony was that the North British itself was eventually compelled to build another dock at Methil, though only because of pressure from Randolph Wemyss. Wemyss was in a strong position to apply pressure, as sixty per cent of the coal shipped from Methil was his, and he had, in all his plans for expansion at Methil, support from the other nearby coal companies.

Resigning from the board of the North British, the laird of Wemyss, working through his own Wemyss Coal Company, sponsored a plan to build a new dock outwith North British control at Buckhaven, a spot which lies on the Fife coast just south of Methil. After complaining that Wemyss thereby violated a pledge which he had given when he joined the North British Board, the railway gave way for fear of worse to follow. After obtaining parliamentary powers in 1907 the North British embarked on another massive investment at Methil which neither it nor outside observers expected to be profitable. This attitude towards Methil dock-development was rooted in Burntisland optimism, which had forecast that the earlier Methil docks would be failures.[23] Randolph Wemyss did not live to see the third dock, for he died in 1908 aged only fifty, leaving behind perhaps the most remarkable record of industrial achievement of any of his house. The third dock at Methil, on which he had set his heart, was opened as late as January 1913.

This was mainly because of the very great technical difficulties which the contractors, Robert McAlpine and Sons of Glasgow, ran into in the course of building a new sea wall, which was an essential preliminary to the construction of the dock itself. The site of the new dock lay to the east of the existing docks. A site to the west would have been more convenient, but the Wemyss Coal Company enforced prior claims. Thereafter treacherous foundations and fierce storms delayed completion of the sea wall until late in 1910. By July 1911 a forty-four acre dock and its gates were completed. The rest of 1911 and 1912 were devoted to installing six hydraulic hoists and to completing dockside buildings and structures, including railway lines and storage yards. These storage yards were eventually capable of storing 30,000 tons of coal.[24]

For all the buoyancy of the Fife coal trade, there was only room for investment on the scale that occurred at Methil harbour in one port in the county. That was why internecine strife between the Fife coal ports was so bitter. Leven, the early developer fell clean out of the race. Dysart was already a moribund port by 1880 and declining into the status of a suburb of Kirkcaldy. There were no significant developments of new wet docks in Alloa or Inverkeithing in the late nineteenth century.[25] Even Burntisland, for all the North British money poured into it, fell behind Methil in the early twentieth century. The full measure of Randolph Wemyss as a port promoter can be gathered from two sets of statistics.[26] One is the record of employment and output in mining in Fife as a whole in certain years:

Year	Number Employed	Coal Output (Tons)
1886	7,525	2,295,926
1887	7,558	2,585,412
1892	11,308	3,573,818
1897	11,945	4,077,818
1902	16,933	6,134,171
1906	23,574	7,783,459
1907	23,099	8,530,043
1908	25,447	8,412,855

The other is the tonnage of coal shipped from Methil in these years:

Year	Coal Shipped (Tons)
1886	35,000
1887	219,884
1892	810,545
1897	1,090,324
1902	1,759,041
1906	2,797,257
1907	2,823,720
1908	2,559,500

The falling off in 1908 reflected a general slackness in the British economy, but it is quite clear that the growth of coal shipment through Methil between 1886 and 1908 greatly outpaced the overall expansion of coal production in Fife. It is equally clear that the growth of Methil's exports was levelling off towards the end of the period, and this was the justification for the campaign for the third dock. By 1913 it had become, to use a contemporary analogy, the 'Cardiff of Scotland'.

OTHER PORTS AND CONCLUSION

Between 1870 and 1914 the history of investment in port

Coal drop, Methil Docks. This photograph was taken in 1970

Burntisland Docks *c.* 1900. A good example of a coal port with its specialised handling equipment

facilities in the Firths of Forth and Tay shows a higher degree of selectivity than ever before. Cyclical depressions in trade and industry apart, the period was one of general prosperity. The years preceding the outbreak of war in 1914 were particularly good ones for most ports. Yet in this, the last age of extensive dock construction, such major developments as new docks or big wharves were confined to a very few harbours. This was all the more significant in that the railways still constituted the main alternative transport system competing with ports for medium-distance hauls. British trunk roads had stagnated after the coming of the railways. Apart from horses, the only common source of power on late nineteenth-century roads was the clumsy and slow steam engine. It was only after legislation in 1896 that petrol-driven motor cars, and petrol or steam-driven lorries began to appear in any numbers on British roads. Few manufactured products have improved as rapidly as the petrol motor lorry between 1900 and 1914, and between 1909 and 1914 existing roads were extensively re-surfaced with 'tarmac', but road haulage did not seem a serious threat to Scottish ports on the eve of the First World War.[27]

Tayside shows very clearly why port development was becoming so very selective. Only Dundee could afford extensive development, and this was primarily in aid of a single bulk import—textile fibres. In 1907 Dundee's total imports were valued at £5,707,282. Exports were a fraction of this at £970,269, and of the imports jute accounted for £3,990,106 by value, while jute goods accounted for £799,804 by value of exports. Dundee was a textile fibre port. The advantages of bulk-handling, and the availability of railway connections to the rest of the region ensured that Dundee completely dominated jute imports. Montrose and Arbroath remained small ports with an imbalance of imports over exports. In 1906, for example, Montrose's imports were worth £324,892, while exports were valued at only £23,859. Furthermore, of those imports, flax accounted for £266,901 by value. Arbroath was in a broadly similar situation. In 1907 imports there were valued at £166,821, of which £148,944 was accounted for by flax, while exports were worth a mere £6,632. Both Arbroath and Montrose had remained what they had been before the regional jute boom. They were small ports with a steady import of flax, hemp, and wood, and a more unpredictable import of grain, fodder, and fertiliser. Their exports were almost entirely agricultural. Both had retained more vitality than Perth which remained, after its unfortunate over-commitment to expansion, a financial problem and a purely agricultural port.[28]

This pattern of significant development largely confined to a single port, and largely based on a single bulk commodity was equally true of the coal ports of Fife. By the late nineteenth century Fife was fairly ringed with small ports left behind by events. Culross had been stranded on the shores of time for centuries by then, but Kincardine-on-Forth was heading for the same sort of limbo because of the collapse of its distilling, brewing, coal-mining, and ship-building industries. Inverkeithing harbour was too shallow, and those of St Andrews and Leven too silted for contemporary shipping. The Tay bridge had deprived Tayport, as the Forth bridge Burntisland, of much ferry traffic. Only Kirkcaldy, Burntisland, and Methil survived as significant harbours. Of these Methil was incomparably the most vital. Its excellent facilities, built primarily to export coal, also attracted a fair volume of imports. In 1907 its exports, mainly coal, were valued at more than four times its imports. Even so, the volume of flax, hemp, oil-seed cake, paper-making material and wood imported was impressive. Burntisland, which in 1908 was behind Methil as a coal exporter, though not by a great margin, had a significantly smaller volume of imports. They were only about a tenth of exports by value, and their value was approximately a third of those of Methil.[29] By 1913 Methil had opened yet another dock.

Kirkcaldy is in some ways a very good example of what was happening in the Fife ports between 1870 and 1914. The harbour of Kirkcaldy had undergone major improvement in the middle of the nineteenth century, after which the town maintained its traditional trading links with the northern lands of Europe, whilst developing new industries and new contacts. At one point, for example, the Ravenscraig Chemical Works in Kirkcaldy was sending cargoes of pitch to Rouen in France and Cadiz in Spain. In the 1870s and 1880s a whole swarm of ambitious plans for dock extension were proposed and turned down as too costly. It was only with the continued growth of the Kirkcaldy linoleum manufacture in the 1890s that further development at the harbour became a feasible proposition. A great deal of the linoleum produced in Kirkcaldy was shipped to London. Demand for shipping space was therefore strong. Local shipping lines did very well, especially one owned by a J. R. Stocks who in due course rose to be Provost of Kirkcaldy. It was Provost Stocks who set in motion a serious agitation for another dock, on the grounds that both trade, and the size of ships, were increasing. Apart from its own linoleum industry, Kirkcaldy was acting as the harbour for nearby paper mills. The omens were propitious.

Provost Stocks did not live to see the new dock, which was begun in 1906 and completed in 1909. It had a depth of twenty-one feet at spring and fifteen feet at neap tides. The longest of its six quays was 500 feet long, and ships of 290 feet length and 47 feet beam could use it. An adequate array of cranes, including one specially designed for coal ships, completed the equipment. This was to be the last major development at Kirkcaldy harbour. The linoleum industry had passed through its period of most rapid growth by 1908, leaving Kirkcaldy a relatively minor part. In that year the tonnage of outgoing vessels was 56,143, and that of vessels entering 29,024. Without an underlying economic dynamic, Kirkcaldy harbour could scarcely hope to grow further.[30]

On the southern shore of the Forth development was largely concentrated on Leith and Grangemouth. East from the Forth bridge at Queensferry lay a string of moribund harbours, mute tributes to the vigour of Leith. Neither Cramond just west of Leith, nor Musselburgh just east had any pretensions left by 1900. Further east a whole string of small harbours maintained a shadowy existence. Dunbar still exported some corn, fish and potatoes, and imported a little coal, and timber. Prestonpans had a very limited export of coal, bricks, tiles, and salt. Port Seton and Cockenzie lacked the modern handling machinery to export the coal of the immediately adjacent collieries, let alone the coal from the Tranent collieries a mile or two inland. None of these harbours had quite sunk to the level of the little harbours on the north bank of the Tay between Perth and Dundee. These small ports like Kingoodie, just west of Dundee, Powgavie south of the village of Inchture, Port Allan near the village of Errol, and Inchyra, not far from Perth, had become ghost ports by 1912, overgrown with weeds disturbed only by a seasonal flurry of activity due to a cargo or two of coal or lime coming in, or a cargo of grain or potatoes going out.[31]

The reasons for the decline of the smaller ports were clear enough. Rising costs necessitated mechanical handling to secure a quick turn-round of vessels, but only the larger ports could afford the expensive equipment required. On top of this the steadily increasing size of ships placed a premium on ports which had, or could afford to build very expensive docks. In some ways Granton, a mile or two along the coast to the east of Leith, was an exception to the rule that the big ports were becoming increasingly dominant. Like Methil, it was an exception which proved the rule, without rendering it untenable.

It was the Duke of Buccleuch who filled the role of wealthy sponsor for Granton, as Randolph Wemyss had sponsored Methil. Even after losing most of its ferry traffic Granton was a potentially profitable port because of the demand for coal-exporting facilities generated by the development of the Lothian coalfield. In 1912 the harbour was still tidal, being formed by two great breakwaters over 3,000 feet long between which a pier 200 feet wide ran out for 1,700 feet. Dredging helped to ensure that even at low water during spring tides, there was a depth of thirteen feet. The harbour was well endowed with steam cranes, including special coal cranes and tips capable of loading 110 tons of coal an hour.

Exports were dominated by coal but also included machinery, castings, and whisky. Imports were more varied including timber, iron, grain, cement, china clay, and esparto grass. In 1909 a significant development occurred when the Anglo-Saxon Petroleum Company opened a depot at Granton, from which a very substantial import of petroleum was to grow. In 1909 Granton cleared 456,585 tons of shipping.[32]

Granton enjoyed rail connections with both the Caledonian system and the North British, yet it maintained its autonomy. In this it was doubly fortunate. It was fortunate that Leith had not been willing to pay the price needed to tempt the ducal house of Buccleuch into a sale. It was also fortunate compared with Bo'ness, which in the late nineteenth century became enmeshed in financial trouble and railway politics. The North British had a natural interest in Bo'ness, since Grangemouth was owned by the rival Caledonian. Unfortunately the harbour authorities at Bo'ness mismanaged the finances of the port to the point where they became utterly dependent on North British loans. The railway then began to behave as if it owned the port, which it did not, and the upshot was a fierce quarrel, which must have amused the Caledonian, through whose harbour of Grangemouth the North British perforce shipped much coal. In 1896 the liabilities of Bo'ness Harbour Commissioners stood at over £460,000, while their assets were under £1,000. Grangemouth had little to fear.[33]

Indeed between 1870 and 1914 Grangemouth pursued a steady course of expansion of trade and extension of facilities. The town itself became a burgh in 1872, by which time the volume of traffic was pressing against existing dock capacity. With plenty of easily-excavated marsh areas with underlying clays to hand, Grangemouth was in a position to expand. In 1882 the Carron Dock had been opened. Within ten years the expansion in traffic through the port had rendered the situation as bad as ever. Delays to shipping were endemic. The town itself grew from 1,488 people in 1841 to 8,386 in 1901. Its overseas trade was quite out of proportion to its

size because of its links with the Glasgow area, and these
links remained very important, even if the Forth and Clyde
Canal, Grangemouth's original transport link with the west,
was increasingly replaced by rail transport. By 1906 Grangemouth was clearing over two and a half million tons of
shipping per annum. In that year it opened a new dock
christened the Grange Dock. With this dock Grangemouth
passed into a new stage of port development. Hitherto the
harbour had used the mouth of the Carron river as its own
entrance, despite drawbacks of accessibility and size. Now,
at the cost of extensive reclamation on the muddy foreshore,
Grangemouth had not only a new dock, but also a new
entrance cut in reclaimed land south of the river. Coal continued to dominate Grangemouth's exports, as might be
expected of a port whose owner, the Caledonian, also owned
much of the Lanarkshire coalfield in the centre of Scotland,
but the port also exported chemicals and pig iron. Timber
and grain were the biggest inward items.[34]

Between 1870 and 1914 significant developments occurred
only in Dundee, Methil, Grangemouth and Leith. Each of
these ports had a clear regional paramountcy. In the case of
Dundee and Methil that paramountcy was closely linked to
a functional paramountcy in handling one bulk item.
Dundee was a port based on the import of jute. Methil was
a port based on the export of coal. Grangemouth and
Leith, though both very concerned with the export of coal,
had the great advantage, and opportunity for diversification
of trade, which sprang from their special relationship with
major conurbations. Leith was the port of Edinburgh:
Grangemouth the eastern port of Glasgow. One feature was
common to all four ports. They tended to attract such a
high percentage of the capital needed to maintain dock and
handling facilities within their distinct coastal regions, that
their growth effectively ensured that nearby ports would
either not grow at all, or grow relatively slowly. There was a
general air of prosperity about all four major ports on the eve
of the European war, but two of them had nearly all their
eggs in one basket.

CHAPTER V

From the First World War
to the Second

THE APPROACH OF WAR

In the decades immediately prior to 1560 the ports of the
Forth and Tay, and their hinterlands, suffered extensively
from the effects of war. Scotland, France, and England
were locked in a complex struggle over the future of the
Scottish realm, and the great firths were natural lines of
approach for French or English forces seeking to contact
their respective Scots allies. Amphibious warfare was widely
practised while religious factors, in this age of the
Reformation, both added to the fanaticism and complicated
the politics of these wars. After 1560, however, protracted
naval and amphibious warfare never again ravaged this
coastline for decades on end. By the late eighteenth century
seaward defence had become a care of the past for a
population living under a stable Hanoverian regime which
disposed of the greatest fighting navy in the world. It was
therefore a salutary shock to a widespread complacency
when, during the war of the American Revolution, the
American naval commander John Paul Jones brought his
hostile squadron into the Firth of Forth. In that year of
1779 rich towns like Leith and Kirkcaldy lay helpless before
an absurdly small naval force commanded by a Scotsman
from Galloway who had become an ardent American rebel.
Only a severe storm, provoked it is said by a particularly

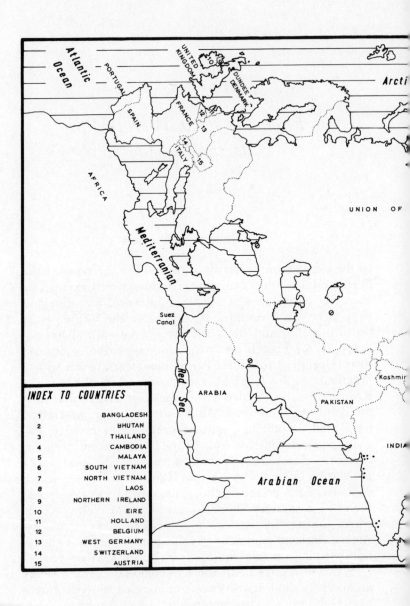

INDEX TO COUNTRIES

1	BANGLADESH
2	BHUTAN
3	THAILAND
4	CAMBODIA
5	MALAYA
6	SOUTH VIETNAM
7	NORTH VIETNAM
8	LAOS
9	NORTHERN IRELAND
10	EIRE
11	HOLLAND
12	BELGIUM
13	WEST GERMANY
14	SWITZERLAND
15	AUSTRIA

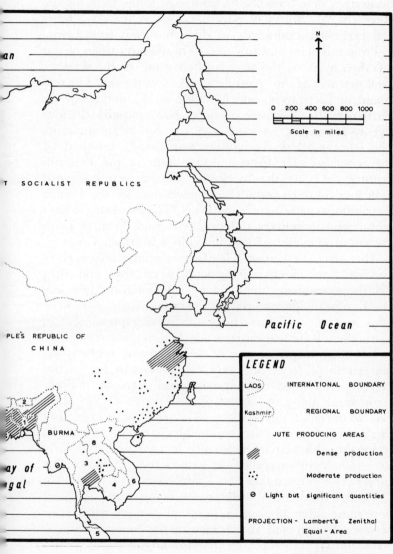

N

0 200 400 600 800 1000
Scale in miles

T SOCIALIST REPUBLICS

Pacific Ocean

PLE'S REPUBLIC OF
CHINA

LEGEND

LAOS   INTERNATIONAL BOUNDARY

Kashmir   REGIONAL BOUNDARY

              JUTE PRODUCING AREAS

              Dense production

              Moderate production

⊖ Light but significant quantities

PROJECTION - Lambert's Zenithal
             Equal - Area

BURMA
ay of
gal

World Trade in Jute

blunt appeal, in broad Scots, addressed to the Deity by the Reverend Mr Shirra of Kirkcaldy, saved the day. Jones was propelled southwards, to glory, but away from Leith.[1]

From this point onwards a series of wars or threats of war left their mark on this stretch of coastline, in the shape of land defences against possible attack from the sea. The tiny island of Inchgarvie, which stands in the middle of the Forth near the Queensferry passage, was equipped with four twenty-pounder guns soon after the American squadron had left the Forth. Inchgarvie was already crowned by the remnants of a fortress prison built in the sixteenth century. In 1781 the Inchgarvie battery was re-formed with four fourteen-pounders, in good time for the French Revolutionary and Napoleonic Wars.[2] Those wars left further monuments to military archaeology behind them. In Leith the fort of 1779 vintage was joined by a Martello Tower.

After 1815 the United Kingdom enjoyed a long spell of freedom from external danger. Between 1815 and 1914 British governments fought many colonial wars, but only one European one, and that in the distant Crimea between 1854 and 1856. Yet starting with a widespread fear of marauding Russian·cruisers—which never materialised— in late 1854, the latter part of the nineteenth century was marked by a series of waves of enthusiasm for coastal defence which led to unprecedented feats of military engineering along the shores of the Forth and Tay. It is easy to sneer at this activity as a series of 'scares', but there was often a quite reasonable basis for alarm. In retrospect, this activity gradually merged with the early twentieth-century naval rivalry with Germany which unlike earlier crises did not fade away painlessly.

The first massive and widespread wave of coastal fortification came after 1859 as a result of a diplomatic crisis between Britain and the France of the Second Empire. Napoleon III had rapidly expanded French naval power. He had fortified Cherbourg in a manner which suggested that he envisaged it as an important potential base in a future naval war against Britain. Sabre rattling by minor representatives of this cynical and opportunistic French regime called forth a massive response in Britain. Volunteer rifle units, and volunteer artillery units were formed all over the land. Partly to provide outlets for the enthusiasm of the latter, Lord Palmerston's government created a chain of artillery forts to guard vulnerable points on the British coasts. Scotland had its share of these, including a radical re-construction of the ruined castle at Broughty Ferry, just east of Dundee. Here a young architect with a brilliant career ahead of him, Robert Rowand Anderson, constructed on behalf of the War Office a coastal fort whose main armament was composed of huge sixty-eight-pounder, smooth-bore, muzzle-loading cannon.[3] These monsters, designed to control the bar of the Tay, were already obsolete when mounted. They were identical with weapons installed at a coastal battery at Fort George in the Moray Firth in 1850–1.[4] Inevitably, the rapid progress of military technology in the late nineteenth century, allied to continuing diplomatic tension with France, Russia, and then Germany, led to a continual re-equipment and extension of coastal defences, both in the Tay and in the Forth.

In the Tay Broughty Ferry Castle was soon supplemented by another battery at Buddon Ness, a few miles to the east. In the Forth Inchgarvie was by 1900 quite outgunned by other batteries. For example, at that date the island of Inchkeith, lying four miles out from Leith and well suited to cover that port with battery fire, mounted a formidable weight of metal in three forts. Four ten-inch guns weighing eighteen tons apiece were the core of the garrison's fire power. Furthermore, the Inchkeith defences were supplemented by a strong battery on Kinghorn Ness, the nearest point on the Fife shore, a couple of miles distant.[5] A later observer was to remark that the Firth of Forth, with its succession of powerful batteries planted along the shores from Dunbar to Dalmeny on the south, and from Crail to Burntisland on the north, was virtually impregnable against naval attack.[6]

This fact was undoubtedly one consideration behind the

155

decision of the British government to site a major new naval dockyard in the Forth. The site chosen was close to the traditional safe anchorage of Saint Margaret's Hope, about thirty miles from the mouth of the firth. It was sheltered on the east, up to a point, by the promontory on which North Queensferry stands, and therefore lay upstream from the great railway bridge whose two central spans rested on the island of Inchgarvie. In 1900 the future site of Rosyth Naval Dockyard was marked only by a sixteenth century castle rising from a rocky islet lying just offshore, but linked to the shore by a causeway. The decision to establish the base was taken in 1903 by the Conservative government led by Arthur Balfour. A couple of years later the Admiralty purchased 285 acres of foreshore, with another 1,184 acres of hinterland, from the Marquis of Linlithgow. This great enterprise was part of a major re-appraisal of the basic assumptions of British naval strategy. A new northern repair base for battleships was part of a re-orientation of the naval power and diplomatic alliances of the United Kingdom in the light of the rising naval might of the German Empire, which from 1897 had been pursuing an ambitious programme of warship construction. Of course, Germany had both trade and colonies to protect, but it was a platitude amongst those in charge of Germany's naval preparations that the focal point of their efforts around 1905 should lie in ships of the line and torpedo boats.[7] Such a navy was clearly meant to fight the Royal Navy in the North Sea, not to patrol the remoter coasts of Africa. In so far as government circles in Germany were rational about the naval rivalry with Britain, they probably saw their new fleet as a deterrent calculated to dissuade the British from interfering in a major power struggle in Europe. This was an unrealistic hope, and naval rivalry merely exacerbated British suspicion of Germany. Even so, few politicians faced up to the full and grim implications of the military, naval, and diplomatic confrontation implicit in Britain's understanding with Germany's rivals, Russia and France. After 1906 a new Liberal government reduced the battleship-building programme of the Balfour regime to a dangerous level, while work at the new site at Rosyth proceeded at a very slow pace.

Despite a small army of navvies established in a shanty community known locally as 'Tin Town' from 1909, Rosyth was not fully operational as a naval dockyard until March 1916. War broke out in August 1914, but prior to March 1916 Rosyth had been capable of only minor activity. This was making haste slowly with a vengeance. There were a variety of factors explaining the delay. First, the British government, though deeply suspicious of the new Imperial German Navy, was not finally clear in its own mind that Germany rather than France and Russia was the likeliest foe in the next naval war until after a major diplomatic crisis over the affairs of Morocco in 1905. That crisis set the seal on Anglo-French co-operation against excessive German demands. Secondly, there was a distinct enthusiasm for economy in naval expenditure after the change of governments in Britain in 1906. Thirdly, and perhaps most significant of all, there proved to be considerable difficulty in constructing a dock complex at Rosyth, because of the geology of the site. It proved difficult to excavate in clay deposits in the land purchased by the Admiralty. The resulting problems enabled an engineer called Bell who was involved on the job to give his name to a significant new theory in civil engineering, but this was small comfort to the government or, especially after 1914, the Royal Navy.[8]

The War and its Aftermath

From what has already been said, it will be clear that in some ways the most dramatic developments during the First World War amongst the ports of the Forth and Tay were likely to occur at Rosyth. At the outbreak of war the main base for the British Grand Fleet was at Scapa Flow in the Orkney Islands, but from the end of 1914 the anchorages available in the Forth off Rosyth were being used by

Admiral Beatty's squadron of battle cruisers. As the war progressed anti-submarine defences in the vicinity of Rosyth were strengthened, and more and more use was made of the river anchorages off Rosyth. It was not, however, until April 1918 that the anti-submarine measures incorporated in the outer defences of the Forth were considered sufficiently effective to justify the transfer of the entire Grand Fleet to the Forth. By that date the naval dockyard at Rosyth had at last entered on its primary function— the refitting and repair of warships. It was to Rosyth that Admiral Beatty's flagship the *Lion* was towed after it sustained severe damage in the British victory over German battle cruisers at the Battle of the Dogger Bank early in 1915. It was in Rosyth Naval Dockyard that most of the repairs to British capital ships were executed after the great fleet engagement known as the battle of Jutland, which was fought in the middle of 1916.[9]

Rosyth was, however, a very exceptional harbour for which war was a blessing. The outbreak of peace alone could restrict the scope of its work. For almost all other ports on the east coast of Scotland the outbreak of a war during which the North Sea was a main combat zone could not but be disturbing. On top of the disruption of economic life and loss of merchant shipping by government requisition and enemy action common to all British ports; the ports of the Forth and Tay suffered unique handicaps due to their geographical position. It was significant that the trade of Glasgow and the other Clyde ports increased relative to that of all other Scottish ports during the war. To avoid the dangers of the long voyage around the northern parts of Scotland ships which in peace would have gone to Aberdeen, Dundee, or Leith, discharged their cargoes at Glasgow. Jute was increasingly unloaded at Glasgow and transported to the manufacturing areas. A temporary wartime transit trade grew up in several commodities. Coal from the Fife and Lothian mines was sent through Glasgow for shipment in large quantities during the war, instead of being shipped in traditional fashion through the east coast ports. When it is remembered that the trade of the port of Glasgow fell substantially in absolute terms, despite the increase in the relative significance of the port during the war, some idea may be gained of the losses suffered by the east coast ports.[10]

Precision is difficult, because for security reasons the government soon ceased to publish figures for individual ports, but it is clear that the effect of the war on the volume of trade in the ports of the Forth and Tay was felt with increasing severity, but over a substantial period of time. Thus the General Manager of Dundee Harbour, who had reported that the financial year ending in May 1914 had seen some decline from the dizzy heights reached by harbour revenue in the boom year 1913, was more concerned with disorganisation of trade than with stoppage in his report for 1915. After initial panic, flax and jute cargoes were coming through to the port, even if they came in concentrated bursts of arrivals which overwhelmed port facilities. There was talk in Dundee of 'the inestimable privilege of carrying on business in a country whose government holds command of the seas'.[11] This was, however, before the German Admiralty unleashed unrestricted submarine warfare around the British Isles. Shipping losses soared until efficient convoy techniques were evolved. Some other counter measures taken by the British and their allies, like the vast minefields which eventually sealed not only the Straits of Dover, but also the stretch of sea between the Orkney Islands and the Norwegian coast were probably much more menacing to friendly shipping than to German submarines. The latter appear to have slipped through the mines of what was called the Northern Barrage with great success. All in all, the North Sea by 1918 was a hostile environment for traditional maritime traffic.[12]

Some measure of the disruption caused to normal coastal trade during the war may be gleaned from the records of the Dundee Perth and London Shipping Company. Between 1914 and 1918 the company lost three of its original six steamers, and every one of its vessels was at one time or other requisitioned for national service. A very skeletal skeleton service was maintained on the firm's east-coast routes when ships were available, but it was a hazardous as well as an intermittent business.[13] The Firth of Forth experienced, if anything, even wider extremes of fortune during the war than the Firth of Tay. In the early months of the war that firth was crowded with an unprecedented number of merchant ships, including an unusual number of small foreign sailing ships, to the point where the pilot services available were strained to breaking point.[14] Thereafter the Royal Navy made more and more extensive use of the facilities offered by the Firth of Forth, until the combined Grand Fleet itself moved to the Forth on 12 April 1918. The hazards to normal shipping in this great volume of naval activity were underlined by such incidents as the blowing up of an Anstruther fishing vessel on the minefield defending the mouth of the Forth.[15] By the end of the war Kirkcaldy harbour had been taken over by the United States Navy which more or less closed the port to ordinary shipping, apart from a skeleton service to London.[16] Leith docks were largely taken over by the British Admiralty. The port had in 1913 been on the verge of starting work on another extension involving in the first instance the reclamation of fifty-seven acres of foreshore on the west or Newhaven side of the docks. The war effectively paralysed this programme. Government policy was, in general, to use existing transport facilities like docks and railways ruthlessly to further the war effort, with minimal allowance for wear and tear, let alone development. It was only in 1918 that the commissioners responsible for Leith docks could envisage a renewal of construction work within a finite time.[17]

The drastic distortion of trade by the war cannot be said to have ended with the hostilities, which in western Europe came to an end with an armistice agreement on 11 November 1918. On the contrary, the immediate post-war period was marked by a spectacular economic boom, followed by a sharp slump. On a national level the boom may be said to have started around April 1919, and to have reached a peak round about midsummer 1920.

Sail and steam in Alloa harbour in the late nineteenth century

The harbour at St Andrews c. 1870. Note the herring boats at anchor and the timber on the quay

Thereafter most of the indicators of economic activity showed a downward trend, most notably the figures for employment.[18] For the ports of the Forth and Tay these vicissitudes were all the more extreme because in 1918 their normal commercial activity had fallen to a very low ebb due to a combination of friendly and hostile naval activity. On top of this, a very high percentage of their pre-war trade had been with either enemy countries like Germany, or neutrals whose trade was much affected by the war, like the Scandinavian countries. After the German declaration of unrestricted submarine warfare in the seas around the British Isles on 31 January 1917 trade between Britain and Denmark and Sweden virtually ceased. Trade between Britain and Norway was more stable, but it was subject to considerable vicissitudes during the war, and not only because of German submarines. In 1916, for example, the British government had placed an embargo on coal exports to Norway in a successful effort to persuade Norway to stop exporting copper pyrites or copper ore to Germany.[19]

Economically, the year 1919 has been described as a 'breathing space', but for Scottish east-coast ports it brought a dramatic improvement in commercial activity as compared with 1918, albeit levels of activity at all ports were below those which had been achieved in 1913. As early as 1919 a significant difference emerged in the experience of the major, as compared with the minor ports. Comparisons are difficult, for between 1914 and 1919 severe inflation affected the British economy to the point where in 1919 the pound bought only approximately a third of what it had in 1914. Nevertheless, it does seem that Leith, Grangemouth and Dundee had by 1920 recovered not far short of the volume and value of trade which had been theirs immediately before the war. Taking millions of pounds at current prices (i.e. with no allowance for changing monetary values) the import and export trade of Dundee in 1913 was worth £9.2 millions, and in 1920 the same total came to £18.7 millions. For Leith the figure for 1913 was £22.6 and for 1920, £44.8. For Grangemouth the figures were £9.0

and £15.1 respectively. Even admitting that due to inflation the higher figures for 1920 were probably below those for 1913 in real terms, it is clear that a very substantial recovery had occurred, especially from the near paralysis of say 1917.[20]

The experience of the minor ports was, however, quite different. Extreme examples were Perth, Arbroath, and Montrose. Perth, whose imports and exports had been worth approximately £21,500 in 1913 failed to reach a figure of £2,000 for total value of imports and exports in any year between 1919 and 1921. Arbroath experienced a similar collapse of trade, while Montrose was just marginally better. Other ports did better, of course, but none of the Forth or Tay ports displayed the buoyancy of Leith, Grangemouth, or Dundee. Bo'ness, for example, whose combined exports and imports in 1913 had been worth approximately £800,000, was handling less than £550,000 of imports and exports in 1920. For Burntisland the figures for 1913 and 1920 were both approximately £1,300,000. Once allowance is made for inflation, it is clear that the figures for 1920, which after all was a boom year for the national economy, are not very impressive. In the case of Burntisland the main trouble was that coal exports never reached the high 1913 figures. Methil was also affected by an irreversible decline in coal exports. In 1913 over 2,500,000 tons of coal had been exported from there. By 1919 the figure was over 950,000 tons, but it fell back to a little over 500,000 in 1920, recovering to nearly 800,000 in 1921. Kirkcaldy harbour experienced a similar, and in the event a long-term decline in staple imports and exports. In 1913 that port imported over 11,000 tons of cork for the local linoleum industry, and exported over 100,000 tons of coal. By 1920 the figures for cork imports were approximately 4,700, and for coal exports just over 48,500.

The overall figures for some of the smaller ports do occasionally conceal a more cheerful underlying trend. Granton, for example, though very hard hit by the decline in coal exports, did show a steady growth in petroleum imports between 1919 and 1921. Nevertheless, it would be fair to say that the performance of the smaller ports of the Forth and Tay during the immediate post-war boom gave little grounds for optimism over their long-term future. When the boom burst and turned into a slump in 1921 they suffered an even greater relative collapse of trade than the major ports. This was traumatic, for the import and export trade of Leith, Grangemouth, and Dundee was slashed by over a half between 1920 and 1921.[21]

THE SMALLER PORTS, 1922–39

From what has already been said it will be clear that by 1922 the smaller ports of the Forth and Tay were not attractive propositions from the point of view of further investment. By and large, their existing facilities were more than adequate for the volume of trade passing through them. Indeed, in the peculiar case of Rosyth the repair and refitting facilities available greatly exceeded post-war naval requirements, with the inevitable result that in 1926 the dockyard was placed on a care and maintenance basis. A skeleton staff sufficed to look after a naval asset which was only fully re-activated early in 1939.[22] It is therefore hardly reasonable to enquire why further extensive development failed to occur in the smaller ports of the Forth and Tay between 1922 and 1939. There was, of course, a recovery in trade after the 1921 slump, but even at the peak of the subsequent recovery in 1927 the unemployment rate in Britain was just under ten per cent. After the collapse on the American stock exchange in 1929 world economic activity and world trade experienced unprecedented depression. The really important question is why more of the smaller ports of the Forth and Tay did not become, like Rosyth, fossils.

Certainly the basis of some of the most important nineteenth-century trades in the smaller ports had either vanished or been severely eroded by the inter-war period. Montrose is a good case in point. At one stage in the nineteenth century its timber imports had been extremely large, and much of the timber was worked in Montrose before being re-exported. All this depended on the lack of development of woodworking industries in Scandinavia, for which there were sound historical reasons. Water-driven sawmills had spread from Germany to Scandinavia as early as the sixteenth century, but due to a general fear of over-exploitation the sawmill industry only established itself on any scale in Norway. In Sweden and Finland legislation restricted its development. The coming of steam power gave the wood processing industries of Britain a fresh advantage over potential Scandinavian competition. Until 1850 the economies of the Scandinavian countries were over-whelmingly agricultural, short of capital for industrial development, and desperately short of workmen with any mechanical tradition. Sweden was a partial exception to this, but Norway was not. After 1870, however, all the Scandinavian countries entered a phase of much more rapid industrialisation, with a great deal of investment being directed into steam-driven sawmills and other woodworking equipment.[23]

As Montrose's textile industry has tended to be small and shrinking in the twentieth century, the port was left without any real major staple. Between 1918 and 1939 it imported sawn wood, fertiliser, and flax, while exporting very little apart from agricultural produce. As early as 1905 the trustees of the harbour had decided to cease to retain a tug in the port, on the ground that the volume of shipping hardly justified the expense. Throughout the inter-war period the total value of imports and exports was un-impressive. In the decade before 1930 they were usually worth between £100,000 and £150,000 annually, but in the decade to 1939 the figure slumped to under £45,000. Imports always greatly exceeded exports in value and volume. Fortunately Montrose was a relatively cheap port to maintain. It had little expensive handling equipment, only one dock, and riverside wharves automatically dredged by the current.

Arbroath, the total value of whose imports and exports throughout the period from 1918 to 1939 was generally well below half that of Montrose, was another harbour for which stagnation in development was inevitable. Like Montrose, there was no very elaborate complex of docks and handling equipment requiring maintenance, while there was a very active fishing fleet. The fishermen made full use of at least part of the facilities of an under-used port. Perth, the value of whose trade in the inter-war period was a mere fraction of that of Arbroath, maintained a rather shadowy existence as a port. The worst year of all was 1937 when the total value of imports and exports failed to reach double figures, but 1937 shared that unsavoury distinction with 1933; 1935, when the combined total reached £19 was quite good in comparison. The figures for 1938, giving a total of nearly £2,500, were more respectable but not very encouraging.[24]

With such low volumes of trade, due to recurring depression, and the relatively low cost of labour natural in an age of mass unemployment, there was little premium on modernisation of facilities in the smaller ports. Up to the middle years of the 1930s it was quite common for German sailing ships to visit a small Fife port like Crail. They would bring cargoes of timber, and in the season they would load cargoes of potatoes. Manoeuvring a sailing ship of any size into that harbour was a considerable feat. The ship would tie up to a buoy outside the harbour prior to being pulled into the port by hawsers assisted usually by the ship's own auxiliary engine.[25] On the southern shore of the Forth in the early 1930s it was still possible to see a schooner waiting offshore for a favourable tide to enable her to sail with her cargo of salt into the old tidal harbour of Cockenzie.[26] A very ancient maritime technology based on wind, tide, and relative poverty was still just alive in the Firths of Forth and Tay on the eve of the Second World War.

Interestingly enough, the smaller ports of the Forth which depended heavily on coal exports usually managed to avoid the catastrophic decline in business which affected ports like Arbroath and Perth. Their overall performance never matched the boom years just before the First World War, but this was a reflection of a general decline in British coal exports. The amount of coal exported from Britain fell from 61.7 million tons in 1924 to 35.9 million tons in 1938. The latter figure was not quite half the 1913 figure.[27] Nevertheless Methil, the most capital-intensive and specialised of the Forth coal ports managed to maintain an average annual export figure of roughly three million tons of coal between 1911 and 1935, the war years only excepted. By 1938 the figure had fallen because world trade was entering yet another depressed phase. Even so, at 2.8 million tons of coal, the volume of exports was impressive. Methil was Scotland's leading coal-exporting port in the inter-war period, and in every respect something of an exception amongst the ports of the Forth and Tay.[28]

Though the other coal ports of the coast did not match Methil's performance, they managed to retain a reasonable volume of trade. Bo'ness experienced severer fluctuations than most, but this was partly because it was so close to the rival major port of Grangemouth. Throughout the 1930s Bo'ness still managed to export an average of nearly 150,000 tons of coal, despite a fall to only 60,000 tons in the bleak year 1931. Burntisland managed to export about four or five times as much coal annually as Bo'ness in this same period, without experiencing anything like the same degree of fluctuation.[29] Granton had perhaps the most interesting record of all. During the First World War it had been almost entirely taken over by the Royal Navy as a mine-sweeper and destroyer base. Between 1919 and 1937 the Duke of Buccleuch, who still owned the port, embarked on an ambitious programme of wharf reconstruction. As a trawler harbour and as an importer of esparto grass and petroleum as well as an exporter of coal, the harbour flourished in the 1930s. Its coal exports included a large element of coke from the nearby Edinburgh Corporation Gas Works. In 1932 the harbour became a private limited company, with the Duke as chairman. In 1937 His Grace inaugurated a new carrying-belt coal-loading plant with a capacity of 600 tons per hour, based on a new reinforced concrete jetty 450 feet long, and copied from a similar installation on Tyneside.[30]

That most of Granton's coke exports went to Denmark, Sweden, or Germany, helps explain the comparative vigour of the Forth coal ports in the 1930s. Their traditional markets lay in northern Europe. Coal and coke were in the 1930s much the most important single category of goods imported into the Scandinavian economies, despite the extensive utilisation of hydro-electric power in those lands. It was a condition of trade agreements made in 1933 between the United Kingdom and Denmark, Norway, Sweden, Finland, and Iceland that each of these countries should buy a certain agreed percentage of their coal requirements from the United Kingdom. As a result about half the coal imported into Sweden in the period 1933-9, and some three-quarters of that imported into other Scandinavian countries in the same period was of British origin.[31] Economic historians tend to decry the significance of these Anglo-Scandinavian trade agreements, on the grounds that the German and Polish coal they excluded from Scandinavia simply swept British coal exports out of other markets like Italy. For the coal mines and coal ports of the Forth, however, there can be no doubt that the agreements were an important factor helping them to retain traditional markets.

THE MAJOR PORTS, 1922-39

Throughout the inter-war period Leith remained incomparably the most important port on the east coast of Scotland. The town of Leith itself was re-incorporated into Edinburgh in 1920, but Leith docks remained under the control of Leith Dock Commission, a statutory body numbering fifteen which by this time was composed of representatives from the town council of Edinburgh, Edinburgh Chamber of Commerce, Leith Chamber of Commerce, Edinburgh Merchant Company, and Leith shipowners and dock ratepayers. This body came increasingly under fire from radical critics for its extremely cautious approach to the question of further dock development. The ambitious schemes adopted in 1913, for which an extension of powers had been sought in 1918, had by the 1920s been unmistakably shelved. Partly this was because after the hectic post-war boom, when in 1920 exports and imports at Leith reached a total value of nearly £45 million at current prices, the trade of the port had settled down again. The total value of trade at the docks in 1913 and 1914 had averaged £23.5 million. Between 1921 and 1930 the average total annual value at current prices was about £25 million. Allowing for inflation, it is clear that the situation was not auspicious for further dock-extension.

By 1933, however, there was a fairly vigorous agitation going on with a view to forcing Leith Dock Commission into a substantial new construction programme. As the value of trade through the docks was in the early 1930s roughly half of what it had been in the 1920s, the timing of this agitation may seem curious. In fact it was the depression of trade which gave edge to the agitation as its principal spokesman, Mr David Dryburgh of Newhaven made clear. Unemployment in Leith in the 1930s was very high. It was said that at times one man in three or four was unemployed. The local trade unions saw in a massive new dock extension scheme the possibility of work for their members and a stimulating inflow of cash and credit for the local economy. They could and did reinforce their arguments with several very good points. There were certain long-standing deficiencies in the facilities at Leith, notably in the provision for the Newhaven fishing fleet. Secondly, it could be argued that Leith docks were falling behind nearby rivals in terms of relative efficiency and modernisation. Thirdly, it was pointed out that as a consequence of the depressed economic climate money was cheap and a body with a good credit rating like Leith Dock Commission could easily raise funds for a large construction programme.

It is not easy to assess the full weight of the second argument. There had been no significant dock development since the Imperial Dock was opened in 1904. The only substantial building undertaken by Leith Dock Commission in the early 1930s was the erection of a great new reinforced concrete grain elevator warehouse at the Imperial Dock. It was served by two pneumatic ship-discharging plants, and the silos of its grain storage section had a capacity of 20,000 tons. It represented a total cost of £250,000 when it was opened in 1934. Nevertheless, it was essentially a replacement and improvement job, for it was built in place of a grain warehouse destroyed by fire in January 1930. It could be argued that in other respects the docks at Leith were out of date compared with, say, Grangemouth. At Leith the dock gates were open only from five to six hours in twenty-four, whereas at Grangemouth the gates were open for fifteen hours in twenty-four. A captain who just missed high tide and the gates at Leith could lose a lot of time and money. It was true that certain berths at Leith could be reached during twelve hours out of the twenty-four, but these were the preserve of the London steamers. It could also be argued that the trend in merchant shipping was towards larger and larger ships with, inevitably, deeper draughts. Both at Grangemouth and at comparable ports in the North of England in the 1930s big efforts were being made in most harbours to secure a depth of not less than thirty feet at low water. In Leith the depth available in the biggest dock— the Imperial—was well under thirty feet.

The upshot of much debate and crossfire was that early in 1935 Leith Dock Commission approved in principle a new dock development scheme. By 1936 it had been agreed, despite criticism from Leith Dock Ratepayers Association, to embark on the first stage of construction, at an estimated cost of £500,000. All the new development pivoted on the bay between Leith and Newhaven where a great new breakwater enclosing over 250 acres of water was to be the essential preliminary. Between a long west breakwater, and a shorter east one, well over 2,000 feet of breakwater was envisaged. Thirty acres of foreshore were to be recovered. Not only did Leith experts visit Holland to study the latest developments in Dutch land-reclamation and dyke-building techniques, but Leith Dock Commission also brought over a significant number of Dutch workmen who applied their own land reclamation methods such as 'thatching' reclaimed land with willow stakes, reeds, and wire. Despite sceptical comments about the dock complex which was supposed to arise within the breakwater, and predictable conflicts with riparian proprietors like Lord Rosebery during the search for suitable Forth sand for the works, the project was well advanced by 1939.

Trade was reasonably buoyant in 1936 and 1937. The introduction of tariff protection for British agriculture after 1931 undoubtedly depressed Leith's traditional import of foodstuffs, while coal exports failed to match the vigour of those of smaller Forth ports, but with the general recovery in world trade, Leith was more prosperous. Imports of grain during 1936–7 totalled 416,459 tons. This was the highest figure ever recorded with the exception of 456,704 tons in 1912–13. Part of the trouble with coal exports was that, though exports to Scandinavia stood up well, much of Leith's traditional coal export was to parts of Europe outwith Scandinavia. There was a small decline in the total value of imports and exports in 1938. Then came 1939 and the Second World War.

At its outset Hitler's war was not marked by a naval confrontation in the North Sea comparable to that of 1914. Leith Dock Commission was therefore very angry when the Admiralty issued an order suspending work on Leith dock extension. Works like these could not be suspended without a high risk of damage by wave action. By 1940 the order had been rescinded, but the damage was done. The principal contractor had exercised his right to refuse to renew his obligations, and war had once again paralysed the extension of Leith docks.[32]

On the surface, the history of the port of Grangemouth between the wars does not appear very different from that of the port of Leith. Like Leith Grangemouth was taken over by the Royal Navy during the First World War, but earlier and with more drastic consequences for the local economy. The population of the town actually fell by over a thousand during the war. As with Leith, the 1920s saw a fall in the volume of trade after the peak of the post-war boom in 1920, and the 1930s saw a futher fall, particularly in the mid-1930s. In total annual value the trade of Grangemouth was usually between a third and a half of that of Leith in the inter-war era. What was truly significant in the history of Grangemouth between 1922 and 1939 was the rise of a whole new range of industries, whose full effect on the prosperity and status of the port was really only felt after 1945.

Grangemouth had, of course, begun to develop as an oil-importing port before 1914. Although the firm involved was called the British Petroleum Company, it was in fact German. Its assets were taken over by the Admiralty for the benefit of the Royal Navy in 1914, and were sold after the war by the custodian of enemy property to the Anglo-Persia Oil Company. That company was the predecessor of the modern British Petroleum. By 1934 there were several oil storage and distribution firms with installations in Grangemouth. Apart from the Admiralty, these included the Ebano Oil Company, the Medway Oil Company, the Power Petroleum Company, Ross Creosote and Oil Fuel Storage, and Russian Oil Products. More significant still, in 1924 Scottish Oils Limited—then part of the Anglo-Persian organisation—opened a refinery for the treatment of imported crude oil at Grangemouth. The products were motor spirit, kerosene, and fuel oil.[33]

Parallel with this development came that of a dyestuffs industry. It began in a small way in 1919 when a firm called Scottish Dyes Limited, founded by the Scot James Morton in 1915 to manufacture vat dyestuffs in Carlisle, chose Grangemouth as the site of its new factory. It was attracted by the good rail, road and sea connections of the port and by the availability of water and labour. Vat colours were complicated to make but extremely reliable or fast when applied. By 1930, within this limited range, Scottish Dyes were making nearly 100 colours and 200 intermediates. The might of the German dyestuffs industry, however, ensured that their British rivals could only survive by amalgamation. In 1926 Scottish Dyestuffs amalgamated with the British Dyestuffs Corporation, though it kept its own name. Two years later British Dyestuffs became one of the four great firms which united to form Imperial Chemical Industries Limited, and before long the name Scottish Dyes was replaced by I.C.I. Dyestuffs Division.[34]

The population of Grangemouth grew to nearly 12,000 by 1931, but thereafter industrial and general expansion flagged. The development of oil importation led to the installation of specialised equipment at the docks, but there were no other major developments between 1919 and 1939. The foundations of Grangemouth's two main modern industries—dyestuffs and petroleum chemicals—had been laid. Neither, however, generated a great volume of business for the harbour, which was still very dependent on imports of timber, and exports of coal. Coal exports were not very buoyant. Timber imports were more reliable. Grangemouth was represented in the syndicate of British wood merchants who bought the entire Russian production of sawn softwood in 1929, 1930, 1931, and 1932. It is true that after the economic agreements reached by representatives of the states of the British Empire and Commonwealth at Ottawa in 1932, there was a hostile tariff against non-Empire timber, but the building boom of the 1930s to some extent offset the impact of this measure.[35]

The port of Dundee in the inter-war period had a completely different experience from that of the port of Grangemouth. Grangemouth saw the emergence of new industries which, in the long run, had a vast growth potential and which were likely to benefit the harbour with bulk imports of raw material. Dundee simply carried its Victorian pattern to a logical, if extreme, conclusion. It is true that the percentage of United Kingdom flax and hemp imports reaching Dundee fell from 30.5 in 1853 to 11.3 in 1938, but the percentage of United Kingdom jute imports entering the harbour of Dundee rose from 57.3 in 1853 to 98 in 1939. Even more striking was the increase in the percentage of jute reaching Dundee direct from India: in 1853 the figure was 3.5; by 1939 it was 90, and Dundee was the only significant port in the United Kingdom for jute imports. The big jute ships almost never belonged to the port of Dundee by 1939. They usually stopped off on their voyage from India to unload some raw jute at Continental ports, and some coarse Indian jute textiles at other British ports, before entering Dundee.

In sheer bulk the trade of Dundee reached a zenith at this period, and the size of ship carrying the staple import grew steadily larger. The docks were no longer adequate for these. The Camperdown and Victoria Docks, for example, were by the 1930s used mainly by the smaller ships engaged in the North Sea and coastal trades. Medium-sized vessels in the Baltic, Scandinavian, and Mediterranean trades preferred the wharves, when these were not pre-empted by jute boats. Even amongst the wharves, there was a high degree of selectivity, for the old Western Wharf, which remained a timber structure, could not cope with the demands of modern unloading machinery and motor traffic. The favoured berth for the jute liners, which were by the 1930s very often upwards of 11,000 tons gross, was the King George the Fifth Wharf. The first section of this wharf had been built in 1913–5. A second section of 255 feet was constructed in 1924–6, by which time the total cost of the wharf, with its electric cranes and other handling equipment was £225,000. After the closure of a shipyard in 1928, it proved possible to extend the wharf by another 574 feet in 1931–2. Because of the need to float the largest jute liners at the lowest tides the depth alongside this wharf was dredged to twenty-eight feet at low tide by 1938.[36]

The industrial history of Dundee in the inter-war period was in fact a very unhappy one, with staggering unemployment in the textile industry which was so unhealthily dominant in the local economy. Even in 1940, after the start of the Second World War, the high point of unemployed in Dundee was 9,613 and the low point 6,459. An attempt to attract industry to Dundee in the inter-war period was led by the town council and more particularly Treasurer Frain. Despite extensive publicity, it came to nothing. Perhaps the motto selected for the campaign— 'Do it at Dundee'—deserved no better fate. Be that as it may, it is clear that Dundee harbour, by simply taking a larger share of total British jute imports, managed to do relatively well in a depressed local economy.[37] However, the long-term prospect was not good, for there was little hope of further expansion in jute. Of the three major ports of the Forth and Tay between 1922 and 1939, Dundee seemed to do better than either Leith or Grangemouth, but it was to reap a bitter harvest after 1945, just when Grangemouth was reaping the benefits of economic change.

CHAPTER VI

Shipowning and Shipbuilding in the Forth and Tay

INTRODUCTION

The history of shipowning and the history of shipbuilding in the harbours of the Forth and Tay are best treated as two distinct stories. There has often been an intimate connection between the two spheres of activity, but it has never been a necessary connection. This was demonstrated at an early stage by the experience of the ports of the Forth and Tay in the seventeenth century. Though Scotland had a reputation for shipbuilding in the sixteenth century, very few Scottish ships were built at home by the second half of the seventeenth century. Indeed a small shipyard at Leith is the only fully proven example of continuous construction between 1660 and 1707. During the civil strife of the central decades of the seventeenth century it is clear that both shipowning and shipbuilding fell to a low ebb on the east coast of Scotland. Dutch shipping established a firm grip on what coastal and overseas trade of value survived. When, after 1660, Scots shipowners re-established themselves on the important coastal and foreign trade routes, they tended to do so with ships bought abroad. The mass-produced small wooden ships available at very low prices in Holland and Norway could and did undersell anything Scottish shipyards could produce.[1]

175

Shipowning

Inevitably, shipowning in this region in the late seventeenth and eighteenth centuries was deeply affected by the general state of the regional economy. Most ships did not represent a vast investment of capital. In the late seventeenth century £100 sterling laid out shrewdly could secure a respectable trading vessel, perhaps not in her first youth, but fit for North Sea voyages. Fifty tons was a respectable size of ship. With the expansion of the regional economy, within the framework of a highly protectionist British state, the eighteenth century saw a great expansion in both overseas and coastal trade, and in the number of ships owned in the harbours of the Forth and Tay. By 1800 most of these ships were Scottish built. Leith ships engaged in extensive overseas commerce, and even Dundee had a trade with the colonies of British North America before 1776, but many of these ships were engaged in relatively short-range coastal trade. Montrose, for example, in 1789 had fifty-three ships of 3,543 tons mostly engaged in coastal trade, bringing coal from the Firth of Forth and exporting sail-cloth, salmon, and agricultural products.[2] A detailed shipping list for Dundee in 1822 survives, and it underlines how little matters had changed since the late seventeenth century, except in terms of volume of activity. In 1822 158 ships belonged to the port of Dundee, with a total tonnage of 16,572. Coasters outnumbered vessels in foreign trade, though the latter were larger on average than the coasters. Fifty tons was a small but still respectable ship. The vast majority of vessels lay between 70 and 200 tons burthen. Ownership seems to have been widely spread through the mercantile community, partly because ownership did not necessarily represent a massive financial commitment. By far the biggest ships on the register were the highly specialised whaling vessels, some of which were nearer 400 than 300 tons. Whalers were, however, a very small proportion of local shipping, for only ten ships were thus employed.[3]

There were legal, as well as economic and social barriers

Crail harbour. Note the crane inserting booms in the entrance

Dysart harbour in the late nineteenth century. Note the Norwegian ship

to the formation of shipowning companies pooling the resources of a number of capitalists. Under English law the Bubble Act of 1719 restricted the right of incorporation to companies which could obtain it by Royal Charter or by parliamentary legislation. Only after the Joint Stock Companies Act of 1856 was it relatively easy for a company in the United Kingdom to secure incorporation, with its three main benefits: transferability of shares, the separate legal personality of the company, and limited liability for the shareholders. The legal position in Scotland between 1719 and 1856 was debatable, but in practice there were easy ways of obtaining incorporation, and the Scots law on partnerships and unincorporated companies gave them transferability of shares, and the right to a legal personality. English legal concepts tended to erode the liberalism of Scots commercial law, but for a time there was even a species of limited liability for unincorporated Scots companies. All this made substantial shipping companies possible in Scotland, without really encouraging their formation.[4] In fact, it seems that sheer necessity was the main reason for the formation of the earliest significant shipping companies in the Forth and Tay. A need for expensive, specialised equipment; a need to maintain regular services with several boats; and technological factors like the coming of steam power, and the general increase in the size of ships, especially for long-distance overseas trade, all seem to have played a part.

In the early nineteenth century the overseas trade of Leith tended to decline in comparison with that of Glasgow and the other Clyde ports. By 1820 there was real depression in the overseas trade of Leith, apart from the trade between Leith and the Dutch and North German ports. On the other hand, Leith coastal trade with London was buoyant, while a new and valuable long-range trade was just opening between Leith and the British colonies in Australia. It is no accident that the same small group of men can be found promoting in 1820 the London, Leith, Edinburgh and Glasgow Shipping Company, and in 1822 both the Leith, Hamburg and Rotterdam Shipping Company and the Australian Company of Edinburgh and Leith. These promoters were mainly Leith shipowners and Edinburgh merchants anxious to restore the prosperity of their port. For a trade like that with Australia, involving large ships and very lengthy voyages, a strong corporate organisation capable of bearing the financial strain must have seemed appropriate. In fact, by 1833 the Australian Company had been wound up.[5] Nevertheless, it helped found a vigorous new trade route. Scottish exports ranged from thousands of emigrants to cargoes of William Younger's Strong Ale, which started to arrive in Australia, often on Leith ships, in 1856.[6] In return, Australia exported primary products, including wool, which soon became an important raw material for the Scottish Border textile industry.

The great Bell Rock Lighthouse off the mouth of the Tay, built by Robert Stevenson as early as 1807–11, is a tribute to the contemporary importance of the coastal shipping it primarily safeguarded. Leith too had major coastal shipping interests, especially in the highly competitive passenger trade to London. In the late eighteenth century ships sailing from Leith to London were usually brigs of 160–200 tons, heavy in build and with only one small cabin. They remained in harbour until a full cargo was obtained, so their time of departure was vague. By 1790 most people preferred to journey from Leith to London on the fast light smacks whose main function was to pick up cargoes of salmon at Berwick and transport them to the London market. The profits made out of passenger traffic were large enough to encourage the Leith and Berwick Shipping Company to establish its headquarters in Leith in 1791, in order to offer a service of fast light smacks between Leith and London. These ships still picked up cargoes of salmon at Berwick, but sailing arrangements clearly subordinated this function to the maintenance of a regular scheduled passenger service. By 1802 the Edinburgh and Leith Shipping Company had entered into competition, with six fine smacks devoted exclusively to the trade between Leith and London. In 1812 the old Leith and Berwick Company metamorphosed itself, with additional financial backing, into the London and Leith Old Shipping Company, which operated six smacks on the run between Leith and London. Two years later, in 1814, the Edinburgh Glasgow and Leith Company entered this already crowded field. The size of the sailing smacks continually grew. Whereas in 1800 few reached 100 tons, by 1824 none was under 130 tons, and several were nearly 200 tons. An average voyage lasted four days, which matched the rate of coach travel until a regular mail coach began to run between Edinburgh and London in a couple of days. Nevertheless, the smacks remained competitive for they were more comfortable than the coach, and for anyone with any amount of luggage, they were much cheaper.

The introduction of steam power on the passenger service between Leith and London was delayed until 1821 by fears that steamships could not operate profitably enough to yield a reasonable return on the considerable investment required. However, in a competitive and profitable trade it was inevitable that an attempt would be made to exploit the speed and regularity possible with steamships. In 1821 the London and Edinburgh Steam Packet Company was formed, with very heavy financial backing. In 1821 it put into service the *City of Edinburgh* of 420 tons equipped with two 40 horse power engines. This ship was followed by the *James Watt* of 449 tons in 1822, and the *Soho* of 510 tons in 1823. Carrying nearly a hundred passengers, these vessels cut the trip to London to just over two days. The need for financial strength to cope with the problems of a rapidly changing technology in this competitive trade had already by 1820 produced a tendency to amalgamation amongst companies.[7]

The history of shipping services between the Tay and London in this period shows similar forces at work. The Dundee Perth and London Shipping Company formed in 1826 was a fusion of two earlier companies. These were the Dundee and Perth Shipping Company, which had been established in 1798, and the Dundee and Perth Union Shipping Company, which had been established in 1819.

The new company formed in 1826 disposed of nineteen ships and lighters, and its capital was valued at £38,045. All these vessels were sailing ships or barges. Those on the London run usually made the trip from the Tay to London in about six days. It was only in 1832 that the Dundee Perth and London Shipping Company decided, after fierce disputes in the directorate, to order steamships. By 1834 the company had taken delivery of two 399 ton paddle steamers built on the Clyde by Robert Napier and called the *Dundee* and the *Perth*. These two ships cost £18,000 apiece. Despite this price Robert Napier lost heavily on the contract.[8] Some measure of the rapidly escalating cost of remaining competitive on the east-coast routes may be gathered from a comparison of this £36,000 order with the first ship built for the Dundee and Perth Shipping Company. This was almost certainly the 101 ton wooden smack the *Lord Duncan*, launched on the Tay in 1799, but retained in the company fleet for only a short time. Those were the days when a brigantine of 143 tons was considered such an exceptionally big ship to be built at Dundee that her launch attracted a large and excited crowd. The coming of the railway inevitably eroded the profitability of coastal passenger services, but up to about 1840 even quite short-range coastal services could be highly profitable. The heavily patronised service on the Tay between Perth and Dundee is a good example. Steam packets were introduced on this run a good decade before they appeared on the route between the Tay and London. Significantly, the competition between the earliest steam packets running between Dundee and Perth was so frantic that rival crews came to blows, and passenger safety was endangered.[9]

Apart from the long-distance trades, including whaling, and the very important coastal passenger routes, shipowning in the harbours of the Forth and Tay in the first half of the nineteenth century was not dominated by large companies. Partly this was because of the enduring vitality of the sailing ship as an economic carrier of freight. The early steamships were expensive to run. They were an economic proposition only in trades where objects of very high value compared with their weight had to be conveyed speedily and regularly. People and mails were the obvious examples. As late as 1837 there were only 668 steamships in the whole United Kingdom, averaging a mere 120 tons apiece. For short and medium distance hauls a relatively modest investment in a sailing ship was often enough to secure a steady flow of business. This point is well illustrated by the history of the trade between Leith and the most northern parts of Scotland —the Orkney and Shetland Islands. Until very well into the third quarter of the nineteenth century the bulk of the fish exports of Orkney and Shetland and the grain exports of Orkney were carried in smacks and schooners which also carried the multifarious imports of the islands. These ships were usually owned by small island companies like the Zetland New Shipping Company.

Sailing ship design changed repeatedly in the nineteenth century, and this last-named company was quick to take advantage of the development of the clipper type of ship, with its long sharp bow, hollow lines, and raked masts. The clipper design was the answer of Aberdeen shipbuilders to the challenge of the steamship on the east-coast routes. Alexander Hall and Company of Aberdeen built for the Zetland New Shipping Company the famous clipper-style schooner *Matchless* which entered service in 1846 and was able to trade regularly between Lerwick and Leith, despite steamship competition, as late as 1882. Indeed, early attempts to operate steam packets between Leith and Aberdeen or Leith and the Orkney and Shetland Islands tended to founder on the absence of a heavy regular passenger traffic. What saved steam navigation on this northern route was the policy of the Board of Admiralty in the late 1830s under a Whig government, when it was decided to turn over the carriage of mails from state-owned steam packets to private enterprise. It is no coincidence that the first regular steamship service between Leith and Orkney and Shetland was established in 1838 by the Aberdeen, Leith, Clyde and Tay Shipping Company, which that year secured a mail contract between Leith and Lerwick, the principal town of the Shetland Isles.[10]

Shipbuilders continued to produce new and more efficient sailing ships throughout the nineteenth century. Many clipper ships, for example, were composite in construction. That is to say they had wooden hulls on iron frames, as well as very often having iron lower masts. The iron-hulled sailing ship was a logical development from this compromise, as was a tendency towards simpler sail plans which could be handled by smaller crews. Nevertheless, improvements in steamer engines and design from screw propulsion to the much more economic triple expansion engine, steadily eroded the competitiveness of sailing ships. Several Leith firms which had started in a small way before 1840, and which had built up a modest level of prosperity on the basis of sailing ships between 1840 and 1870, burgeoned into major shipping lines in the first great era of the steamship as general freight carrier, an era which only dawned after 1870 and perhaps only after 1880. The partnership of William Thomson and Company is a very good example. Its origins can be traced to 1839 when William Thomson and his brother Alexander bought a minority share in the small vessel *Carrara*, in order to safeguard supplies of marble from Italy for their modest business as marble cutters in Edinburgh. From this trade William Thomson progressed to holding a stake in ships which transported Alloa coal to Canada, whence they returned with cargoes of timber for Leith. Soon the partnership of William Thomson and Company was operating tramp sailing ships in the Far East as well as on the North Atlantic. The ships of this firm, soon known as the Ben Line, did not include a steamer until 1871, and the second steamship added to the line only joined it in 1875. However, their triumph was inevitable because, despite their high costs, they were more profitable than sailing ships. Only steamships could use the Suez Canal, opened in 1869, and this fact, allied to their greater efficiency, clinched their dominance in such bitterly competitive fields as the China trade.[11]

A glance at another important Leith shipping firm, the Leith, Hull, and Hamburg Steam Packet Company, shows a similar pattern. Founded as a very small coastal venture in the 1830s, it was re-constructed after 1853 with fresh capital and a policy of developing steamer services with Hamburg and Baltic ports. With the rise of the steamship, the company grew, acquiring new partners and capital until in 1880 the company was incorporated under the Joint Stock Companies Acts, thereby securing the benefits of limited liability. By 1890 it owned twenty-six vessels trading to England, Germany, Scandinavia, and Russia, and in the year ending May 1889 its ships paid fifteen per cent of the total tonnage dues on shipping received by Leith Dock Commission, while over twenty per cent of the total dock dues on goods paid at Leith was paid on goods conveyed by the company's steamers. The Scandinavian trade was particularly vigorous after 1867, for in that year the last preferential duties on Canadian timber in the British market were removed. This pattern of an early interest in an Atlantic trade succumbing to an emphasis on the North Sea closely allied to the expansion of steamer traffic can be found in other Leith shipping companies, notably George Gibson and Company. Rooted originally in the West India trade, this company became a pioneer of steamer services between Leith and Hamburg and Rotterdam in the 1850s. By 1890 it could claim to have pioneered steamship communication with the Netherlands, having opened a trade with Antwerp in 1864, Amsterdam in 1877, Dunkirk in 1878, Ghent in 1880, and Harlingen in 1889. The great prize at stake was, of course, bulk food imports into Leith, but there was also a big tourist traffic.[12]

To some extent the high levels of profitibality which had helped to create the fourteen shipping firms functioning in Leith in 1886 were based on relatively low labour costs. Seamen on the east coast of Scotland had a record of militancy going back to a great strike during the era of the French Revolution. Nevertheless, they remained un-organised and weak until very late in the nineteenth century. Wages were low. In the 1840s able-bodied seamen on the east coast of Scotland were known to accept £2 per month, and until Samuel Plimsoll's successful parliamentary agitation of the 1870s, overloading of ships to the point of danger was quite common.[13] In Leith itself there was undoubtedly acute social tension between an aristocracy of rich shipowners and merchants, many of whom had opposed even Plimsoll's limited objectives, and the mass of the population. An all-pervading Liberal political ascendancy, and such extraneous issues as Irish Home Rule sufficed to mask the sharpness of this conflict.[14] Only in 1887 was the National Seamen's and Firemen's Union formed. In 1890 the employers established their own Shipping Federation, at first as an undisguised strike-breaking organisation, and it was only after a series of bitter struggles that the seamen's union, led by Havelock Wilson, achieved formal recognition by the employers. The great strikes of 1911 marked a decisive turning point.[15]

The history of shipowning on the Tay shows intriguing differences from that of shipowning at Leith. Certain trends are broadly similar, from the dispersed pattern of early shipowning, to the expansion of many firms between 1870 and 1900, on the basis of the achievements of the steamship. Yet a complex of firms comparable to the major Leith shipping lines never arose on Tayside. In particular, Dundee shipowners never seemed able to secure predominance in the very large trade created by imports of jute fibre from India. The much smaller trade in Baltic flax remained in local hands, though no great process of concentration occurred in the ships that carried it. Had major textile firms elected to diversify permanently into shipping, circumstances might have been different. As it was, a few local flax or jute magnates, like George Armitstead, later Lord Armitstead, were both shipowners and fibre importers. It was wholly appropriate that Armitstead, who had been born in Riga of mixed British and Russian Jewish parentage, should be a major flax importer for his own merchant business, chairman of the Dundee and Arbroath Railway in 1856, and a pioneer of direct steam communication between the Tay and Baltic.[16] However, he was an exceptional man in every way, and most of the big textile firms were slow to follow his example.

Before the 1860s, of all the substantial Dundee jute firms only Gilroy Brothers was making a serious effort to ship jute between Dundee and India in their own ships. During the American Civil War boom the Lochee firm of Cox Brothers began to follow a similar policy, but it is significant that neither of these major firms diversified into shipowning on a large scale for more than a few decades. There was no reason why they should. The business was a risky and specialised one. One of the Gilroy boats, for example, burned out due to spontaneous combustion in her coal. Nor was Dundee a particularly good base for an India trade, due to the difficulty of finding outward cargoes. It was better to leave the business in the hands of established lines in London, Liverpool, and Greenock. Interestingly enough, one of the Gilroy captains, Charles Barrie, launched an independent shipping line of his own in 1881 in the shape of the Dundee and Calcutta Line of Clippers. Barrie, later Sir Charles Barrie, specialised in big iron sailing ships until 1894, when he ordered a 5,650 tons steamship the *Den of Airlie*, which proved the ancestor of a succession of steamships famous all over the world as the Den Line.

The history of Charles Barrie and the shipping enterprise he founded is a microcosm of the history of shipowning on the Forth and Tay. Barrie started as an apprentice aboard the *Sutlej*, a wooden ship of 782 tons completed at Dundee in 1854 for Bailie William Clark, then a leading shipowner in the town. After sundry adventures in Australia, New Zealand, and South Africa, he entered the service of Gilroy Brothers, from which he progressed to his own lines of sailing and then steam ships. The last of his sailing ships was sold in 1908, and his steamship fleet was sold in 1917, his firm surviving as shipbrokers. That the sale of the Barrie fleet was part of a larger trend may be deduced from the fact that Dundee, which had achieved representation on the

General Committee of Lloyd's Register of Shipping in 1887, had lost it again by 1919 because of the sharp drop in tonnage owned in the port during the First World War.[17] The reasons for this drop are not far to seek. Between them, heavy losses of tonnage to German submarines, and the needs of an economy geared to total war, had created a shipping shortage, with accompanying high prices for vessels, by 1917. This particular boom looked like fading with peace, but it was artificially prolonged, partly by port congestion, which immobilised a great deal of tonnage, until 1920. During a period when the operation of vessels on ocean routes involved high risks, it was tempting for provincial shipowners to sell out at a good price. Unfortunately, coastal shipping had emerged from the war in bad shape. Many coastal vessels were lost between 1914 and 1919, and the railways after 1919, partly due to government policy, could seriously undercut coastal shipping freight rates. Not much wonder provincial shipowning entered the doldrums.[18]

The big Leith shipping lines proved more resistant to elimination by absorption, but they were by no means all in good financial shape, even in 1919. The Ben Line persisted until that date in the common nineteenth-century practice of regarding each ship as a separate financial unit divided into sixty-four shares. The holders of these shares, who in a family firm would normally be mostly members of the owning family, expected an immediate distribution of the profits of each voyage. Reserves of working capital were hard to come by, and overdrafts had to be guaranteed against the personal fortunes of the managing partners. Inevitably, the Ben Line became a limited liability company in April 1919, after which it faced two decades of violently fluctuating world trade. In 1932–3 the net profit of the company was £30. Despite this sort of result, a fleet of eleven vessels with a total deadweight of 64,500 tons in 1919 had become a fleet of twenty vessels of 145,750 tons in 1939.[19] A similar pattern can be seen in other major shipping lines with interests in eastern waters. The Peninsular and Oriental Line, which between 1914 and 1932 was dominated by an

Arbroath man, James Mackay, Lord Inchcape, also built many new ships in the inter-war period. The ships were either ordered in the post-war boom or in the period 1925–30, when shipbuilding costs were low. After 1930 survival rather than expansion was the keynote, and dividends were not much heard of.[20]

Lord Inchcape's career is a reminder that able entrepreneurs from the Forth or Tay often made their careers in shipping in major ports outwith their native region. The Clyde attracted Paddy Henderson, a man from the East Neuk of Fife who went on to found one of the bigger Glasgow shipping lines, while other men were drawn from Tayside shipping offices into London ones. John Stewart, a clerk in the Dundee shipbrokers' office of Messrs Machan originally, is a good example. Captain George Duncan invited him to go to London to co-operate with him in founding the famous Empire fleet of sailing ships. By 1877 Stewart resigned from his position under Duncan to found the John Stewart Line, famous as the last line to operate foreign-going, square-rigged, cargo-carrying sailing ships registered in Great Britain.[21] In the light of all this, and in view of the depressing history of shipowning on the Forth and Tay after 1919, and more particularly after 1945, it requires an effort to remember that in the first decades of successful steam navigation the Forth was a metropolitan area in the shipping world, exerting a strong influence over much of the north of Europe. Indeed, in the early 1850s the development of steam navigation in Norway owed much to a sense of outrage that a Leith line could secure mail contracts from the Norwegian Department of the Interior.[22] Furthermore, Grangemouth and then Leith attracted one of the great Norwegian shipowners, Christian Salvesen, to make his career in them.

The Salvesen enterprise was always rather different from other Scots shipping firms. For a long time it maintained close links with the southern part of Norway from which the family had come, and whereas in 1914 the Arctic whaling industry of the Tay was on its last legs, the

Antarctic whaling enterprises of the Salvesen family were thriving and prosperous. Equally contrary to the general trend, the Salvesens did not join in the rush to order new tonnage after 1919. On the contrary, they reckoned that their fleet had been over-expanded during the war, and chose to sell several vessels at a profit, which greatly strengthened the capital reserves available to meet the subsequent depression. When Christian Salvesen and Company did buy tonnage between 1919 and 1939, it was often in the shape of relatively old and cheap ships. Indeed when they ordered a new ship from the Clyde yard of D. and W. Henderson in 1934, this was their first new building, apart from whale catchers, for forty years. Though the firm did try to compete in the Baltic trade in the 1930s, showing real suspicion of cartels and the cruder forms of subsidy, profit margins on its main export commodity, coal, and its main import commodity, timber, were very low in the decade before 1939. Oil imports were a better proposition, but by 1939 it could be said that Christian Salvesen and Company was keeping its merchant fleet in being in the hope of better days, and with the help of its more lucrative whaling operations.[23]

The impact of the Second World War on the shipping lines of the Forth and Tay was physically very severe. The enemy powers pursued a ruthless campaign against British shipping for a longer period, and with a wider range of weapons than had been the case during the First World War. The Ben Line alone lost fourteen vessels in its own ownership during the war, not to mention several government vessels lost when under Ben Line management, and severe poundings from bomb and shell which could cripple ships even if they failed to sink them.[24] The experience of Christian Salvesen and Company was, if anything, more traumatic. Not only did the firm lose many ships, but it also saw a whole component of its whaling fleet—the floating factories—wiped out. In another sense, however, the war was not such a dramatic turning point in the history of shipowning in the region as the First World War. Local lines had started to sell out to compaines based on major English ports long before 1914. However, the process accelerated beyond recognition between 1914 and 1919. Nothing comparable occurred between 1939 and 1945. There was a new and rather fussy tidy-mindedness around in government circles immediately after 1945, and this mentality swept away several anachronisms, like the retention of some authority over pilotage in the Forth by the master mariners of the Trinity House of Leith,[25] but by and large it was the remorseless working of very long-term economic factors which continued to erode the shipowning traditions of the Forth and Tay after 1945.

In so far as that erosion reflected the pressures of alternative means of transport, it represented an absolute loss to the ports of the region. The extension of air services, and the spectacular expansion of road transport, were particularly damaging to coastal shipping. The shipping line which maintained regular services from Leith and Aberdeen to Orkney and Shetland, for example, experienced competition for light and valuable cargoes, like people, newspapers, and mail, from private air operators several years before 1939.[26] Despite this the company managed to survive, changing its name to the North of Scotland, Orkney and Shetland Shipping Company in 1953, but surrendering its independence, if not its name, by amalgamation with the great organisation known as Coast Lines Limited in 1961. Coast Lines in the 1950s also took over some services operated by the Dundee Perth and London shipping line.[27] By 1955 the managers of that firm were arguing that their competitive margin over road and rail was tiny, and that costs were becoming prohibitive. They argued that thirty-two per cent of gross freight earned per ton, was absorbed by handling charges, mainly dockers' wages. Carriage to and from the docks swallowed another twenty per cent, leaving forty-eight per cent to cover the costs of operating the ships, administering the business, and earning a reasonable profit. In 1955 the directors believed they could still retain and attract traffic by investing in a specialist Dutch-built, two-deck ship, but in 1961 they suspended their two-century-old London service.[28] The ships of lines like the Arbroath and London had been shadows of a shade long before that, while financial pressures rendered the foreign-going ships of the Dundee Loch Line and the Dundee Gem Line a mere memory. Surviving shipping firms on Tayside by 1960 were nearly all in agency or brokerage work.[29]

Obviously, the superior financial resources of at least some of the Forth-based shipping lines placed them in a stronger position after 1945. Even so, by the 1950s the dominant note in shipowning circles in the Forth, even in Leith, was one of contraction. The smaller shipping lines of the Forth went the same way as those of the Tay, sometimes faster. By 1956, when the Dundee Perth and London had yet to succumb to road and rail competition to the point of completely abandoning ships, the Carron Line of Grangemouth, another coasting organisation, had already disposed of its last vessel.[30] The J. M. Piggins fleet of coasters based on Montrose was a post-war casualty, but then so was the Matthew Taylor fleet of Methil.[31] Amongst the larger Leith lines, fleets like those of the Ben Line and Christian Salvesen and Company were reconstructed after the war, but there was a definite worsening of prospects in the 1950s, and Salvesen was eventually to abandon its whaling activities. The experience of the Currie Line of Leith is instructive. It was the successor of the old Leith, Hull, and Hamburg Steam Packet Company. As such, it straddled both the coastal and overseas trade worlds. After 1945 it wisely elected to concentrate on the latter. In 1951, during a good period of trade, the line ordered an 11,000 ton freighter from the shipyard at Burntisland. Shipping rates slumped shortly afterwards, leading to cancellation of the order.[32]

It is easy to argue that it does not matter to any given port just who owns the ships frequenting it. Equally clearly, the continuous increase in the size of merchant ships was bound to outstrip both the physical capacity of smaller ports, and the capital resources available to ship owners in them. There is, however, more to the decline of shipowning in the Forth and Tay than this. Ultimately it reflects two deeply disturbing trends. One is an absolute contraction in certain parts of the shipping industry, notably coasting, and the other is the steady reduction of even the biggest ports on the coast to a peripheral and, in the pejorative sense, provincial status.

SHIPBUILDING AND SHIPBREAKING

If it is clear that there was very little shipbuilding in this region in the second half of the seventeenth century, it is equally clear that by the late eighteenth century there was a great deal, and it was widely dispersed round the coast. Just how early in the eighteenth century shipbuilding began to develop is a moot point. There is not a great deal of positive evidence of shipbuilding before the second half of the century, though this may be partly due to the fact that for the smaller wooden vessels of the period no yard was required. Thus at Eyemouth tradition simply pointed to a stretch of beach where it was said sloops and barques had been built in the eighteenth century. These would have been small trading vessels, for as far as is known all local fishing boats were built at Berwick until 1841.[33] Craftsmen, imported timber, and a stretch of beach were the only essentials. After the ship had been launched, very little sign of the work would remain. Nevertheless, snippets of evidence like the petition of the shipmasters of Dundee in 1720 that James Watt, anchorsmith be granted a free burgess ticket on the ground that he was the only shipsmith in the town,[34] suggest that it was only after 1750 that serious development occurred.

Entries in the volumes of the *Old Statistical Account of Scotland* show that by the 1790s some form of shipbuilding was conducted at nearly every port on the Forth and Tay. At the larger centres specialist facilities and long-term accumulations of capital and skill in the shape of permanent yards were emerging. Of the parish of North Leith in 1793 it was said that the principal manufacture in the place was shipbuilding. A number of fine vessels of between 200 and 300 tons had lately been built. There were five master builders, who employed about 152 carpenters, whose wages were about 1s. 10d. (nine new pence) per day each. There were a few more specialised craftsmen like anchorsmiths and within the last sixteen years two dry docks had been built. One was retained by the proprietor, the other let at £130 per annum.[35]

By the early nineteenth century the specialised ship-building yard was common in the larger ports. There were several in Dundee, all clustered together on what had been the shoreline of medieval Dundee, from Yeaman Shore in the east to the line of Dock Street in the west. Unfortunately the improvement of the harbour and the coming of the railway between them ruined the access of these yards to the Tay, forcing a few yards further west, and most of them much further east. It was, however, on the old sites that major technical and managerial experiments were conducted in the early decades of the century. The technical experiments involved the manufacture and installation of marine steam engines, and the manufacture of iron hulls. In both, the firm of J. and C. Carmichael was a pioneer, engining the first steam ferry on the Tay, the *Union*, which was built by Brown at Perth. Later, in their yard at the Seabraes, a site now marooned from the river by many acres of railway sidings, the Carmichaels became the second yard on the Tay to produce iron ships. The first was Macfarlane of Perth in 1836.[36] Iron hulls did not in fact win general acceptance in Dundee yards before the later 1850s. The Carmichaels, who sprang from the millwright tradition of rural Scotland, were increasingly absorbed by social and business connections with Dundee textiles. Their excursion into shipbuilding was brief, but significant, for both iron hulls and the marine steam engine had a great future ahead of them.[37] The same could not be said for the remarkable experiment in co-operative principles represented

The whaler *Active* beset in ice in the Spitzbergen Sea, 1894

Newhaven fishwives of the nineteenth century displaying their traditional dress
and the creel in which they carried their fish to Edinburgh

by the New Shipwright Building Company of Dundee, which began operations in 1826. This firm represented a reaction by the Dundee Shipwright Provident Union Society to a lock-out by the employers, who were anxious to reduce wages, which were averaging about £1 a week. Some workers secured ground for their own yard which built ships of up to 195 tons until it succumbed to trade depression around 1851.[38] It was usually the case in Scottish shipbuilding throughout the nineteenth century that employers found it easy to import strike-breaking labour from elsewhere in times of depression. Wages in shipyards in Dundee in 1868, except for specialists like rivetters, were much what they had been in 1826.[39]

As early as 1850 the pull of the Clyde was felt by eastern shipyards. The great firm of Alexander Stephen and Sons, which started shipbuilding in Aberdeen, moved by stages down the coast, acquiring yards in Arbroath and in 1842 in Dundee. Then in 1850 it took the great leap to the Clyde, which soon became much its most important centre of activity. By 1894 the Stephen Yard in Dundee had been sold to the Dundee Shipbuilders' Company.[40] Undoubtedly, the great concentration of metallurgical and engineering expertise in the hinterland of the Clyde enabled the yards on that river to pioneer many major developments in nineteenth-century shipbuilding from the steam engine and the iron hull to the steel hull and the steam turbine. Between the expertise of Aberdeen yards specialising in clipper-built sailing vessels, and the large and dynamic Clyde shipbuilding industry, Leith had rather a thin time of it.

Until about 1840 it looked as if Leith might remain a major shipbuilding centre. In that year Messrs Menzies of Leith contracted for and launched two steamers larger than any afloat. However, orders fell off, and soon there was widespread redundancy among Leith shipyard workers. The firm of Messrs S. and H. Morton of Leith, specialists in the manufacture of patent slips, began to manufacture iron ships, but after launching a few steamers, a sailing ship, and

193

one or two dredgers, the trade petered out temporarily. Both in Leith, where there were six graving docks in 1868, and in Granton, which invested in a patent slip in 1852, the tendency was for shipyards to specialise in repair work. This was lucrative enough to keep the yards going, but it tended to be seasonal, many ships being regularly laid up for repair work over the winter.[41]

From the northern shore of the Forth to Montrose there were more than twenty shipyards active in 1869, exclusive of small yards building only fishing boats. The bigger yards were well scattered. Montrose had three: J. and D. Birnie, Strachan and Company, and J. Petrie and Company. Arbroath had the Arbroath Shipbuilding Company, while Dundee had no less than five yards. These belonged to Gourlay Brothers and Company, Alexander Stephen and Sons, the Tay Shipbuilding Company, the Dundee Shipbuilding Company, and Brown and Simpson. There were four shipbuilding firms active in Perth, as well as two at Tayport. Newburgh had a yard, as had Dysart, Kinghorn, and probably Limekilns. Inverkeithing had two. Between them, these yards launched at least thirty ships in 1869, of which by far the biggest was the 2,645 ton passenger cargo steamer *Scotland* built by Keys of Kinghorn for London owners. Already by 1869 some of the smaller yards specialising in wooden ships were in trouble. The principals of Messrs Dickie of Tayport, for example, emigrated to San Francisco before the year was out. The Scrimgeour yard at Newburgh was in financial difficulty, having to sell its last and largest ships, the brigantines *Leander* and *Racer* (227 and 260 tons respectively) at a loss. Immediately after this the yard closed.[42]

It is easy enough to see that with the steady increase in the size of merchant ships many of these smaller yards were doomed. The depth of the Tay at Perth, for example, restricted the size of vessel which could be built there. What was much more disturbing was that by the early twentieth century there were signs of permanent contraction in shipbuilding even in the larger ports. Ironically, the late nineteenth century was a time of quite exceptional activity in the bigger shipyards of the Tay and Forth. In Leith in 1883 there were seven shipyards, some of which were mainly engaged in repairing and refitting vessels. However, in 1882 thirteen iron steam vessels with a tonnage of 16,250, and one sailing vessel of 1,032 tons were launched at Leith. In addition to these, the same year saw the building of four yachts of 1,699 tons. Between 1877 and 1882 fifteen wooden steam trawlers were built in Leith.[43] The level of activity on the Tay in these years was equally impressive. Output was dominated by a couple of big Dundee yards, Gourlays and the Caledon. The latter yard was a comparative newcomer. Its owner, W. B. Thompson, was in business in Dundee as a marine engineer at Tay Foundry, Stobswell, in the late 1860s, but it was not until 1874 that he acquired his own yard. The name Caledon was a tribute to an early order for a yacht from the Earl of Caledon. Thompson proved a dynamic businessman with a flair for publicity. He soon progressed from the first ship launched from the Caledon in 1874—the 178 ton *Ilala*—to much bigger ships like the 3,382 ton *Ailsacraig* launched in 1889.[44]

By 1908 Gourlays, the other big Dundee yard, was in liquidation. Technical change in the shipbuilding industry had compelled it to re-equip its yard at heavy expense. A slump in shipping freights and consequently shipbuilding after 1907 meant that Gourlays could not carry the weight of debt they had incurred.[45] The rapidly-changing technology of the twentieth century placed a premium upon substantial financial resources, which only major shipyards could hope to dispose of. During the post-war boom of 1919–20 there were rumours that a major outside shipbuilder was considering opening a yard on the Tay, but the rumour faded as boom became slump, and an inexorable process of concentration resumed. By 1936 it could be said that ship building in Dundee was now concentrated in one establishment, but that that establishment was as well equipped as any in the country. The establishment was the Caledon, and in the six berths it possessed in 1936 vessels of up to

530 feet long could be built.[46] Ship repairing was a less hazardous field of operations in the troubled 1930s, and Leith in 1937 had several yards specialising in repair work, of which two of the best-known were George Brown and Sons and Menzies and Company. As in Dundee, however, only one big shipbuilding yard had survived. This was the establishment of Henry Robb Limited, whose success may be measured by the fact that they contrived to launch nine vessels in the first ten months of 1936.[47]

The only exception to this tale of steady contraction both lay on the northern shore of the Forth. In the East Neuk of Fife many small shipyards survived in an era of rapid technological change because that change hardly affected them at all. The small wooden boat remained ideal for local fishing, and that was what they produced. In 1947 one of these firms, J. N. Miller and Sons celebrated its bicentenary under the same family. The other exception was a more normal shipyard—the Burntisland Shipbuilding Company Limited. Its output and labour force in the early 1950s greatly exceeded that of all the East Neuk yards put together. Founded in 1918, it launched its first ship in 1919, concentrating at first on smallish tramp steamers and coastal colliers. It survived the difficulties of the 1930s to have a potential gross annual output of 28,000 tons in 1937. By 1939 the firm was poised to expand its capacity in the light of war demand, and its capacity was increased to 55,000 tons. 1942 saw the acquisition by the Burntisland Shipbuilding Company of the engineering and shipbuilding complex of Hall, Russell and Company of Aberdeen.[48]

After 1945 British shipyards enjoyed a strong position in the international market, mainly because Germany and Japan had ceased to be serious competitors. The Burntisland yard, for example, was producing a little under 40,000 tons of shipping a year around 1950, mostly for customers in Norway, Portugal, Argentina, and Egypt. Indeed, the record of steady expansion between 1919 and 1950 of the Burntisland Shipbuilding Company was really only matched by the two Fife shipbreaking yards sited in Inverkeithing and Rosyth. Before 1939 one of these yards had benefited by the scrapping of German warships once scuttled in Scapa Flow, but subsequently raised. After 1945, in a world hungry for scrap metal, both did very well.[49]

By the 1950s the three big shipyards of the region still looked healthy. Henry Robb Limited, for example, had over 1,000 men on his payroll in 1957, and in that year the firm laid the keel of a ship of some 6,000 tons, the largest ever built in Leith.[50] The Caledon yard launched three ships, each over 8,000 tons, in 1957. This total compared quite well with the seven ships totalling over 30,000 tons, which the Caledon had launched in 1951. Burntisland launched four ships with a total tonnage of over 30,000 tons in 1957, as compared with six and approximately 19,000 tons in 1951.[51] Nevertheless, certain underlying trends were disturbing. From the mid 1940s to the mid 1950s demand was high enough for the availability of raw material, especially steel, to be the main check on the volume of production in Scottish yards. After June 1952 there was a steady decline in orders, which resulted in a sharp trend towards a lower level of overall activity after 1958.[52] Foreign competitors, notably German, Dutch, Swedish, and Japanese yards, were back in force. The low levels of wages which had undoubtedly helped nineteenth-century Scots shipbuilders were a thing of the past, especially after 1951 when the Confederation of Ship-building and Engineering Unions, like so many other British unions, entered on a more militant phase.[53] On top of this, there were radical changes in the type of ship in demand, which meant that Scottish yards had to adapt and invest as never before. Like the west coast yards, the yards of the Forth and Tay were not in too good financial shape to face testing times ahead.

CHAPTER VII

Fisheries of the Forth and Tay

The fisheries of this region can roughly be divided into three main categories. These are the herring fishery, the white fishery (including salmon, lobster, and crab), and the whale fishery. Historically, the development of whaling and herring fishing from the ports of the Forth and Tay have much in common. Both fisheries grew at the expense of an existing Dutch industry, and both were assisted at a critical stage in their development by government subsidies. The inshore fishery for salmon, lobster, crab, and white fish always remained firmly in local hands. Nevertheless, it is convenient to deal with whaling as a distinct phenomenon, for, always based on a very few ports, it differed radically in nature from any other form of fishing, and its history is a completed story. In roughly two and a half centuries the whaling industry of the Forth and Tay has moved from nothing, through periods of dramatic expansion and drastic slump, back to nothing. The inshore and herring fisheries have had a much more continuous history, and have left many more permanent marks on the pattern of harbour facilities in the region.

WHALING

European whaling in the seventeenth century was carried out in Arctic waters, mainly off the coasts of Spitzbergen

199

and Greenland. It was dominated by the Dutch. There were several reasons for this, including the very strong maritime traditions of the Dutch based on their key position in the carrying trade between northern and southern Europe, but the decisive factor was probably the availability of capital. Though to modern eyes seventeenth-century whaling seems an inexpensive exercise in all save man-power, it was by contemporary standards very capital intensive. The wooden sailing ships from which the whales were hunted by open rowing boats using hand-thrown harpoons, had to embark on a very long voyage to reach the cold waters where alone a big enough whale population survived to make hunting them an economic proposition. Furthermore, whaling was always a very risky business in which ships were often lost, or returned without a catch or 'clean' to use the whalers' term. Only the Dutch both possessed adequate capital for such a large-scale enterprise, and were willing to put that capital to the hazard of Arctic whaling. At the end of the seventeenth century their whaling industry employed 260 ships and 14,000 seamen, reaching its peak with a run of very big catches in the halcyon years between 1675 and 1690. Thereafter the Dutch whale fishery entered into decline, until by the end of the eighteenth century it employed only about fifty ships. The basic causes of this decline were over-fishing of accessible waters, and competition from other nations.[1]

Among those nations Scotland was by the second half of the eighteenth century a significant force. State subsidies, originally introduced in 1733, and increased in 1740 and 1749, undoubtedly played a key rôle in persuading Scottish shipowners to embark upon whaling. Between 1750 and 1788 alone Scotland drew nearly a million pounds from the British Treasury in the shape of whaling subsidies. Leith was early off the mark, for in 1750 a group of Edinburgh merchants sent a ship to the whaling from Leith, and to encourage the trade many Edinburgh ladies undertook to have their hoops and stays made from whalebone brought home by Leith ships. By 1754 a group of influential burgesses had united to form the Dundee Whale Fishing Company, though the first period of rapid growth in the Dundee whale fishery did not come until the 1780s. As late as 1788 Leith with six whaling vessels and Dunbar with five led the list of Scottish whaling ports, while Dundee with three was well down the list, below ports like Peterhead. Still, by 1825, the Scots whaling industry had expanded further and the combined whaling industries of Dundee and Peterhead alone were over half the size of that of Hull, the leading English whaling port.[2]

It was shortly after this that the Scottish whaling industry had to face a major crisis. State subsidies were withdrawn in 1824, but this did not curb the growth of the industry. Kirkcaldy, for example, which had entered Arctic whaling late with two ships in 1816, had nine ships with a combined tonnage of over 3,000 engaged in whaling in 1828. In 1833 Kirkcaldy's whalers brought home 900 tons of whale oil and 60 tons of whalebone, with a combined value of £30,000.[3] After 1835, however, whaling from the port went into permanent decline. The reason was a general crisis in whaling, due to changes in contemporary technology. Whale oil had many uses ranging from lighting and soap to paint-making and lubrication, but the substitution of coal gas for whale oil in lighting severely reduced demand for whale oil. The resulting fall in prices was sharpened by competition from imported American oil produced in great quantities from sperm whales by the Nantucket whalers. Even the price of whalebone suffered from substitutes like flexible steel. By 1837 it seems that the only British whaling fleet that could be described as being in a flourishing condition was that of Peterhead, and this was mainly because the Peterhead ships devoted a great deal of attention to sealing.[4]

The combination of whaling and sealing was to prove in the long run very important, but the revival of the whaling industry on the east coast of Scotland south of Montrose was due to technological developments in the late 1850s. The most important of these was the introduction of the steam engine, which began when engines were installed in the Dundee whaler *Tay* in 1857, and which became standard when Stephen's built the *Narwhal* in 1859 as a steamship, with auxiliary sail.[5] This judicious combination of steam and sail allowed for endurance and power to smash through pack ice. Though expensive, the new steam whalers could fit in two seasons' fishing in a year. In spring they hunted seals off Newfoundland or Greenland, while in summer they whaled in the Davis Straits between Canada and Greenland. By 1873 the Dundee whaling fleet comprised ten ships, all steamers, ranging from 270 to 439 tons. The Dundee Company and the Tay Company between them owned over half the ships. That whaling survived the depressed 1830s is attested by the fact that these ten ships had been built at various times between 1847 and 1867, and four were sailing vessels converted to steamers. Their crews were paid by a blend of free provisions, monthly pay, and bonus payments depending on the catch.[6] After 1865 there are no returns for whalers sailing out of Kirkcaldy, while Leith had dropped out of the picture even earlier.

The resurgence of whaling in this region was therefore centred entirely on Dundee. There were a variety of reasons for this. One was undoubtedly the development of the process of batching jute fibre in order to make it easier to work. This was done by treating newly-opened bales with a mixture of water and whale oil. Prices for whale oil naturally rose under this stimulus, and suitable mineral oil substitutes did not emerge until the 1920s and 1930s. Another factor was the exceptional interest which the firm of Alexander Stephen displayed in the development of the design of whaling vessels. Although not the originators of the idea of applying steam to whaling vessels, they were amongst the very first shipbuilders to grasp the importance of this. Furthermore the firm participated in the whaling industry itself, showing particular interest in the sealing side. William Stephen, who controlled the Dundee yard and operated its ships, was a pioneer of the Newfoundland seal fishery at a time when the Greenland seal fishery was in decline due to excessive exploitation.[7] Iron-hulled sealing vessels were used in the Newfoundland seal fisheries, and many of them were built in Scottish yards, but the predominant tradition in the Dundee yards was that whalers and sealers were wooden-hulled. One interesting consequence of this was that when the Royal Geographical Society commissioned W. E. Smith to design a ship to take an expedition to the Antarctic in the early years of the twentieth century, Smith selected Stephens' old yard in Dundee, then owned by the Dundee Shipbuilding Company, to build the vessel. It had been agreed that the ship should be wooden-hulled. She was engined by Gourlays, christened the *Discovery*, and when she was launched in 1901 much of the Dundee whaling tradition was embedded in her.[8] Ahead of her lay a long career, starting with the tragic death of her first commander, Captain Scott.

The new steam whalers operating out of Dundee made a brilliant start in the early 1860s, partly because the American Civil War was raging between 1861 and 1865. In the course of it Confederate privateers seriously disrupted the American whaling industry, previously a serious rival of the Scottish one. However, as early as 1875, when there was a very poor season from which the majority of Dundee whalers returned with no whales and relatively few seals, there was talk of over-fishing in Arctic waters. A closed seaon for part of the fishing year to give whale populations a respite was called for.[9] It came by international agreement in 1878, and the 1880s were good years for the Dundee whalers. By the 1890s, however, the industry was beginning to collapse under the dual pressure of falling yields and tumbling prices for whale and seal oil. Mineral oil continued to undermine the price of whale oil. Whalebone prices remained quite high, but it became more and more difficult to catch whales. It was in 1860 that the *Dirkje Adema* earned the melancholy distinction of being the last Dutch vessel to catch a Greenland whale.[10] In 1872 Dundee was Britain's leading whaling port, but a combination of economic pressures and a dwindling whale population steadily eroded the Dundee whaling industry. In the 1880s it was reckoned in Dundee that it cost between £5,000 and £6,000 to send an average whaler out for the season. Not less than four full-grown whales, plus a reasonable yield of seals were required to make the voyage profitable.[11] Too many Dundee whalers were coming home 'clean', in the whalers' sense of the word.

There were occasional freak successes quite late in the day. In 1910, for example, the Dundee whaler *Diana* caught a shoal of whales which were trapped in a bay of ice in Lancaster Sound off Baffin Bay. Seven whales were caught in what proved the last bonanza of the Dundee Arctic whalers.[12] Norwegians proved that by a radical use of new techniques like the explosive harpoon and powered catcher, it was possible to make whaling pay, even with falling oil prices. Such radical re-equipment was beyond the Dundee industry. Firms like the Tay Whale Fishing Company were becoming very agitated about the poor financial results of whaling as early as 1884, and after the loss of their ship the *Intrepid* in 1885 the directors of that company seem to have confined their activities to renting shore facilities to other whaling companies, like the Arctic Fisheries Limited. Even this side of the business was faring badly by 1913, because Dundee whaling was nearly dead. The Tay Whale Fishing Company was wound up in 1920.[13] By then the industry was quite extinct. The last Dundee whalers, commandeered by the state to carry ammunition to Russia, had mostly foundered in 1914 as their seams opened under a dead weight of cargo they had never been designed for.

By then, however, whaling in the region had found a new centre in Leith. Significantly, the only Scots firm which proved capable of adopting the full range of new Norwegian whaling techniques was the half-Norwegian one of Christian Salvesen. The first whaling ventures with which this firm was associated, were aimed at Arctic waters. These were the traditional hunting grounds of Scots whalers, and a Dundee expedition to the Antarctic in 1892 had been a failure. After

1914, though Dundee whaling was dead, there was an obscure relationship between Peterhead and Dundee and Baffin Island, where Scots' 'free traders' poached on the trading territory of the Hudson Bay Company, dealing extensively with the natives until Hudson Bay men moved in to assert their rights in the 1920s.

Christian Salvesen and Company first became involved with whaling indirectly, by acting as commission agents for the sale of whale oil in Scotland. The firm had a close connection with the father of modern whaling, the Norwegian Svend Foyn. They not only sold his oil, but they also supplied him with coal. By the late nineteenth century the Arctic whaling had reached a stage when the only substantial stock of whales left were the finner whales, which were too fast in the water to be caught by traditional methods, and which sank when killed. Svend Foyn developed a combination of the steam-powered catcher vessel, and an efficient gun-fired explosive harpoon. His catchers could 'play' a whale, haul its carcass to the surface, and inflate it by means of a steam pipe to make it buoyant. On the strength of these new techniques there was a boom in Norwegian whaling which eventually tempted Theodore Salvesen, a son of the founder, to persuade his father to risk some of the firm's capital in whaling. The entry of the Salvesens into Arctic whaling more or less coincided with anti-whaling legislation in Norway, pushed through by rival fishing interests. By 1904, therefore, the Salvesen whaling operations were based on a station at Millburn Brae in the Shetland Islands. Most companies involved in whaling were by 1905 trying to maximise their yield of oil by using such devices as the steam boiler known as the Kvaerner Cooker, to extract oil from blubber. Even so, Salvesens and other whaling companies were malodorous and unwelcome guests in Shetland, accused by locals of fouling the shores with whale offal.

It was inevitable that Salvesens should turn to Antarctic whaling. The Norwegians had developed the full range of devices necessary for success in this area. Apart from the

FROM ESK TO TWEED

catcher, with its cannon and explosive harpoon, they had created the modern factory ship, with its stern slipway up which whales could be dragged by the fearsome 'whale claw'. Starting from about 1905, the Norwegians were able to confirm their ascendancy in this pelagic whaling in the Antarctic during the First World War. Christian Salvesen and Company broke into Antarctic whaling in 1909, turning to the use of the factory ship in 1911. Even before the First World War the firm controlled the biggest single whaling group in the world.

After the First World War Antarctic fishing came more and more to dominate the whaling industry. By the 1930–1 season Antarctic whaling accounted for about ninety-seven per cent of world production of whale oil. To some extent this was a reflection of the depletion of Arctic whale stocks, but it also reflected major developments in Antarctic whaling. Notable amongst these was. the movement of the whaling teams into the pack ice itself, where higher rates of kill could be obtained than by hovering on the edge of the pack ice. To operate successfully in this new and dangerous environment, however, more sophisticated equipment was essential, and there were significant improvements in such spheres as wireless communication. By 1927 the Salvesen ships were fully committed to the ice fishing. There was a steady expansion in both the area and the scale of operations until by the early 1930s factory ships of over 20,000 tons were normal, and both they and their catchers were oil-burning.

Inevitably, oil prices were affected by the international economic depression after 1931, and it proved extremely difficult to stabilise prices by restricting output. New nations like the Germans and Japanese were entering the whaling field in the late 1930s, and they were not prepared to restrict their efforts. All the same, by dint of constant modernisation the Salvesen whaling enterprises remained generally profitable, with the odd exception, in these bleak years. The firm's hunting techniques were the most modern in the world, and nobody could approach the thoroughness of their carcass utilisation. After the complete rupture caused by war between 1939 and 1945, the firm had a splendid tradition on which to build in a world where whale oil commanded excellent prices, and where German and Japanese rivals had been eliminated. Margarine manufacturers in particular were prepared to pay well for whale oil, so the Salvesen fleet was rapidly reconstructed around two new factory ships as a prelude to the last really successful whaling era. That era lasted until 1951. After 1951 Christian Salvesen, like most other whaling firms, considered that the industry was in decline and built no more whaling tonnage.[14]

As late as 1955-6 the Salvesen fleet processed about 4,300 whales and employed, at sea and on land, about 1,900 men,[15] but by 1963 the firm had withdrawn from whaling. It was the end of an old song on the Forth and Tay. Falling oil prices could to some extent be covered by other whale products, but not falling catches. The great blot on the Salvesen whaling record was the foul state in which men had to live and work at their principal South Atlantic shore base, Leith Harbour in South Georgia. Apart from that they were reasonable employers, paying high wages, albeit to crews which always contained far more Norwegians and Shetlanders than Leith men.[16] Except for the odd street name like 'Whale Lane' the once-great whaling industries of the Tay and Forth have completely faded from the scene.

The Other Fisheries of the Forth and Tay

Compared with whaling, the other fisheries of the Forth and Tay have left a more enduring mark on the region. They have been the basis of the existence of a host of long-lived specialist fishing communities, and from the needs of those communities have sprung many interesting harbour developments. In considering all other fisheries, however, it is essential to recognise the unique problems and importance of the herring fishery. At the same time it must be remembered that until well on into the eighteenth century most fishermen from the Tay and Forth simply did not participate in the herring fishery. Most fishing communities were built on the catching of white fish like cod, ling, or haddock; on salmon fishing; or on fishing for lobsters, crabs, oysters and mussels. Most fishing communities clearly took what they could from inshore waters. Few had much capital at their disposal. Fishing was therefore normally conducted from small, open boats, which dared not venture far from shore. For such vessels even a rudimentary man-made harbour was not absolutely essential. A sheltered stretch of beach on which small boats could land and be unloaded before being dragged ashore well above the high-tide mark, was sufficient. Quite a few small 'harbours' never developed beyond being a slightly improved beach, usually protected by natural rock formations. Thus, though the burgh of Crail in Fife has a complex harbour history, there were half a dozen landing places in the neighbourhood, all associated with fishing and classed as 'creeks' of Crail for customs purposes, which never seem to have acquired significant harbour works. Redheugh shore in Berwickshire contrived to have a long history of white, salmon, and herring fishing, not to mention smuggling, without any serious harbour works. The narrow, sheltered tidal beach there was simply improved by straightening its rock sides and removing the bigger boulders from the bottom of the anchorage.[17] Berwickshire also includes the fishing village of Ross which contrived to have a very active inshore fishery in the middle of the nineteenth century, without any benefit of artificial harbour works. Boats were drawn up on the shore, which was approached by several natural creeks in the rock. About 1850 the village sent significant quantities of cod, ling, haddock, and salmon to Edinburgh by sea, while lobsters and crabs were shipped alive in smacks to London.[18]

Only very small boats could operate out of such natural creeks. Of necessity most fishing communities maintained

A Newhaven fishing boat outward bound for the fishing grounds *c.* 1900

'Reddin' the lines at Broughty Ferry near Dundee in the late nineteenth century. The girls are baiting the hooks with shell-fish while the boy coils the baited line so as to make it easy to 'shoot' it overboard at sea

some form of harbour works, ranging from a wooden jetty to piers and breakwaters. Some of these fishing harbours existed in the medieval period. There is, for example, reference to one at St Andrews in 1222. The exposed nature of the coast meant, however, that the establishment of harbour works, and their subsequent maintenance, was often no light task. The small fishing harbour of Cove in Berwickshire is a good example, for although this tidal inlet has a recorded history as a port dating from the seventeenth century, it acquired artificial harbour works only in 1831. Attempts in the 1750s and 1820s to build harbour works were wrecked by storms before completion.[19] A certain measure of prosperity in the fishing community was therefore essential for the maintenance, let alone the extension of fishing harbours. Unfortunately, at the end of the eighteenth century, there were few signs of prosperity among the fishing communities of the Forth and Tay.

On the Tay the larger towns like Dundee and Arbroath played little part in the industry, which they left to small, specialised communities, like that of Auchmithie, the tiny hamlet perched on high red cliffs above an inlet north of Arbroath. These fishing communities supplied the market for fish in the larger towns and, according to an observer writing in 1785, supplied it very inadequately. The many small fishing harbours of the Forth had a reputation for white fishing, as well as major markets like Bo'ness and Edinburgh at hand. These Forth fishermen used mainly small boats with keels about fifteen feet long. They cost under £5, though their equipment and fishing lines cost twice as much again. By the 1790s there were general complaints of decline in the inshore fishery. Haddock stocks do seem to have fallen, though cod, turbot, and whiting were still abundant.

Ironically, there had been an elaborate system of state intervention and subsidy in Scottish fisheries from 1749. It was based on concern at the continuing ascendancy of the Dutch in the herring fishery of the east coast of Scotland. In practice this attempt to sponsor a rival Scottish herring fishery was largely vitiated by the fact that most of the schemes and subsidies were based on a slavish imitation of Dutch methods. The normal Dutch fishing vessel or 'buss' was a ship of about fifty tons costing approximately £700. Such a scale of operations was well beyond the capacity of most east-coast fishing communities, even given state subsidies. In Shetland the only effect of attempts to discourage the Dutch was to deprive the locals of a vast floating market, without compensating them with a great new herring fishery. Nor was it really necessary to copy Dutch methods, which were governed by the fact that for Holland the North Sea herring fishery was bound to be a long-distance operation. The burgh of Crail in Fife had, in the first half of the eighteenth century, developed into an important centre for small boats active in the herring fishery. Boats from the Tay joined boats from the Forth there, being supplied with nets by the townspeople in exchange for a share of the catch. The smaller boats of the east coast, however, were not eligible for support from public funds until after 1786. By then the herring fishery of Crail was in relative decline. The harbour of the burgh after 1750, like so many other fishing harbours of the Forth, appears to have been in poor repair.[20]

It was only after 1815, when the inevitable disruptions caused by the French Revolutionary and Napoleonic Wars were over, that a trend towards increasing productivity and prosperity set in in the fishing harbours of the Forth and Tay. The annual reports of the Board of Trustees for Fisheries and Manufacturers in Scotland inevitably recorded short-term fluctuations in catches, but by the 1820s there was clearly an overall trend towards expansion, especially in the herring industry. Yet, as the Board of Trustees themselves pointed out, there was an irony in the statistics. Only substantial boats qualified for government subsidy based on tonnage. Such boats contributed only a small share of the total catch.[21] Nearly all herring were being caught by small boats which did not qualify for tonnage subsidies. As early as 1819–20 the herring

fishery of the east coast of Scotland was employing 2,429
boats, mostly small, manned with 11,008 fishermen, and
giving employment to 10,968 coopers, packers, and general
labourers.[22] Most of this employment was generated by
quite small, open boats, for until 1855 nearly all the boats
used for sea fishing on the east coast of Scotland by
Scotsmen were open vessels, with no sort of protecting
decking, even on the forecastle. This was true of the
majority of vessels long after 1860. Yet they not only
supplied a home market, but also exported a great many
fish to the northern parts of Europe.

The herrings were either pickled to produce white
herrings or, less often, smoked to produce red herrings.
Various government bodies were authorised to assist fishery
harbours involved in this fishery, so here was a basis for
state-aided improvement in the fishery harbours of the
Forth. By 1831 the Commissioners for the Herring Fishery
were helping to improve the harbour of Cellardyke in the
East Neuk of Fife. The aim here was to improve the
shelter available for fishing boats, and to smooth the rocky
bottom of the harbour. On the other side of the Firth of
Forth the Commissioners for the Herring Fishery were
simultaneously sharing with the local landowner the cost of
erecting the boat harbour at Cove in Berwickshire.[23] As
time went on there were signs of parliamentary hostility,
on Free Trade principles, to the structure of control and
assistance surrounding the herring industry.[24] Before this
criticism had any serious impact, however, the state had
made very substantial contributions to the development of
the fishing harbours of the Forth. As the herring fishery
was by far the best channel of government benevolence,
it was important that the nineteenth century saw the
development of the herring fishery in the Forth itself into
a highly significant industry.

It was quite impractical for boats from the Forth ports to
confine themselves to the Forth herring fishery. Throughout
the year there are a sequence of herring fisheries sweeping
down from Icelandic waters to the southern end of the

North Sea. Contemporaries tended to think in terms of great shoals moving down through consecutive fishing areas. It is a picture which modern research has largely destroyed, for we now know that the individual fisheries tend to involve different groups of fish. Those that constitute the East Anglian fishery, for example, probably originate in the central parts of the North Sea, off the Dogger Bank.[25] None the less, it was a great boon to ports like Eyemouth and Granton, and those of the East Neuk, to have a great fishery on their doorstep. And in the middle of the nineteenth century it really was spectacularly successful; 1841 was a very good year, but then so were 1843 and 1849; by 1850 the reputation of the Forth fishery was such that several large decked English boats were conveyed by railway from Whitehaven to the Forth, complete with crews and gear. Normally, however, the railway was more significant for its promise of swift access to markets. In 1849 the Commissioners for the British Fisheries were helping to finance a new sea wall at Dunbar, and in 1851 they were assisting in the enlargement of Buckhaven harbour in Fife, though they paid tribute to the enterprise of local fishermen who had raised £3000 amongst themselves to set the harbour improvements in motion.[26]

Self-help was, of course, only one side of the coin. The fishing harbours of the East Neuk could and did squabble furiously amongst themselves in the late 1850s over the prospect of government funds for a harbour of refuge in the area.[27] Nevertheless, self-help remained an important feature of the fishing communities. By and large the fishermen owned their own boats and gear. The precise arrangements varied from one part of the coast to another, but generally the boat was held in shares, graded by rank, amongst the crew. Fife was an exception, for there it was normal for the boat to be owned by the skipper, while the rest of the crew provided the nets and gear.[28] In such a context, it is possible to understand the achievement of the fishermen of Saint Monance, who in the 1860s and 1870s financed a very considerable improvement in their harbour entirely on their own initiative. They realised by 1861 that the rapid increase in the number and size of fishing boats, and the enhanced profitability of fishing due to the coming of the railway, made an extension of their harbour facilities very desirable. By pledging themselves to regular payments they secured, serviced and repaid a loan of between £11,000 and £12,000 from the National Bank.[29] Nearby harbours could scarcely afford to ignore the achievement of Saint Monance, so it is not surprising to find Anstruther and Pittenweem following suit, albeit with more of an eye to outside assistance. In the case of Pittenweem the prospect of the approach of the East Fife Railway was a major stimulus.[30]

Gone were the days when the improvement of an East Neuk harbour like Pittenweem depended on the state of the coal trade, and the generosity of the local landed proprietor.[31] What did continually stretch the financial capacity of the fishing communities and the physical capacity of their harbours was the growth in the size of boats. Until well after 1860 open boats were dominant, and of these perhaps the most famous was the relatively large type known as the 'Skaffie'. Increasingly, however, the herring shoals tended to be found further and further offshore. Bigger types of boat, half-decked or fully decked, like the 'Baldie', 'Fifie', and 'Zulu', had to be designed. The 'Zulu' was a particularly fast sailer, with a sharply raked stern, a big sail set well forward, and a straight stem. To simplify the handling of gear on these bigger boats, steam winches were introduced. By 1900 the vessels involved in the Forth fisheries were often over fifty tons, and with gear could cost £1,200.[32] The smaller shipyards of the Forth which specialised in fishing boats had and have a great reputation for this size of vessel. Even after 1945, for example, the ships of the Shetland fishing fleet, if not built on the Moray Firth, have tended to come from the Forth, notably from the East Neuk or Cockenzie.[33] This was not the only fringe-benefit that the fishing towns of the Forth derived from their predominant industry. Musselburgh saw the establishment of the first machine-made fishing net industry in the 1820s, due to the genius and persistence of one James Paterson. During the 1850s cotton was substituted for the heavier hemp in fishing nets, and by 1867 Messrs J. and S. Stuart, heirs of Paterson, were doing a thriving business in herring, salmon, mackerel, pilchard, and sprat nets. The next biggest contemporary net manufacturer was N. and N. Lockhart of Kirkcaldy.[34]

The transition which most fishery harbours of the Forth and Tay had difficulty in making was the transition to steam trawling. The white fishery was until late in the nineteenth century almost exclusively a line fishery. Herring were usually caught in drift nets. Then from 1882 steam trawling became established in Aberdeen. The catches of haddock and halibut made by the Aberdeen trawlers rapidly claimed a very large share of the increasing catches of that port. Further north, in Fraserburgh and Peterhead, the steam drifter established itself as the dominant boat in herring fishing. There was a sharp rise in the cost of individual boats. In Dundee, never a great fishing port though in the late nineteenth century it had several notable fish-curing firms, it was thought that the herring fishery would largely be confined to ports having a sufficient depth of water to admit steam drifters at all states of the tide. Here it was felt was an opportunity for the new fishery harbour built after 1902 at Carolina Port east of Dundee docks, for this was the only fishery harbour between Aberdeen and the English border which met the criterion of being able to cope with such drifters at all states of the tide.[35] A trawling company was formed, but it is a measure of its failure that by 1931 the most significant single fishing out of Dundee was the Tay sprat fishing, employing fourteen very small boats.[36] By the 1930s it was in fact clear that the only port in the Forth or Tay which was going to benefit from the new methods and bigger fishing boats was Granton, which despite its tidal nature became an important base for the Forth trawlers. After 1945, despite the establishment of a Herring Industry Board with its head offices in Edinburgh, the herring industry of Scotland as a whole, and the Forth in particular, contracted sharply. Guaranteed markets and grants for new vessels could not compensate for English competition and the complete collapse of the old herring fishery in the Forth in the ten years after 1947.[37] The herring shoals were just not there to be caught.

Technical change tended to accelerate, partly because the state subsidised it. Fife fishermen were relatively slow to effect the change from sail to steam. As late as 1910 nine out of ten fishing craft in the county were sailing ships.[38] However, the transition from sail to steam and motor propulsion was effected in the inter-war period. After 1945 the Herring Industry Board was willing to subsidise trawler construction. This really only helped Granton, for trawling was increasingly centred on Aberdeen and Peterhead, and even in the north-east of Scotland smaller fishing harbours like Boddam were in decline.[39] After 1953 the White Fish Authority was prepared to make generous grants to finance boat construction. The result was a considerable measure of re-equipment in inshore fishing. This was not confined to the boats themselves. New fishing techniques like seine nets and ring nets became commoner without banishing the drift net, the trawl net, and even the hand line. In the midst of all this change one phenomenon remained constant—the increasing dominance in Scottish east-coast fishing of the ports of the north-east.[40]

The endless work of maintenance, and a surprising volume of development which occurred in the fishing harbours of the Forth and Tay, especially after 1955, was increasingly dependent on state subsidisation. Before 1955 funds were made available on a modest scale from the Development Fund, under legislation of 1909, and from the Piers and Quays Fund, under legislation dating from 1824. After 1955, however, the bulk of the cost of a vigorous programme of repair and development came from the state. Most of the East Neuk ports participated, as did Arbroath and Dunbar, but the most ambitious programme of all was probably at Eyemouth, where the harbour was remodelled

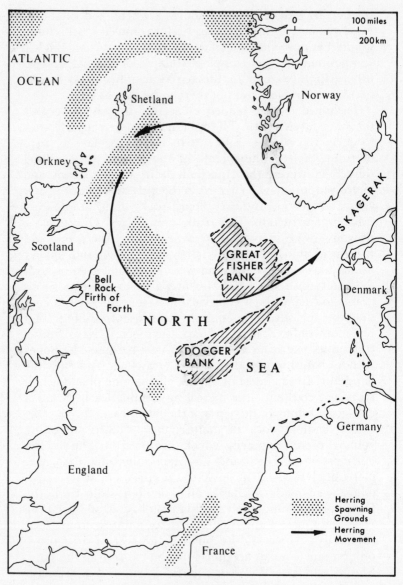

Herring Fisheries of the North Sea

and a new fish market built at a cost of roughly £450,000. The inshore fisheries of the Tay and Forth were still healthy, and were to enjoy a boom after the extension of British fishing limits, but the real dynamic behind most of this construction was Section Two of the Fisheries Act 1955.[41] Inshore fishermen could defend a high degree of state subsidisation on social grounds. They could argue that they were numerous and disproportionately important in a Scottish economy short of alternative employment. The government subsidised other groups for the sake of social stability.[42] The herring fishermen argued that the economics of their industry were hopelessly distorted by very large subsidies to farmers, some of whose products were substitutes for those of herring fishermen. As long as the government kept these agricultural products cheap by artificial means, it owed the herring fleets a subsidy.[43] Clearly, the relations between the fishing industry and the government were complex.

Grangemouth Docks 1969

N

500
Metres
0

Principal Sheds
Railheads served by dockside lines
Swing Bridge
Storage Tank

T.S.F.   Tank Storage Farm
O.D.   Oil Depot
C.C.   Container Compound
B.D.   Bitumen Depot
W.L.I.
E.L.I.   West and East Lead in Jetties

RIVER FORTH

EASTERN CHANNEL

ENTRANCE LOCK

JETTIES

No2A

No3

No4

No5

T.S.F.

COMMON LEADERS
OIL BERTH
T.S.F.
T.S.F.

O.D.

GRANGE DOCK

32 TON TRANSPORTER CRANES

C.C.

B.D.

GRANGE BURN

RIVER CARRON

WESTERN CHANNEL

CARRON DRY DOCK

CARRON DOCK

MIDDLE DRY DOCK

OLD DOCK

JUNCTION DOCK

STATION RD.

BONESS

ROAD

Postscript: The Ports since 1939

The outbreak of the Second World War in 1939 was followed by a more immediate and severe interruption of normal trading through the Forth and Tay ports than had occurred after 1914. World depression had already confirmed the end of the great age of dock expansion which had lasted since 1800. Between 1939 and 1945 only the specialist naval harbour of Rosyth expanded its range of activities and work-force. By 1948 post-war redundancy had cut that work-force by thirty per cent to about 7,500.[1] During the war Grangemouth docks were entirely taken over by the government. Of the coal ports only Methil retained most of its pre-war trade, and this was because convoys assembling in the Forth bunkered there.[2]

After 1945 timber imports remained scarce and government-controlled. Major softwood importers like Brownlee and Company of Grangemouth had to make inroads to their slender reserves in 1946 and 1947, while employees were intermittently on short time. Coal exports were slow to revive, though productivity and profitability in the Lothian pits in 1946 was above the United Kingdom average.[3] After 1945 a much higher percentage of Scottish coal production was consumed at home. In 1951 a commentator remarked on the general decline in prosperity of the Forth ports apart from Leith and Methil.[4] The former remained the most important harbour. In the year ending

May 1948 some 450 vessels with a gross tonnage of 1.1 million entered it. In 1949 1.45 million tons of coal were exported from Methil alone, so the pattern was one of concentration. In the Tay the pattern was dominated by a steady decline in jute imports at Dundee as the local textile industry contracted. The new light engineering industries which sprang up in the city provided little business for the docks.[5] Everywhere costs were raised by the much stronger bargaining position which the dockers had established during the war and consolidated under the National Dock Labour Board after 1945. Even if the Attlee government was strong enough to use troops against a major dock strike, the days of cheap dock labour were gone.[6]

Not surprisingly, the General Manager of Leith docks said in 1946 that extravagant port extension plans were likely to prove economically unsound. By 1948 Leith's trade was only forty-four per cent of the 1938 figure. Apart from re-equipment projects the only new development in Leith before 1952 was the dredging of a deep channel and the creation of quays to service the new Rank flour mill to the west of the dock complex.[7] Burntisland compensated for the loss of its coal trade by importing 100,000 tons of bauxite annually for the British Aluminium Company works there.[8] Alone amongst the Forth and Tay ports Grangemouth expanded rapidly after 1945. By 1951 its imports, at current prices, were nearly seven times the 1938 figure in value, while its exports were eight times the 1938 value. The petroleum refineries and chemical works created before 1939 began to prosper and expand and plastics became an important local industry.[9]

A problem which affected both Grangemouth and Leith was the escalating size of cargo ships, and especially of oil tankers. The British Petroleum Company overcame the lack of natural deep anchorage in the Forth and Tay by opening in 1951 a deep-water tanker terminal at Finnart on Loch Long on the west coast and by running a fifty-seven mile long crude oil pipe-line from Finnart to Grangemouth.[10] Leith could scarcely solve its problems this way, so it lobbied the Ministry of Transport until in 1964 that body agreed to lend Leith Docks £600,000 for a modernisation programme ensuring access at all tides for ships of 40–50,000 tons.[11] In comparison, the opening by Shell-Mex-B.P. in 1960 of an oil jetty at the Stannergate east of Dundee docks, was a minor event.[12]

In the smaller ports and in the shipowning and ship-building industries decline continued. Inflation plus one unfortunate contract closed the Burntisland Shipbuilding Company in 1969 after a history of half a century since its foundation in 1918 by the brothers Wilfrid and Amos Ayre.[13] Metal shipbuilding in the Forth and Tay was then confined to the Robb Caledon firm, with yards at Dundee and Leith, neither notably profitable nor trouble-free.[14] Coastal shipowning virtually vanished. In 1969 only twenty-four of 169 vessels entering Perth harbour were British.[15] In 1951 only twenty-five ships entered Alloa dock. More and more of Alloa's imports came by road from Grangemouth and by 1970 Alloa harbour had been closed as redundant.[16] Bo'ness, also too close to Grangemouth, shared Alloa's fate. Its export of coal and import of pit props faded to nothing before closure. In the Tay, Tayport was abandoned as a railway harbour but survived precariously as a timber-importing harbour owned by a single firm. Perth alone flourished due to low costs based on its cheap tidal harbour and its exclusion from the National Dock Labour Scheme.[17]

Official or semi-official reports on the regional economy like *Oceanspan* which was published by the Scottish Council in 1970 forecast a 'European' future in which Forth ports would export goods manufactured in central Scotland from raw materials imported at deep anchorages in the Clyde.[18] By 1973 it was clear that this reasoning was facile rather than sound. Scotland had always been part of Europe, nor had entry into the European Economic Community notably stimulated her economy. In 1970 a mixed academic and bureaucratic parentage produced *Tayside: Potential for Development*. This report started from a hypothetical increase of 300,000 in what was actually a declining regional population. Even so, it saw no need for expansion in harbour facilities.[19] In 1968 *The Grangemouth-Falkirk Regional Survey and Plan* did forecast further expansion at Grangemouth docks, but the prophecy merely registered existing trends.[20]

Containerisation, or the loading and unloading of cargo in large standardised boxes handled by special quayside machinery had by 1969 become an essential attribute of the twenty main United Kingdom ports, including Leith and Grangemouth.[21] Competition was such that there was no room for a third container port in the Forth and Tay, especially after new road bridges were opened in 1964 and 1966 respectively. In Dundee the Tay Bridge approach roads crossed the infilled King William and Earl Grey Docks and the West Tidal Harbour.[22] The ability of Leith to embark after 1966 on a programme involving deepening the Imperial Dock and turning the West Harbour from a tidal into an enclosed basin hinged largely on government subsidy.[23] In 1971 the new Conservative government threatened to adopt more rigorous criteria for harbour financing.[24]

In practice this government reneged on most of its electoral pledges, including the ones about curbing indiscriminate subsidisation of uneconomic enterprises, with a rapidity worthy of its Labour predecessor. The east-coast ports could take further comfort from the development in the late 1960s of a major boom in offshore drilling for oil in the northern parts of the North Sea. Aberdeen was strategically placed to benefit from this. The Forth ports were too southerly, though most of the oil was to be taken to Grangemouth by pipeline when landed.[25] In the Tay, Dundee experienced some spin-off in the shape of oil-rig servicing facilities based in its harbour, but by 1973 Montrose was the only port of the region deeply affected by the oil boom. The long straggling fishing village of Ferryden on the south bank of the River Esk opposite Montrose was rendered unrecognisable by massive civil engineering works designed to create major facilities for oil producers. Elsewhere in the Forth and Tay, however, it seemed unlikely that oil would prove the fairy godmother capable of extricating ports from the network of problems created by a long history and a changing present.

Notes and References

Notes and References

CHAPTER I

1 For the geological background see Walker, F. *Tayside Geology* (1961);
Stamp, L. Dudley. *Britain's Structure and Scenery* (Fontana ed. 1969),
ch. 23; McAdam, R. 'Mining', *Scientific Survey of South-Eastern
Scotland* (British Association 1951), 113-9; and Campbell, R.
'Geology', ibid., 185-99.

2 McManus, John. 'The Hydrology of the Tay Basin', *Dundee and
District* (British Association 1968), 107-24; and 'Bottom Structures
of the Tay and Other Estuaries', *Scottish Geographical Magazine*, vol.
82, no. 3 (1966), 194-7; Cadell, H. M. *The Story of the Forth* (1913).

3 'Report by Thomas Tucker upon the Settlement of the Revenues of
Excise and Customs in Scotland, AD MDCLVI', and 'Register
Containing the State and Condition of Every Burgh within the
Kingdom of Scotland, in the year 1692', both *Miscellany of the
Scottish Burgh Records Society* (1881). The quotations are from Tucker's
preface, and from the state and condition of Dysart. Before 1773
government records recorded tons burden, deadweight tonnage or
carrying capacity. All three terms are synonymous, and this tonnage
was the one which did and does concern shipowners, who therefore
used it in their mercantile contracts. Measured tonnage is a different
concept worked out by shipbuilders for pricing their work, and in
ships of conventional English build in the seventeenth century
carrying capacity was usually about three-quarters of measured
tonnage. In eighteenth-century ships the two measurements are
often closer. After 1786 all official statistics are in measured tonnage,
and therefore not strictly comparable with earlier ones, but as
tonnage figures in this book are invariably used merely for purposes
of crude comparison, adjustment has not been deemed necessary,
and they are given as they occur in the sources. For further discussion and bibliography of this topic see Davis, R. *The Rise of the
English Shipping Industry* (1962), 7, footnote 1.

4 Defoe, Daniel. *A Tour through the Whole Island of Great Britain* (Everyman ed., n.d.), vol. 2, 300.

5 Christie, Guy. *Harbours of the Forth* (1955), 22–3.

6 Smout, T. C. *Scottish Trade on the Eve of Union 1660–1707* (1963), 140–2; Lythe, Sidney. *Life and Labour in Dundee from the Reformation to the Civil War* (Abertay Historical Society Publication no. 5 1958); and McNeill, W. A. 'Papers of a Dundee shipping dispute, 1600–1604', *Scottish History Society Miscellany X* (1965), 55–85.

7 Figures from 'Returns of Stampmaster of Linen Cloth Stamped in Scotland by Counties', in Hamilton, Henry. *An Economic History of Scotland in the Eighteenth Century* (1963), appendix V.

8 Warden, Alexander. *The Linen Trade* (1864), 584.

9 'Imports into Dundee, From 1815 to 1863', ibid., 633.

10 Fraser, Duncan. *Montrose Before 1707* (1967); *Old Statistical Account of Scotland*, vol. 5, 23–49.

11 Turner, W. H. K. *The Textile Industry of Arbroath since the Early Eighteenth Century* (Abertay Historical Society Publication no. 2 1954); *Old Statistical Account*, vol. 7, 340–52; and vol. 21, 199–204.

12 Lenman, B. and Gauldie, E. 'The Industrial History of the Dundee Region from the Eighteenth to the Early Twentieth Century', in Jones, S. J. (Ed.), *Dundee and District* (1968), 162–73.

13 Warden, Alexander. *The Linen Trade* (1864), 578–632; *Old Statistical Account*, vol. 8, 192–250.

14 Ibid., 'Council Book 1716–1742' and 'Shoremaster's Account Book', both in Dundee City Archive, VIII A and D 1800 resp.

15 *Old Statistical Account*, vol. 18, 489–540.

16 Smout, T. C. *Scottish Trade on the Eve of Union 1660–1707* (1963), 136–7; Pryde, G. S. *The Burghs of Scotland* (1965).

17 Hamilton, Henry. *An Economic History of Scotland in the Eighteenth Century* (1963), 253.

18 Stephen, W. *The Story of Inverkeithing and Rosyth* (1938), ch. VII; *Old Statistical Account*, vol. 12, 502–24; vol. 16, 513–33.

19 Ibid., vol. 18, 1–61.

20 Ibid., vol. 12, 229–44.

21 Ibid., vol. 2, 423–33.

22 Ibid., vol. 8, 453–4; vol. 13, 428–80; Chalmers, Peter. *Historical and Statistical Account of Dunfermline* (1864), section XIII.

23 *Old Statistical Account*, vol. 10, 131–49.

24 Ibid., vol. 11, 546–59; Duncan, A. I. R. 'The Domestic Architecture of a Fife River Port prior to 1810: Kincardine-on-Forth', *Proceedings of the Society of Antiquaries of Scotland*, vol. XCVII (1965–6), 300.

25 *Old Statistical Account*, vol. 8, 592.

26 *New Statistical Account of Scotland*, vol. 8, 397.

27 Smout, T. G. *Scottish Trade on the Eve of Union 1660–1707* (1963) ch. VII.

28 Robertson, D. *The Bailies of Leith* (1915); Russel, J. *The Story of Leith* (1922).

29 Irons, J. C. *Leith and its Antiquities* (1887), vol. 2, chs XIII–XV.

30 Robertson, D. *The Bailies of Leith* (1915); Irons, T. C. *Leith and its Antiquities* (1887); Malcolm, C. A. 'The Growth of Edinburgh, 1128–1800', *Scientific Survey of South-Eastern Scotland* (1951), 65–72.

31 *Old Statistical Account*, vol. 6, 559–76; 601–2.

32 Ibid., vol. 14, 558.

33 Lindsay, J. *The Canals of Scotland* (1968), ch. 1.

34 Campbell, R. H. *Carron Company* (1961).

35 *Old Statistical Account*, vol. 18.

36 Ibid., vol. 17, 489–97.

37 Ibid., vol. 17, 61–88; *Ordnance Gazetteer of Scotland* (1885), vol. III, 227–31.

38 *Old Statistical Account*, vol. 10, 83–99; vol. 16, 1–49.

39 Ibid., vol. 5, 440–5; 474–9.

40 Graham, A. 'The Old Harbours of Dunbar', *Proceedings of the Society of Antiquaries of Scotland*, XCIX (1966–7), 173–90.

41 *Old Statistical Account*, vol. 12, 43–60.

42 Elder, J. *The Royal Fishery Companies of the Seventeenth Century* (1912); Hamilton, Henry. *An Economic History of Scotland in the Eighteenth Century* (1963), ch. IV; Lythe, Sidney. 'The Dundee Whale Fishery', *Scottish Journal of Political Economy*, vol. 11 (1964), 158–69.

43 *Old Statistical Account*, vol. 6, 546.

44 Ibid., vol. 9, 439–58; vol. 17, 537–42; vol. 4, 369–77; vol. 16, 243–4; vol. 3, 77–88.

45 Ibid., vol. 21, 467–70; Lindsay, J. *Canals of Scotland* (1968), 186–7.

CHAPTER II

1 Dyos, H. J. and Aldcroft, D. H. *British Transport* (1969), ch. 1; Parkinson, C. N. (Ed.). *The Trade Winds* (1948), ch. 2.

2 *Old Statistical Account of Scotland*, vol. 3, 112–8; *The New Statistical Account of Scotland*, vol. 2, 318–36; for Smeaton see Smiles, S. *Lives of the Engineers* (1861), vol. 2, ch. 5.

3 Stephen, W. *The Story of Inverkeithing and Rosyth* (1938), 89–90.

4 Smiles, S. *Lives of the Engineers, loc. cit.*

5 *New Statistical Account*, vol. 9, 758–9.

6 *Ordnance Gazetteer of Scotland* (1885), vol. 3, 211.

7 *New Statistical Account*, vol. 2, 140–1.

8 Irons, J. C. *Leith and its Antiquities* (1887), vol. 2, ch. 18; *New Statistical Account*, vol. 1, 767.

9 Minutes of Committee of Corporation of Edinburgh, 2 November 1799 and 6 January 1800, copies in Scottish Record Office (hereinafter SRO) GD229/1/1.

10 Ibid., August and May 1807, SRO, GD 229/1/2.

11 *New Statistical Account*, vol. 1, 767–8.
12 Ibid.; Irons, J. C. *Leith and its Antiquities* (1887), vol. 2, ch. 18.
13 Robertson, D. *The Bailies of Leith* (1915), ch. 14.
14 *Report of the Treasurer's Committee to the Town Council, Respecting the Ecclesiastical Revenues of the City of Edinburgh* (1835); *Report by the Lord Provost's Committee concerning the Patronage and Management of the University of Edinburgh* (1835); *Report to the Commissioners for the City Improvements* (1830).
15 Curious, Peter. *Peep into Leith Harbour* (1833).
16 *Dictionary of National Biography*, vol. 11 (1909), 367–9; Labouchère, H. *Report to the Chancellor of the Exchequer re the Affairs of the City of Edinburgh and Port of Leith* (1836), copy in SRO GD 229/13/38; *Report by a Committee of the Trustees for the Creditors of the City of Edinburgh of the Reasons for Declining the Proposal of Settlement with the City, Contained in a Letter by the Right Hon. H. Labouchère* (1836); *New Statistical Account*, vol. 1, 710–11; 768–9.
17 *Statement by the Commissioners for the Harbour and Docks of Leith* (1847), copy in SRO GD 229/13/17; for railway lines in Leith docks see SRO GD 229/15/2.
18 Norrie, W. *Dundee Celebrities* (1873), 32–5.
19 *The Harbour in 1815* (1815), copy in Lamb 125(5).
20 Stevenson, R. *Report on the Improvement of the Harbour of Dundee* (n.d.), copy in Lamb 305(1).
21 *Proceedings of a Committee of Merchants, Manufacturers, Shipowners, and Others Interested in the Improvement of the Harbour of Dundee* (1814), copy in Lamb 305(2); Minute Book of the Harbour Bill Committee, vol. 2, Dundee City Archive.
22 *Answer by the Committee of Merchants, Manufacturers, and Shipowners to the Magistrates' Letter* (1814), copy in Lamb 305(2).
23 See Tennant, C. *The Radical Laird: A Biography of George Kinloch 1775–1833* (1970).
24 See for example, list of lenders at July 1819 in General Sederunt Book, no. 1, 397, Dundee Harbour Trustees Archive.
25 Beckles, N. I. *The Development of the Port and Trade of Dundee*, unpublished PhD thesis, University of Dundee 1968.
26 *Report on the Harbour and its Revenues—Addressed to the Town Council of Dundee by their Committee* (1829), copy in Lamb 247(7); *Report of a Committee of the Commissioners* (1830), copy in Lamb 305(3).
27 Lythe, S. G. E. and Lee, C. E. 'The Dundee and Newtyle Railway', *The Railway Magazine*, August and October 1951.
28 Hay, G. *History of Arbroath* (1876), part 5, ch. 6; McBain, J. M. *Eminent Arbroathians* (1897), 201–22.
29 *New Statistical Account*, vol. 11, 271–90.
30 *Short Account of the Town of Perth* (1828).
31 *Exposition of Facts and Theories regarding the Improvement of the Tay by a Ship-Owner* (1833).

32 See 'Articles of Roup of a tack of the West Pier and shore of Newburgh Fife 2 August 1775', University of St Andrews, Hay of Leyes Papers (on loan from Messrs Pagan Osborne and Grace WS, St Andrews), nos. 1227–8. I am very grateful to the University Archivist, Mr Robert Smart, for drawing my attention to these papers.
33 Marshall, T. H. *The History of Perth* (1849), 445–9.
34 Hay of Leyes Pps, *loc. cit.*, nos. 1243–73.

CHAPTER III

1 Hamilton, H. *The Industrial Revolution in Scotland* (1932), ch. 11; Baxter, B. *Stone Blocks and Iron Rails* (1966).
2 Stevenson, D. *Life of Robert Stevenson* (1878), ch. 7.
3 Priestley, J. *Historical Account of the Navigable Rivers, Canals, and Railways throughout Great Britain* (1831), 232.
4 Lewin, H. G. *Early British Railways* (1925), 58–60.
5 Priestley, J., *loc. cit.* 247
6 Thomas, J. *The North British Railway* (1969), vol. 1.
7 Douglas, H. *Crossing the Forth* (1964).
8 Lewin, H. G. *The Railway Mania and its Aftermath* (1936), ch. 9.
9 Ahrons, L. H. *Locomotive and Train Working in the Latter Part of the Nineteenth Century* (1952); Sherrington, C. E. R. *A Hundred Years of Inland Transport* (1934), ch. 5.
10 Ellis, H. *The Flying Scotsman* (1962).
11 Lenman, B. 'Mechanical Ferries on the Tay—from First to Last', *Transport History*. vol. 2, no. 3 (1969), 333–4.
12 Prebble, J. *The High Girders* (1956).
13 Diary of James Cox, kindly lent by Cox family. The verse of poetry is from 'The Railway Bridge Of The Silvery Tay', *Poetic Gems Selected From The Works of William McGonagall* (1963), 39.
14 Ms correspondence in 1880 between James Cox, A. B. Gilroy, and the North British directors. This was kindly made available by the Cox family.
15 'The Newport Railway', *Poetic Gems Selected From The Works Of William McGonagall* (1963), 40.
16 Hay, G. *History of Arbroath* (1876), 328.
17 Turner, W. H. K. *The Textile Industry of Arbroath since the Early Eighteenth Century* (1954), 16–17.
18 Article on harbour, *The Arbroath Guide*, 3 January 1953.
19 Harbour Reports and Accounts 1840–8, Arbroath Public Library, Arbroath Room, J 1024–1037/387–12.
20 Peacock, D. *Perth* (1849), 565; Dundee Perth and London Shipping Company, *The History of a Hundred Years* (1926), 18.
21 *Ordnance Gazetteer of Scotland* (1885), vol. 3, 186; Marshall, T. H. *The History of Perth* (1849), 457.

22 Mitchell, D. *The History of Montrose* (1866); *Ordnance Gazetteer* (1885), vol. 3, 57.

23 *Ordnance Gazetteer of Scotland* (1882–5), vol. 4, 416.

24 Ibid., 414–17; Muir, A. *Nairns of Kirkcaldy* (1956).

25 *Ordnance Gazatteer* (1885), vol. 1, 176–7; 403.

26 Owen, D. J. *The Ports of the United Kingdom* (1948), 312.

27 See Minutes of the Joint Committee of the Caledonian, Edinburgh and Glasgow, and Scottish Central Railways, and Forth and Clyde Canal for 1857–9. These were in the British Railway Archive and have been transferred, with the rest of the archive, to the Scottish Record Office. The full reference is SRO/BR/CAL/1/91.

28 *Ordnance Gazetteer* (1885), vol. 2, 211–2.

29 See records of the Select Committee. Copy in SRO/BR/PYB (8)/1/156.

30 *Ordnance Gazetteer* (1885), *loc. cit.*; Oakley, C. A. *The Second City* (1946), 201.

31 Nicoll to Melville, 1 March 1819, Melville Pps, University Library, St Andrews, no. 4564.

32 Malcolm, J. *The Parish of Monifieth* (1910), 211–16; Scott, J. *History of Tayport* (1927), 37–9; Neish, J. S. *History of Newport* (1890), 39–57. The title deeds to Broughty Ferry Railway Harbour are held by Dundee Corporation, and these provide a detailed history of its ownership. They are filed under BFRH/TD.

33 There is a good deal of correspondence on the Forth ferries in the Melville Pps, SRO/GD/51 (5).

34 I owe this point to an unpublished study of Clackmannan Pow executed by Clackmannan Local Studies Unit, and made available to me by courtesy of its director Mr Murray Dickie. I am grateful to Clackmannan County Education Authority and to the County Director of Education Mr Landsborough, for permission to use this material.

35 *Ordnance Gazetteer* (1885), vol. 1, 43.

36 Vamplew, W. 'The Railways and the Iron Industry: A Study of their Relationship in Scotland', in Reed, M. C. (Ed.). *Railways in the Victorian Economy* (1969), 33–75.

37 Beckles, N. I. *The Development of the Port and Trade of Dundee* (1968), ch. 4.

38 Warden, Alexander. *The Linen Trade* (1864), 638.

39 Lenman, B., Lythe, C. and Gauldie, E. *Dundee and its Textile Industry, 1850–1914*, (Abertay Historical Society Publication no. 14 1969), ch. 2 and appendix 2.

40 'Special Report Of Mr George Wallis 1854, Section 1', reprinted in Rosenberg, N. (Ed.). *The American System of Manufacturers, 1854–5* (1969), 209.

41 Semmes, R. *The Confederate Raider Alabama* (1962), 121.

42 Beckles, N. I. *The Development of the Port and Trade of Dundee* (1968), 128–31.

NOTES AND REFERENCES

43 Irons, J. C. *Leith and its Antiquities* (1887), vol. 2, 299–356; *Ordnance Gazetteer* (1885), vol. 2, 480–94.
44 See Abstracts of Accounts of Leith Dock Commission, SRO/GD/ 229/5/16–28.
45 MacDougall, I. *The Minutes of Edinburgh Trades Council 1859–73* (Scottish History Society 1968), Introduction, xvi.
46 Robertson, D. *The Bailies of Leith* (1915), ch. 4.
47 McCulloch, J. R. *A Dictionary of Commerce and Commercial Navigation* (new ed., 1869), 554–6.

CHAPTER IV

1 *Ordnance Gazetteer of Scotland* (1882–5), vol. 4, 485–8.
2 Ibid.
3 Material on Leith docks between 1883 and 1885 in the preceding paragraphs is drawn from Leith Dock Commission Scrap Book 1883–5, SRO/GD 229/12/1.
4 Material on Leith docks between 1887 and 1889 is from SRO/GD 229/12/2.
5 Material on Leith docks between 1889 and 1893 is from SRO/GD 229/12/3.
6 Colston, J. *The Town and Port of Leith etc.* (1892).
7 Irons, J. C. *Leith and Its Antiquities* (1887), vol. 2, ch. 29.
8 Material on Leith docks between 1893 and 1911 is from SRO/GD 229/12/4–5.
9 For Leith docks from 1911 to 1915 see SRO/GD 229/12/6–8.
10 Lenman, B. *et al. Dundee and its Textile Industry, 1850–1914* (1969), ch. 2.
11 Beckles, N. I. *The Development of the Port and Trade of Dundee* (1968), ch. 4.
12 Lenman, B. and Donaldson, K. 'Partners' Incomes, Investment and Diversification in the Scottish Linen Area, 1850–1921', *Business History*, vol. 13, no. 1 (1971), 1–18.
13 Beckles, N. I. *op. cit.*, ch. 4.
14 Thompson, J. H., and Ritchie, G. G. *Dundee Harbour Trust Centenary Book, 1830–1930* (1930).
15 Thompson, J. H. 'Progress and Development of the Harbour', *British Association Handbook* (1912), 357–65.
16 Duckham, B. F. 'Introduction' to Galloway, R. L. *A History of Coal Mining in Great Britain* (1969).
17 Muir, A. *The Fife Coal Company Limited* (n.d.), ch. 1.
18 Goodwin, R. 'Some Physical and Social Factors in the Evolution of a Mining Landscape', *Scottish Geographical Magazine*, vol. 75, no. 1 (1959), 3–17.
19 Carvel, J. L. *One Hundred Years in Coal* (1944).

20 *Ordnance Gazetteer* (1885), vol. 2, 504–5.
21 Cunningham, A. S. *Randolph Gordon Erskine Wemyss. An Appreciation* (privately printed n.d.).
22 Saunders, L. J. 'A Geographical Description of Fife, Kinross and Clackmannan III', *Scottish Geographical Magazine*, vol. 29, no. 3 (1913), 140–1; *Ordnance Gazetteer* (1885), vol. 1, 202–3.
23 See cutting dated 9 January 1883, SRO/GD 229/12/1; also cuttings dated 23 March 1906 and 17 July 1907 in SRO/GD 229/12/4 and 5 respectively; and cutting dated 2 December 1911 in SRO/GD 229/12/6.
24 Hoggan, H. M. C. and Wilson, G. 'Methil Dock', *A Preliminary Investigation into the Industrial Archaelogy of Fife* (Kirkcaldy Technical College 1967), Shipping, section 5.
25 Christie, G. *Harbours of the Forth* (1955); Stephen, W. *The Story of Inverkeithing* (1938).
26 Cunningham, A. S. *Randolph Gordon Erskine Wemyss. An Appreciation* (n.d.), 136–7.
27 Bird, A. *Roads and Vehicles* (1969), ch. 3 and ch. 12.
28 Valentine, E. S. *Forfarshire* (1912), 75–81.
29 Valentine, E. S. *Fifeshire* (1910), 93–6.
30 Lockhart, J. Y. *Kirkcaldy Harbour. An Historical Outline* (Typescript account dated 1940, preserved in Kirkcaldy Central Reference Library); Clark, A. *Kirkcaldy Harbour, Old and New* (Reprinted from the *Fifeshire Advertiser*, 1890); Valentine, E. S. *Fifeshire* (1910), 94.
31 McCallum, A. *Midlothian* (1912), 84; Muir, T. S. *East Lothian* (1915), 70; Macnair, P. *Perthshire* (1912), 139–40.
32 Hannay-Thompson, J. H. *Granton Harbour Edinburgh Centenary 1837–1937* (privately printed, 1937); McCallum, A. *Midlothian* (1912), 89.
33 See evidence before parliamentary committees, excerpts of which are in SRO/BR/PYB (5)/2/4; SRO/BR/PYB (5)/1/70; and SRO/BR/PYB (5)/1/392.
34 Semple, D. 'The Growth of Grangemouth: A Note', *Scottish Geographical Magazine*, vol. 74, no. 2 (1958), 79–80.

CHAPTER V

1 Morison, S. E. *John Paul Jones* (1960), ch. 12.
2 Stephen, W. *The Story of Inverkeithing* (1938), ch. 11.
3 Mudie, F., Walker, D., MacIvor, I. and Coutts, H. *Broughty Castle* (Abertay Historical Society Publication no. 15, 1970).
4 MacIvor, I. *Fort George* (1970).
5 *Black's Guide to Scotland* (31st ed. 1900), 62.
6 *Ward Lock's Edinburgh and District* (11th ed. n.d.), 162.
7 Von Müller to von Tirpitz, 8 February 1905, printed in von Tirpitz, A. *Politische Dokumente: Der Aufbau Der Deutschen Weltmacht* (1924), 15.

The precise phrase used is; 'Dass der Schwerpunkt für uns in Linienschiff und im Torpedoboot liegt, ist klar'.

8 *Ward Lock's Edinburgh and District* (n.d.), 162; Smith, A. *The Third Statistical Account of Scotland: The County of Fife* (1952), 334. I am very grateful to Mr Robert Craig, of the Department of Civil Engineering in the University of Dundee for advice on the engineering difficulties involved in the construction of Rosyth Dockyard.

9 Marder, A. J. *From the Dreadnought to Scapa Flow* (1965), vol. 2, 65, 69, 148, 172-4, 430-5, and vol. 3 (1966), 228; Crutwell, C. R. M. F. *A History of the Great War* (1934), 316.

10 Scott, W. R. and Cunnison, J. *The Industries of the Clyde Valley During the War* (1924), ch. 7.

11 *Dundee Year Book* for 1914 and 1915, Harbour, Jute and Flax sections.

12 Marder, A. J. *From the Dreadnought to Scapa Flow* (1970), vol. 4, chs 3 and 4.

13 *The History of a Hundred Years* (1926), 22-4.

14 Mason, J. *The History of Trinity House of Leith* (1957), 108.

15 Local information.

16 Smith, A. *The County of Fife* (1952), 483.

17 Secretary of State for Scotland, *Leith Harbour and Docks Provisional Order (1918)*. There is a copy of a draft of this, with some relevant correspondence attached, in the Edinburgh Room of Edinburgh Central Public Library, ref. Y/HE/558/L.

18 Pigon, A. C. *Aspects of British Economic History 1918-1925* (1947), ch. 3.

19 Heckscher, E. *et al. Sweden, Norway, Denmark, and Iceland in the World War* (1930); Riste, O. *The Neutral Ally* (1965).

20 These figures are derived from Flinn, M. W. 'The Overseas Trade of Scottish Ports, 1900-1960', *Scottish Journal of Political Economy*, vol. 13 (1969), 220-37, Table 5.

21 Statistics for 1913, 1919, 1920, and 1921 will be found for selected Scottish east-coast ports in the section on individual ports in *Annual Statement of the Trade of the United Kingdom* (1922), vol. 4.

22 Smith, A. *The County of Fife* (1952), 263.

23 *The Northern Countries in World Economy* (1939), ch. 5; Jörberg, L. *The Industrial Revolution in Scandinavia 1850-1914* (1970).

24 The detailed figures for imports and exports at individual ports are derived from the statistics given in vol. 4 of the *Annual Statement of the Trade of the United Kingdom*, which is available throughout the inter-war period.

25 Personal reminiscence of Councillor Hugh Aglionby, Balcomie Links Hotel, Crail. Recorded along with a photograph in *The Courier and Advertiser*, 22 January, 1971.

26 Insh, G. P. *Men, Moods and Movements* (1947), ch. 11: 'A Tall Ship' (dated 1932).

27 Ashworth, W. *An Economic History of England* (1960), 343.

28 Hoggan, H. and Wilson, G. 'Methil Dock', *A Preliminary Investigation*

into the Industrial Archaeology of Fife (1967), section 5.

29 *Annual Statement of the Trade of the United Kingdom, 1930–38.*

30 Hannay-Thompson, J. H. *Granton Harbour* (privately printed 1937).

31 *The Northern Countries in World Economy* (1939), 121.

32 Material on Leith docks between 1922 and 1939 is based on a collection of cuttings from contemporary newspapers in Edinburgh Central Public Library, Edinburgh Room. The reference is Leith Docks: Press Cuttings, Y/HE/558/L.

33 Porteous, R. *Grangemouth's Modern History* (1970).

34 Reader, W. J. *Imperial Chemical Industries: A History* (1970), vol. 1, ch. 18.

35 Carvel, J. L. *One Hundred Years In Timber: The History of the City Saw Mills 1849–1949* (n.d.), ch. 6.

36 Beckles, N. I. *The Development of the Port and Trade of Dundee* (1968), ch. 4.

37 *Do it at Dundee* (n.d.); Wilson, G. *The Making of a Lord Provost* (n.d.), ch. 18.

CHAPTER VI

1 Smout, T. C. *Scottish Trade on the Eve of Union 1660–1707* (1963), ch. 3.

2 Hamilton, H. *An Economic History of Scotland in the Eighteenth Century* (1963), 214–5.

3 *Dundee Delineated* (1822), 78–87.

4 Campbell, R. H. 'The Law and the Joint-Stock Company in Scotland', in Payne, P. (Ed.) *Studies in Scottish Business History* (1967), 136–51.

5 Macmillan, D. S. *Scotland and Australia 1788–1850* (Oxford 1967), chs. 4–6.

6 Keir, D. *The Younger Centuries* (privately printed 1951), 49–50.

7 *The London and Leith Smack and Steam Yacht Guide* (1824).

8 *The History of a Hundred Years* (1926), 1–17.

9 Ingram Mss, Dundee Shipbuilding Records vol. 1, Dept. of History, Univ. of Dundee.

10 Donaldson, G. *Northwards by Sea* (1966), chs 1–2; Parry, A. *Parry of the Arctic* (1963), 189–91.

11 Milne, T. E. 'British Shipping in the Nineteenth Century; A Study of the Ben Line Papers', in Payne, P. (Ed.) *Studies in Scottish Business History* (1967), 345–66.

12 *Leith Pilot Annual for 1890*, 35–9.

13 Johnston, T. *The History of the Working Classes in Scotland* (1929), 361–6.

14 Cooke, A. B. 'Gladstone's election for the Leith district of burghs, July 1886', *The Scottish Historical Review*, vol. 49, no. 148 (1970), 172–94.

15 Powell, L. H. *The Shipping Federation* (1950).

16 See the obituary of Lord Armitstead in the *Dundee Year Book 1915*, 71–5.

17 Davidson, T. M. (Ed.) *In Memoriam. Sir Charles Barrie* (1922).

18 Aldcroft, D. H. 'Port Congestion and the Shipping Boom of 1919–20', *Business History*, vol. 3, no. 1 (1960), 98–106.

19 Blake, G. *The Ben Line* (1956), ch. 11.

20 Divine, D. *These Splendid Ships* (1960), chs 15–17.

21 Laird, D. *Paddy Henderson* (1961); Course, A. G. *The Wheel's Kick and the Wind's Song* (1968).

22 Keilhau, W. *Norges Eldste Linjerederi* (1951).

23 Vamplew, W. *Salvesen of Leith* (1974).

24 *The Ben Line: The Story of a Merchant Fleet at War 1939–1945* (1946).

25 Mason, J. *The History of Trinity House of Leith* (1957), 111–12.

26 Fresson, E. E. *The Air Road to the Isles* (1967).

27 *Sea Breezes*, December 1955, 409.

28 *The Courier and Advertiser*, 15 June 1955 and 20 November 1961.

29 There is a detailed discussion of the shipping firms of Dundee in the Dundee *Evening Telegraph*, 27 July 1957.

30 Ibid., 23 June 1956.

31 *The Courier and Advertiser*, 5 April 1969.

32 *Evening Telegraph*, 14 January 1956.

33 McIver, D. *An Old-Time Fishing Town: Eyemouth* (1906), 276.

34 Lythe, S. G. E. 'Shipbuilding at Dundee down to 1914', *Scottish Journal of Political Economy*, vol. 9 (1962), 219.

35 *Old Statistical Account of Scotland*, vol. 6, 572.

36 Lythe, S. G. E. 'Shipbuilding at Dundee Down to 1914', *op. cit.*

37 Lythe, S. G. E. 'James Carmichael', *Three Dundonians* (Abertay Historical Society Publication no. 13 1968), 1–7.

38 Chapman, D. 'The New Shipwright Building Company of Dundee', *Economic History Review*, vol. 10 (1939–40), 148–51.

39 Johnston, T. *A History of the Working Classes in Scotland* (1929), 372.

40 *A Shipbuilding History 1750–1932* (privately printed for Alexander Stephen and Sons n.d.).

41 Bremner, D. *The Industries of Scotland* (2nd ed. 1969), 74–5.

42 *Evening Telegraph*, 22 February 1969.

43 *Ordnance Gazetteer of Scotland* (1885), vol. 2, 487.

44 The *Ilala* was given yard number 5, but was in fact the first ship launched from the Caledon yard. The four previous yard numbers were given to launches built at the Tay Foundry. The best detailed account of shipbuilding on Tayside in the later nineteenth century is in the Ingram Mss, volumes on shipbuilding, especially the Dundee volumes 4 and 5, which cover the period 1871–90.

45 Lythe, S. G. E. *Gourlays of Dundee* (Abertay Historical Society Publication no. 10 1964).

46 *Dundee Chamber of Commerce Centenary Souvenir* (1936), 78.

47 Oakley, C. A. *Scottish Industry To-Day* (1937), 132.

48 Smith, A. (Ed.) *The County of Fife* (1952), 252–6; *Evening Telegraph*, 12 June 1954.

49 Smith, A. (Ed.) *The County of Fife* (1952), 256.
50 Rees, H. *British Ports and Shipping* (1958), 228.
51 Ingram Mss, Dundee Shipbuilding, vol. 8 and vol. on Burntisland Shipbuilding.
52 Campbell, R. H. 'Scottish Shipbuilding: Its Rise and Progress', *The Scottish Geographical Magazine*, vol. 80 (1964), 107–13.
53 Mortimer, J. E. *A History of the Association of Engineering and Shipbuilding Draughtsmen* (1960), ch. 20.

CHAPTER VII

1 Boxer, C. R. *The Dutch Seaborne Empire 1600–1800* (1965), 108 and 273.
2 Lythe, S. G. E. 'The Dundee Whale Fishery', *Scottish Journal of Political Economy*, vol. 11 (1964), 158–69.
3 Lockhart, J. Y. *Kirkcaldy Harbour: An Historical Outline* (n.d.).
4 Lubbock, B. *The Arctic Whalers* (1937), 342.
5 There are models of both *Tay* and *Narwhal* in the whaling section of the Dundee Corporation Museum at Broughty Ferry Castle.
6 'The Jute and Whale-Oil Trades of Dundee', *The Practical Magazine*, 1874, 167–73 (Copy in Dundee Central Reference Library, Lamb Collection, D7630H).
7 *A Shipbuilding History 1750–1932* (Alexander Stevens and Sons n.d.), ch. 5.
8 There was a very detailed series of articles on Scott's *Discovery* in *Model Engineer*, 131 (1965).
9 Clippings from *Advertiser* dated 20 April 1875 and 23 April 1875, Lamb Collection, D8344H.
10 Shipjer, E. J. *Whales* (1962), 22.
11 'Some Ideas and Information on the Whale Fishery in the Arctic Seas', a paper read before the French Society of Broughty Ferry in 1885 and translated by Mr President. There is a copy of this in the records of the Tay Whale Fishing Company (microfilm in possession of author).
12 Murray, I. 'The Whalers', *Scottish Field*, December 1969, 34–7.
13 Based on minutes of directors' meetings, records of the Tay Whale Fishing Company (microfilm).
14 Vamplew, W. *Salvesen of Leith* (1974).
15 Rees, H. *British Ports and Shipping* (1958), 228.
16 Robertson, R. B. *Of Whales and Men* (1954).
17 Graham, A. 'Archaeological Notes on some Harbours in Eastern Scotland', *Proceedings of the Society of Antiquaries of Scotland*, 101 (1968–9), 200–85.
18 Anson, P. *Fishing Boats and Fisher Folk on the East Coast of Scotland* (1930, reprinted 1971), ch. 5.
19 Graham, A. *op. cit.*

20 Hamilton, H. *An Economic History of Scotland in the Eighteenth Century* (1963), 112–28.

21 For access to a collection of Board of Trustees records, including much fishery material, I am most grateful to Mr Stuart Maxwell of the National Museum of Antiquities of Scotland. The annual Ms statements on the national fisheries between 1819 and 1830 go under various names, from 'General View', to 'Comparative State', to simply 'Account of Fish Caught'.

22 'Report by the Commissioners for the Herring Fishery of their Proceedings, Year ended 5th April 1820', Board of Trustees Mss, National Museum.

23 'Report by the Commissioners for the Herring Fishery of their Proceedings, year ended 5th April 1831', Board of Trustees Mss, National Museum.

24 Vide the speech made in the House of Commons by a Mr White in 1865, in which he denounced the grant for the Board of Fisheries in Scotland as rank jobbery, vide *East of Fife Record*. 16 June, 1865.

25 Hodgson, W. C. *The Herring and its Fishery* (1957).

26 'Report by the Commissioners for the British Fisheries in the year ended 5th January 1849', and also for the year ended 5th January 1851, Board of Trustees Mss, National Museum.

27 *East of Fife Record*, 5 September, 1857; and 19 December 1857.

28 Gray, M. 'Organisation and growth in the East Coast Herring Fishing, 1800–1885', in Payne, P. (Ed.) *Studies in Scottish Business History*, (1967), 187–216.

29 *East of Fife Record*, 12 October 1861; and 28 February 1879.

30 Ibid., 12 October 1861; 18 October 1862; 18 December 1863; 14 April 1865; and 6 October 1865.

31 Loch, D. *Essays on the Trade, Commerce, Manufactures and Fisheries of Scotland* (1778), 2, 47.

32 Anson, P. *Fishing Boats and the Fisher Folk on the East Coast of Scotland* (1930, reprinted 1971), ch. 3.

33 Goodlad, C. A. *Shetland Fishing Saga* (1971), ch. 8.

34 Bremner, D. *The Industries of Scotland, 1869* (1969), 312–19.

35 High, W. 'Fishing, Trawling, and Whaling', *British Association Handbook to Dundee and District 1912*, 326–9.

36 *Do it at Dundee* (n.d.), 36.

37 Campbell, R. H. *Scotland Since 1707* (1965), 322.

38 Valentine, E. S. *Fifeshire* (1910), 90.

39 Aitken, T. M. 'Boddam by the Light', *The Scots Magazine*, April 1971, 46–53.

40 Coull, J. R. 'Modern Trends in Scottish Fisheries', *The Scottish Geographical Magazine*, vol. 84, no. 1 (1968), 15–28.

41 I am very grateful to the Department of Agriculture and Fisheries for Scotland for supplying me with information and statistics on state assistance for fishery harbours on the east coast of Scotland.

42 *Sixth Report from the Estimates Committee, Session 1966–67: Assistance to the Fishing Industry* (HMSO), xx–xxi.
43 Ibid., 183.

POSTSCRIPT

1 Smith, A. *The County of Fife* (1952), 263–7.
2 Porteous, R. *Grangemouth's Modern History* (1970); Bell, R. *History of the British Railways During the War, 1939–45* (1946), ch. 18.
3 Muir, A. *The Story of Shotts* (privately printed n.d.), 60–1.
4 White, H. 'Transport', *Scientific Survey of South-Eastern Scotland* (British Association 1951), 152–61.
5 Carstairs, A. 'The Nature and Diversification of Employment in Dundee in the Twentieth Century', and Campbell, A. 'The Economic Structure of the Tayside Region', *Dundee and District* (British Association 1968), 318–36, and 337–46, resp.
6 For a very shrewd contemporary analysis see Knowles, K. 'The Post-War Dock Strikes', The Political Quarterly, vol. 22, no. 3, 1951, 266–90.
7 Based on the relevant volume of Leith Docks cuttings in the Edinburgh Room of Edinburgh Central Public Library, ref. Y/HE/558/L.
8 Figures from *Annual Statement of the Trade of the United Kingdom*, vols for 1948 and 1951, section 4.
9 Flinn, M. W. 'The Overseas Trade of Scottish Ports, 1900–1960', in Porteous, R. *Grangemouth's Modern History* (1970), ch. 7.
10 The British Petroleum Company, *Finnart Ocean Terminal* (privately printed n.d.).
11 Press cuttings, Edinburgh Central Public Library, ref. YHE/558/L.
12 Beckles, N. I. *The Development of the Port and Trade of Dundee*, ch. 5.
13 Vide obituaries of Sir Wilfrid Ayre in *The Scotsman*, 12 August 1971. and *The Courier* of the same date.
14 Ingram Mss, vol. on Burntisland Shipping. There are many articles on Robb Caledon in the files of *The Courier* in 1970–1.
15 Aitken, J. 'Why our coastal trade is sinking', *The Scotsman*, 3 July 1971.
16 Rennie, R. C. and Gordon, T. C. (Eds). *The Third Statistical Account of Scotland: The Counties of Stirling and Clackmannan* (1966), 501.
17 Aitken, J. 'The Port of Perth', *The Scots Magazine*, New Series, 88, 3 (December 1967), 269–75; *Perthshire Advertiser*, 27 January, 1971; and *The Courier*, 26 August 1971.
18 Scottish Council (Development and Industry), *Oceanspan* (1970).
19 *Tayside: Potential for Development* (1970).
20 *The Grangemouth-Falkirk Regional Survey and Plan* (1968), 2 vols; 'The Grangemouth and Falkirk Regional Survey', *Scottish Economic Development Quarterly Report*, 10 July 1968, 3–6.

NOTES AND REFERENCES

21 Ogg, R. L. *'Throughway' for Boxes*, a supplement distributed with the *Three Banks Review*, 83, September 1969.

22 Borthwick, A. *The Tay Road Bridge* (1966).

23 Press cuttings, Edinburgh Central Public Library, ref. YHE/558/L.

24 Vide Financial Policy for Ports (1971), Cmnd. 4794, 3.

25 Hamilton, A. 'The hard-won picture of North Sea prospects', *The Financial Times*, 26 August 1971.

Index

Index